DATE DUE

MAR 1 5 1996			

DEMCO 38-297

Social Science in the Courtroom

Social Science in the Courtroom

**Statistical Techniques and
Research Methods for Winning
Class-Action Suits**

James W. Loewen
University of Vermont

LexingtonBooks
D.C. Heath and Company
Lexington, Massachusetts
Toronto

KF
8896
.L63
1982

Library of Congress Cataloging in Publication Data

Loewen, James W.
    Social science in the courtroom.

    Includes index.
    1. Class actions (Civil procedure)–United States. 2. Social science–
Research–Law and legislation–United States. I. Title.
KF8896.L63   347.73'5   80–8605
ISBN 0–669–04310–9   347.3075   AACR2

Published simultaneously in Canada

Printed in the United States of America

International Standard Book Number: 0–669–04310–9

Library of Congress Catalog Card Number: 80–8605

To Nicholas and Lucy,

who have brought such happiness to my life, and

to the small band of civil-rights lawyers,

who have brought hope and relief to so many lives.

Contents

List of Figures

List of Tables

Preface

From time to time, legal scholars tell us that the continued use of social science in court will sully or destroy the law. Pure social scientists lament that the practice will distort or destroy social science. A different lament is that social-science findings played a major role in litigation only during the Warren Court era of so-called judicial activism, while the more-conservative judges of the 1980s will find social science much less relevant. Meanwhile, the use of social-science experts in court continues to increase—and for good reason. Social-science findings and conclusions are relevant to the factual side of a wide array of cases. Indeed, the use of social scientists in many areas of litigation is primitive and just beginning. Twenty years ago, Judge John R. Brown wrote, "In the problem of racial discrimination, statistics often tell much and courts listen." [*Alabama* v. *U.S.* (304 F.2d 583, 586, 5th Cir., 1962)] Today this is true, not only in the area of discrimination but also in any area where judgments have to be reached about classes of people, groups of products, or large numbers of documents. As courts are beginning to take note of statistical techniques, law schools are beginning to teach lawyers how to understand and present statistical findings. The questions that remain, then, are these: Will cases go to court with their factual sides well prepared, benefitting from social-science expertise where appropriate? Will judges be familiar enough with social-science methods and statistics to critique incompetent or incorrect presentations? Will attorneys know enough about social science to know when to contact an expert, what kind to engage, and how to work with him or her as a partnership? On the other side of the disciplinary boundary, will social scientists understand what kinds of findings are relevant legally and what are not? And can they learn to present these findings effectively to an audience that may be ignorant of the nuances of research design but that is not stupid about the operation of the social world?

This book is written so that these questions might be answered in the affirmative. Its purposes are to help attorneys learn how and when to use expert witnesses and to help social scientists learn how to become more effective in their courtroom appearances.

Social Science in
the Courtroom

1 Why and When to Use Social-Science Experts

In 1979, Jean Paul Marat commented on the relationship of law to social justice:

> The lot of the poor, always downtrodden, always subjugated, and always oppressed, can never be improved by peaceful means. This is doubtless one of the striking proofs of the influence of wealth on the legal code.

Not a particularly radical statement, and certainly not a Marxist one—Marx was born a quarter century later. Marat's phrasing is merely a jarring way to say what every student learns in the first week of a course in the sociology of law—that is, the legal system usually functions to maintain the status quo.

If there is a U.S. antidote to all this, it would have to include the phrase, "nor deny to any person within its jurisdiction the equal protection of the laws,"[1] because we Americans believe that law is not only an instrument of power wielded disproportionately on behalf of those who already have wealth and prestige but also a route of redress for persons who, owing to their race, sex, poverty, age, or other characteristic, have not been treated fairly. Whole subfields of legal practice, seeking judicial remedy for societal wrongs, have developed—for example, civil rights law, sex- or gender-related practice, poverty law, environmental law, consumer protection, and much of the rest of the area known as class-action litigation.

Until recently, the key elements required to obtain legal redress of unfair treatment, particularly when that treatment amounted to racial, sexual, or other discrimination, were three: a courageous plaintiff, an informed lawyer, and the development of the law. The factual basis of the case was usually clear. In Mississippi, for instance, not one black was a member of the highway patrol in 1968. Discrimination was obvious.

Today, North and South, the factual situation is subtler. No longer does a large company have no women as higher managers, instead, perhaps 17 percent of its management are women, and that proportion may or may not indicate discrimination—other facts must be known to place it into context. Thus, a fourth element is often required today in lawsuits in order to determine if a class of people has been wronged: participation of a social scientist (or several) to make sense of the subtleties in the facts and to counter the inevitable arguments from those in charge of the institution that no discrimination was involved.

1

Social scientists and statisticians can also be crucial to winning other types of suits such as trademark infringement, charges of unfair or monopolistic business practices, and any cases involving large numbers of, for example, people, documents, or cans of clam chowder. Accordingly, parts of this book can profitably be read by persons working on cases ranging from torts to labor law. For example, chapter 9, "Selecting a Defensible Sample," and chapter 10, "Social Surveys," would be helpful to an attorney seeking to prove that two products were packaged so similarly that consumers often purchased the second by accident.

However, the book is especially directed to attorneys, judges, and social scientists who will one day be concerned with a case of alleged unfair treatment, where the treatment is said to result from the person's membership in a class that is usually being treated unfairly. This person may be a father seeking custody of his child in a jurisdiction that has awarded 98 percent of the children in contested cases to the female parent. It may be a fourteen-year-old girl not wanting to read a civics textbook that connotes, through its prose and photographs, that only men can govern. It may be a college sophomore on trial for felony possession of marijuana and who faces a jury in which the youngest member is in her mid-30s. Or it may be a Native-American army veteran seeking employment as a bus driver but unable to surpass the performance of white recent high-school graduates on a verbal-aptitude test. Properly prepared social-science testimony can make the difference between success and failure for each of these plaintiffs—and hundreds of others.

Most cases that cry out for expert testimony go to court without it, however. Also, when social scientists are employed, often they make less impact than they might because their preparation, and that of the attorneys using them, has been faulty. Communication between lawyer, social scientist, and plaintiff can be difficult for disciplinary boundaries are involved. Sociologists now speak an advanced statistical language that can only occasionally be comprehended even by other sociologists; rarely do economists write prose at all; and both groups are put off by legal jargon. Furthermore, researching an issue in order to develop courtroom exhibits and testimony is foreign to most social scientists and places new demands upon them for quick response, near certainty, conciseness, and relevance. On the one hand, social scientists must learn about the legal constraints of the case—for example, what kinds of discrimination are actionable and what are not. Attorneys, on the other hand, must learn something about statistics if they are to interface effectively with the experts they have engaged. They must also learn enough about the social sciences to know what kind of expert to recruit, what the expert probably can and cannot do, and what kinds of data will have to be furnished to the expert for analysis.

There is even a vocabulary problem. Two words in the previous paragraph are typical bones of contention. Social scientists with any feel for syntax believe that *actionable* is an incorrect grafting of a verb suffix onto a noun, while many lawyers believe that *interface* is a barbarous misuse of a noun as a verb. Lawyers and social scientists do not often speak the same language. The purpose of this book is to bridge this gap: to help social scientists see the contributions and the limitations of their role in the courtroom and to show attorneys when social-science expertise can be helpful, how to find it, and what kinds of problems to anticipate. For attorneys, the book has information about using an expert; for social scientists it has information about being an expert.

This chapter describes the essential nature of science, in this case social science, for it is that essence that leads to its narrow but often telling power in legal cases. Then it lists some of the varied kinds of cases appropriate to experts in each social science—anthropology, economics, history, political science, psychology, and sociology, as well as statistics and mathematics. The chapter closes with suggestions on how to locate an expert appropriate to the needs of a given case.

The Source of Social Science's Power to Persuade

Lawsuits, particularly those involving charges of ill treatment, typically involve a factual dispute as well as a legal argument, with parties and witnesses on each side of the courtroom asserting quite different things about the facts and their interpretation. In between, said to be open to persuasion from either side, sits the judge or the judge and jury.

To invent an example, our plaintiff, Mrs. Rephan, lives on an unpaved street in a medium-sized Southern city. She claims her street is unpaved and its drainage poor because she is black and because city officials, themselves white, have discriminated for decades in providing municipal services to black neighborhoods, of which hers is but one example. She has photographs of her street and her drainage ditch, showing obvious deficiencies, under heavy runoff.

What might the city claim in response? Even an unsophisticated reply from the city street commissioner might point out that idiosyncratic conditions, such as floodplain siting or failure of local residents to petition for a special paving assessment, cause or at least excuse the deficiencies on Mrs. Rephan's block.

Now, where do we stand? We have one charge, one counter. The person who was predisposed to believe the black householder will still believe her. The person inclined to believe a city official will still believe the commissioner. Most people, perhaps including the judge, who may never have thought about racial discrimination in paving and drainage before and have no particular knowledge of the matter, will not know whom to believe. Nothing has been proved.

Suppose now that Mrs. Rephan realizes that her claim about her own case, by itself, is not enough. She might contact additional black residents through her church and other organizations; perhaps she locates nine more persons who live on unpaved or poorly paved streets. Suppose that several of them have made specific requests for relief to city officials, without result, and that for each black block, she selects and photographs a paved, guttered, well-drained street in a white neighborhood.

What might the city do in response? Surely it could easily locate ten black residents who owe city officials a favor, over whom the city has some control, or to whom the city has recently been responsive. They could testify effectively to city officials' concern for residential areas regardless of color or income level, and their testimony could be buttressed by the comparison of ten superbly paved, well-drained black blocks, perhaps contrasted with ten narrow, poorly drained streets in white areas.

We would be back to a standstill. Supporters of Mrs. Rephan would claim that the city's blocks and witnesses were not representative of overall conditions in black or white neighborhoods, and the city's attorney would gleefully point out that Mrs. Rephan's witnesses were merely a biased sample of her own friends and associates. Again, the person in the middle has no idea whom or what to believe, and again, nothing has been proved.

However, what if our plaintiff had engaged a social scientist or urban planner who had constructed a total list of all blocks in the city and from which the scientist had taken a truly random sample and sent out researchers to record the street width and type of paving of every block in the sample? What if the results showed, among other things, that 13 percent of all black blocks in the sample were unpaved, compared to less than 1 percent of white blocks, and that black blocks averaged twelve feet less in width, paved or not, than white blocks?

Then the city is up against it. The difference between 13 percent and 1 percent if based on a large sample, could hardly occur by chance but is due to race or something tied to race. The finding possesses what is called *statistical significance*, a term and an assertion that is explained in chapter 4. City attorneys may try to discredit the scientist's work in some way, by topping it with a larger sample of their own, drawn nonrandomly, or by explaining her results by claiming causes such as bond failures or floodplain siting.[2] The city may prevail, but its case is in trouble. A prima facie case of discrimination has been made against it that it must explain or rebut.

Anyone can make a correct statement. I have no doubt, having lived in one middle-sized Southern city for nine years, that Mrs. Rephan was correct about discriminatory municipal services in her city from the beginning. Why, then, must a social scientist go through all the time and effort to take a fairly large and random sample, develop a standard observation sheet, locate each block in the sample, apply to it the observation form, collate and analyze the results, and organize them for courtroom presentation, if she and the plaintiff already know they are right? The answer is that the point is not to know one is right but to prove it to others, using systematic, explicit, public, replicable methods.

The means by which the data were first generated must be able to stand scrutiny. Any sample must be random (or nonrandom for a reason). Any survey questions must be unbiased, and the whole proof, from research design to final product, must be understandable to the lay public. The courtroom result is a presentation of data and conclusions, coupled with an exposition of the methods by which those data were obtained, such that the neutral observer (judge) can understand what has been done, will agree that it was fair, and can visualize doing the procedure himself and coming out with similar results. This is part of what is meant by proof in science, and indeed, our expert's procedures were none too elaborate to prove Mrs. Rephan's point; possible sources of bias in her procedures could still be claimed.

Moreover, the neutral observer, the judge, is probably not neutral at all. He is a pillar of society, a member of the upper or upper-middle class. Probably he is white and male as well. Even though he may be open to new ideas, his mind is subtly biased in many ways to believe that what is is right, so our scientist's best work may be required to convince him that the status quo is operating in a discriminatory way and must be changed.

By making their methods public, social scientists expose their concepts and procedures for the world—laypeople and other social scientists—to attack. Here social science differs from social commentary, from journalism, and from common sense. Only if methods are displayed publicly can other· scientists accept them, and the resulting conclusions, as fair.

What is meant by fair? Much of its meaning can be captured by the phrase, *chance to be disproved.* A study can be deemed fair, then, if it could have come out wrong. To return to our example, Mrs. Rephan's initial sample of ten black residents and their blocks contrasted to ten white blocks was not fair because there was little chance that ten black citizens, recruited by our plaintiff because they had had problems with their streets and with city officials, could have had broader, better streets than ten good white streets, chosen specifically because they were good. Mrs. Rephan's assertion, which could be restated to read, "race (black) is associated with poorer street paving and drainage," has not been fairly tested because it could not have been disproved. Our social scientist's random sample, however, could have show black streets to be broader and better if in fact they were; indeed, it surely would have. She has tentatively proved the assertion, therefore, because she found the association under conditions where, if it did not exist, she would have been disproved.

There is more to proof than this. For one thing, proof is consensual. What happens to a tentative outcome next, if it does not simply sink into that sea of unimportant findings reported in unread academic journals, is that other social scientists working in the same area evaluate its methods, theory, and conclusions. There is sometimes more than one way to interpret a finding, so even if the methods of a study stand up under critique, social scientists may still disagree over the meaning of what has been found. If the methods were fair, however, and if they fairly relate to the concepts under study, then the finding itself will have to be reckoned with.

There is always a temptation, whether researching for the courtroom or for the most abstruse professional journal, to cheat a little—that is, to bias the results in one's favor by subtly biasing one's methods. Thus social surveys, a method widely used in court (for instance, in change-of-venue motions), can be afflicted by what I have come to call Republican-National-Committee questions, items like this one:

> The Soviets now have a combat brigade in Cuba training Marxist revolutionaries for use in South America and Africa. Do you approve of Mr. Carter's decision to do nothing in response to this direct Soviet/Cuban challenge? ____ Yes ____ No ____ Undecided[3]

This statement contains such a loaded prologue that disagreement with it becomes quite difficult. Anyone using this kind of item in court, to prove or disprove a poisoned public atmosphere vis-à-vis a defendant, for instance, would not be proving anything, because she had not framed the question so that disagreement with it was possible. There are subtler ways of cheating, some of which are treated in chapter 14. The point here is that the attorney and social scientist must understand that such research bias must be eliminated or minimized because the methods and interpretations will not be ignored but rather will be subject to harsh scrutiny from the other side's attorneys and perhaps from their expert. Moreover, the social scientist is a professional and must adhere to professional canons in data handling or risk loss of reputation as well as integrity.

What if the results come out wrong? It is unsettling, particularly to attorneys, to imagine that possibility. A new expert may be needed, a more-resourceful methodologist. Or perhaps the expert's most helpful role may be to suggest to the lawyer that the facts simply are not there so the case should be settled or dropped. In the worst eventuality, the other side may even obtain your negative results and use them to defeat you. Ways to deal with negative outcomes are discussed in the next chapter, but there is always a heart-in-the-throat feeling as the lawyer puts part of his case outside his personal control. Precisely because neither the attorney nor the expert can control the outcome, it has persuasive power. And precisely because of this persuasive power, expert testimony, appropriately used, can add a crucial element to a case.

The Role of Statistics

It should be clear by now that the kinds of cases I am discussing and the kind of social science I am recommending deal with classes of people (or things). Hence statistics are involved, whether recognized or not. The following are both statistical statements:

> The mean length of time after hiring before initial promotion is 22.1 months for females, 16.8 months for males.

In the 1970s, some white poll supervisors created an atmosphere of intimidation at the polls by threatening black poll watchers with arrest.

The second is merely vaguer than the first. *Some* is a statistical term, a concept of quantity or number, however imprecise. It follows that most statements we make about the social world, unless they relate to one person only and sometimes even then, are statistical.

Statistical evidence and tests are usually important parts of social-science testimony. Statistics is a branch of mathematics. Therefore, in most simple applications it is an exact study. Accordingly, two statisticians seldom disagree on calculations based on the same formulas and data. This adds to the persuasiveness with which the expert testifies, for she can be asked, "Doctor, would these results show statistical significance no matter who did the calculations?," and the reply will be, "Yes."

Two wide areas for disagreement remain, however. First, questions arise as to which statistical test to use and whether certain assumptions about the data, upon which its use is predicated, have been met. This is a complex matter discussed at length in graduate statistics courses. Second, what additional variables need to be considered and controlled for before causation can be inferred? (Chapter 15 covers this topic.) Different answers to these questions can lead to different conclusions by different experts, sometimes frustrating lawyers and the court.

Many uses of social-science testimony are nonstatistical. Here, disagreement between experts is so common as to be customary, and courts grow cynical about the purchase of expertise by each side. The psychiatrist or clinical psychologist who states that, in her belief, a client is insane and not competent to stand trial, makes a statement about one person, and although it may be couched in statistical language comparing this defendant to others, it is not really a statistical assertion. Any reasonably broad definition of science would include such testimony, and it may be crucial to a case. Owing to the nature of this book, however, as indicated by its subtitle, I shall not treat such uses of social-science experts.[4]

Statistical testimony, based on methodical data collection and analysis, could be relevant to an insanity defense. For example, a social scientist might compare the use and acceptance of this defense for a classes of people—men versus women or whites versus blacks—to make an argument that it is being applied in an unfair and discriminatory fashion. Such analysis is exactly the kind of testimony this book is all about. Since the statistical underpinnings of this kind of testimony are exact and the methods are public, such testimony may be more persuasive than subjective opinion, expert though it may be.

Social scientists are also used by the court and by plaintiffs and defendants to determine remedy. For example, in cases of wrongful death or worker's compensation, economists are often engaged to determine what a victim's life earnings expectancy might be, hence what sort of monetary award she or he should receive. Sociologists and social psychologists may be employed as court-appointed masters to suggest what should be done to remedy the plight of black children in a school system found to have been segregated. Social scientists may be used as observers or monitors by the court or either party to ensure that a remedy is being implemented effectively. Political scientists, regional planners, or sociologists may be assigned by the court to reapportion legislative districts in a state found guilty of illegal gerrymandering. Again, important as these applications of social science are, I do not treat them here, in line with my subtitle—this book is concerned with winning.

Social-science research can also play a role in the out-of-court attempts for redress that precede and often substitute for legal action. For example, our study, showing clear racial disparities in street width and paving, could be used politically by candidates seeking to unite the black electorate and win white support for a change in municipal leadership. The study could also be used in negotiating improvements to avoid protracted litigation. Precisely because careful quantitative social-science studies are persuasive, they can influence the public rhetoric—that vague shared body of attitudes and perceptions about our social system within which political debate takes place.

Social Science and Basic Rights

Social-science research has a complex relationship to legal and human rights. Once a right has been declared, someone deprived of that right does not have to prove, through some kind of social-science reasoning, that the deprivation caused measurable injury. A marijuana defendant, facing a jury from which his or her age peers have been systematically excluded, need not prove that such juries are more likely to convict. It is enough to show the systematic exclusion because Americans have a right to a jury of peers, meaning a reasonable cross section of the community.[5]

In *Brown* v. *Board of Education* [347 U.S. 483 (1954)], the Supreme Court held that segregated schools implicitly and intrinsically stigmatized black children and that black children had a right to avoid that injury. It relied in part, but only in part, on social-science findings in reaching that conclusion. The court also knew that the state laws mandating segregation were imposed by whites upon blacks in order to contain and limit their sphere of opportunities, and the Court held that black students have a right to be free from such state-imposed limitations.[6] What if the social-science studies now came out differently? What if the data now indicated, for example, that segregated schools produce splendid black scholars? Or, to be more pessimistic, what if desegregated schools often resulted in disruption and left black students worse off than before? If 60 percent of all relevant social-science studies concur in this bleak conclusion, must the court now reverse itself and declare separate-but-equal to be legal again?

The social-science literature on desegregation still supports the court.[7] so it is still correct to say that segregation has bad educational outcomes for black children. Today, however, most of that literature is irrelevant to winning desegregation cases. (It might be relevant to remedy.) The right of Afro-Americans to avoid such basic restrictions on their liberty as school segregation must not rest on shifting social-science judgments. If some desegregated schools are an educational mess, courts might order them cleaned up but would not reimpose segregation. Therefore, social-science testimony claiming bad outcomes of desegregation has not often impressed the court.[8]

As we have already seen, however, most discrimination cases are not about whether rights should exist but whether these specific situations represent violations of those rights. Here, social science plays a key role in proving an infringement of a right. Outright open discrimination is rarely encountered nowadays. Rather, the issue is whether certain practices, innocuous on their face, adversely affect a minority. A chain of social-science reasoning, buttressed by data, may be required to prove the racial impact of seemingly nonracist practices.

Social scientists can also provide more general understandings to the court so that judges come to see that a complex of institutional discrimination is built into most of our institutions related to race, sex, age, class, or other characteristics. In effect, such testimony makes available the Myrdal side of the Sumner/Myrdal debate, which holds that racial discrimination is neither natural nor inevitable but is maintained by the continuing acts of persons in major societal institutions.[9]

Cases Appropriate to Each Discipline

Thus, a broad array of cases exists in which social-science testimony has been or might be used. In order to be sure that would-be users of social scientists are at least vaguely familiar with the nature of each discipline, I now discuss some of the kinds of cases that call for the expertise of an anthropologist, economist, historian, political scientist, social psychologist, and sociologist, in that order, followed by a briefer discussion of statisticians, urban planners, and others.

Anthropologists

Anthropology has emphasized the study of premodern societies and cultures. Hence anthropologists have testified extensively in Native-American (American-Indian) rights cases such as land claims and legal attempts to stop Native use of peyote in religious practices.[10] Sometimes these cases hinge upon whether or not the Native-American people can be said to have maintained their existence as a tribe during the decades that have elapsed since an agreement was made.

In other cases, the factual issue is whether a given practice should be viewed as primarily religious, hence protected by the First Amendment. An anthropologists increasingly study modern society, they increasingly use the methods common to sociology and develop specialities such as urban anthropology and political anthropology, similar to fields within sociology. Such anthropologists are potentially interchangeable with sociologists (or political scientists) for courtroom use.

A distinctive emphasis of anthropology is the study of culture. Culture is an interconnected whole, so change in one element reverberates through other areas. It is difficult to prove that introducing practice X will have beneficial (or harmful) effects upon Y, but this kind of argument is important for some cases, and anthropologists are as well equipped as anyone to make it. For example, opponents of the death penalty argue that its existence can actually increase the homicide rate by making murder seen an acceptable way to deal with a problem individual who has resisted other methods or who has done something so outrageous as to "merit" death. A person outraged by the behavior of an ex-spouse, according to this reasoning, might be more likely to kill that person, modeling inadvertently after the state's behavior. Some data suggest as much, such as the fact that most Southern states maintained and used the death penalty often, yet they had higher homicide rates than states in the North. An anthropologist could use cultural analysis to conclude that the death penalty has an antideterrent effect on murder. Again, an anthropologist might be able to establish cultural linkages between subtly sexist company practices and the alleged lack of qualified female applicants for previously male jobs. With regard to "standarized" testing, an anthropologist might be able to show bias against an ethnic group, region, sex, or race, if she is a specialist in regional culture, linguistic differences, ethnicity, or the like.

Economists

Economists testify widely in cases ranging from patent infringement to school desegregation. Most economists are sophisticated data analysts and are conversant with a wide variety of published data sources. Hence they would be useful in cases dealing with employment discrimination, unequal municipal services, budget requirements of welfare families, taxation and assessment irregularities, and many more. Economists are good at marshalling census data and other statistics to show racial- or sex-related differences so they could show that blacks, for instance, face different socioeconomic exigencies than whites. That conclusion, in turn, could support a demand for different recruitment methods for blacks in an affirmative-active program or for the chance to elect black officials in a voting-rights case.

Most economists are not experienced data gatherers, as opposed to analysts, and would not be expert in questionnaire construction or structured observation techniques. Because most economics graduate programs have become so complexly quantitative, some economists know little about the broad field of institutional economics. This means they have little formal awareness of the social world but are highly specialized in, say, monetary policy or microeconomics. Such scientists might be poor choices as experts because they are naive regarding social causation. Also, they may not be widely read in related disciplines outside their field. If trying a case involving discrimination, I would search for an economist with teaching or research experience in the economics of poverty and discrimination, sex roles, or environmental economics. Of course, this would not be a consideration in cases involving trademark infringement, monopolistic business practices, and the like.[11]

Historians

Historians have not been used widely in class-action lawsuits, which seems a pity to me. One reason is that most historians are not well trained quantitatively; they are at the point at which political science was in 1950.[12] Hence, a historian should usually not be the only expert for a case. Every discriminatory practice has a history, however, and a case becomes much more convincing if the assertion of bias or sexism does not strike the judge as a bolt from the blue but is shown to be in line with past practices of the defendant and the community. Similarly, every difference between two groups that affects their present performance or determines their present needs has its roots in the social structure of yesterday. Courts have held that officials have an affirmative duty to eliminate the present effects of past purposeful discrimination. Thus practices having a present discriminatory effect, even though not purposefully discriminatory, are barred if they perpetuate the effects of past discrimination.[13]

For example, suppose we are litigating a municipal services case in a Southern city. We claim racial discrimination, yet city officials can show that street paving and draining are paid for by homeowners, via special assessments, and that they will pave any street when petitioned to do so by a majority of the residents willing to pay such assessments. If we win the case, our victory ironically might merely compel a number of black homeowners to come up with some cash for their streets. Some questions a historian might answer include: What about the older streets? Most U.S. cities initially paved their streets in the first three decades of this century. Was this done by special assessment? (Probably not.) If city officials are all white, when did this begin? (Probably around 1875 to 1890.) What practices caused the end of black elected officials? Can the historian claim that the white officials over the past seven or eight decades have been largely responsive to white needs and interests? If so, then the formal equality of recently identical procedures for paving streets in white and black neighborhoods does nothing to erase the discrepancies continuing from a bygone era.

Moreover, digging up the past sometimes uncovers wondrous nuggets. When was the allegedly discriminatory practice initiated? By whom? Why? Before about 1960, white Americans were much more forthright regarding racism and sexism since it was perfectly alright to express such sentiments. Thus in the floor debates of a legislature enacting a tax law, or in the minutes of a city council discussing a zoning ordinance, you may find astonishingly frank arguments as to its intended effects. In a case in which I was plaintiff, *Loewen et al.* v. *Turnipseed et al.* (488 F. Supp. 1138), we were attaching the refusal of the Mississippi State Textbook Purchasing Board to adopt a revisionist state history book. Newspaper clippings from forty years ago showed that when the legislature first set up the textbook board, its avowed purposes included maintenance of white supremacy—that is, the "sons and daughters of Confederate officers" were supposed to insure that no books that might undermine the "Southern way of life" would ever be approved. Some of this material was later cited by the judge in his opinion. Usually, if an official board has never acted to undo an overtly discriminatory past practice, it can still be found to be perpetuating discrimination today.

Content analysis is a method used by historians (and other social scientists) that has marked courtroom utility. Content analysis is the systematic quantitative study of writing, speeches, photographs, or other productions (films, songs, and so on). It can be used in one area that specifically calls for a professional historian as witness—namely, charges of curricular bias. Many history and civics texts have not kept abreast of the currents of historical revisionism. The white-supremacist view of slavery, Reconstruction, and subsequent race relations, ascendant in history from about 1900 to perhaps 1965, has given way in the academic literature to a more-balanced perspective. However, other than including more coverage of women and nonwhites, most textbooks have not really taken account of this new research, particularly on the state level and in civics texts.[14] Anyone attacking a specific history or civics book for offering a biased and inadequate treatment of nonwhite or female Americans should have little difficulty locating a nearby historian who will attest to its deficiencies.

Political Scientists

Political scientists are obvious choices of lawsuits involving voting rights, jury exclusion, or discrimination by a government body. Like economists, they can marshall socioeconomic data to show differences between two subpopulations and how those differences affect political access. Political scientists are also reasonably conversant with the court and legal systems, the tax system, and the structure of state and local government. They may be less prepared regarding race, sex, age, and the literature of discrimination based on such characteristics, although major exceptions exist. Some older political scientists received their training before quantitative methods became widespread in the discipline; they should be avoided unless their particular knowledge is sought. Modern political scientists know statistics, survey research, and data analysis. Most are perhaps somewhat underprepared in methods of data gathering other than surveys. Otherwise, they are of widespread usefulness in court.

Social Psychologists

Attorneys need to know that psychology is a deeply divided field. Clinical psychologists (and psychiatrists) have little in common with most behaviorists; social psychologists form yet a third group. Clinical psychologists testify widely regarding fitness to stand trial or to be a parent, but they are not usually up to data in statistics and are not central for the kinds of cases this book treats. Behaviorists usually have a good grasp of basic statistics, but they too are not recommended for testifying in court. Often they are naive with regard to social theory. Their work may be quite specialized, and their knowledge of relevant work in political science, sociology, and even social psychology may be scant. Social psychologists, however, are quite useful. Their background in methods and statistics is usually excellent. They are particularly knowledgeable regarding tests and measurement. Sex bias is a major recent concern of social psychology, which now boasts a large literature on topics such as the effects of sexist versus nonsexist reading material on motivation among girls. Social psychologists also know a number of research techniques with great legal utility, such as sociometry, interaction process analysis, and the semantic differential. Many are experienced designers of questionnaires and interview schedules.[15]

Sociologists

Sociology is the most general of the social sciences, bordering upon psychology on one side and on economics and history on the other. Some sociologists are trained as social psychologists; others deal with macrosociology such as changes in the national social-class structure over time. Accordingly, sociologists testify often in class-action cases. Some specialities within the field may be of particular interest. For example, demography, the study of population, is useful when cases involve vital statistics, future population projections, or health care. A lawsuit fighting hospital closure, claiming that the action would discriminate against a certain race or class or neighborhood, might profit from population projections by age and sex, leading to projected hospitalization figures. Demographers can also use census tapes to discuss socioeconomic differences in the population that may result in a discriminatory effect from a law or policy that, on its face, looks neutral. Criminology and penology are fields of obvious courtroom usefulness, as well as race relations and the sociology of women and sex roles. Other fields such as medical sociology, the sociology of education, and political sociology come into play when cases touch upon those areas.

Most sociologists have had some training in statistics and research methods, including data gathering as well as data analysis. Because the field is so broad, however, it is likely that the sociologist who is expert in elegant statistical techniques may not really know much about how to word interview questions; likewide, the criminologist may have had only a single undergraduate course, long ago, in demography. Accordingly, it is important for the expert to consult with colleagues in sociology and in related social sciences when needed. In fact, the greatest weakness of sociologists as expert witnesses is the converse of their strength: they may claim too much. Since they know something about most fields, they may claim to be expert in them all. Sociologists also have inadequate knowledge about the legal process; although they may be political sociologists, they usually know little about such formal matters as the statutory limits and requirements affecting a public office.[16]

Statisticians

If there is such emphasis on statistics, one might reasonably ask, what about using a statistician in court? Statisticians are used widely. For class-action suits of the kind we will be discussing, however—suits involving assertions about groups of individuals—I recommend against statisticians. This is an overgeneralization. However, a social scientist with up-to-date knowledge of statistics and research methods is as capable as a statistician to apply the fairly simple statistical tests that are usually involved in courtroom testimony. Also, the social scientist has the advantage of an additional field of expertise, whether in resource economics or penology, that may be tied to substantive areas of her testimony. Moreover, some statisticians, coming from a background in mathematics departments, have only a lay understanding of the social world. They may not think to control for a variable that would never be overlooked by a political scientist or sociologist. On cross-examination, they may make statements that are counterproductive as well as theoretically indefensible. The same problems can afflict other mathematicians and computer experts.

Educational Researchers

Researchers in education may be useful. By this term I mean to include persons with doctorates in education, many of whom teach in colleges of education and themselves study educational institutions, testing and measurement, educational psychology, and teaching methods. Any complaint against a school district, university, or other educational program might benefit from such an expert. Many educational researchers are also broadly competent in statistics and research methods so they should also be considered for cases outside of education itself. For instance, a case arguing for the availability of legal services to a penitentiary population made use of testimony regarding the average reading-difficulty level of law books.

Urban Planners

Urban planners have several social-sciences-based competencies that make them prime candidates for courtroom use. They are expert users of census and other community data. Many of them know statistics, survey design, and other research methods. They usually know about the municipal and state governing processes, and their specialized knowledge about things such as zoning, traffic flow, and shopping patterns can be crucial.

Other Scholars

Scholars from other areas also may be useful. Some people in departments of U.S. studies, Afro-American studies, communications, epidemiology, public administration, and business have research and statistical training, and that list is not exhaustive.[17]

Locating the Right Expert for the Case

Although we have seen how some kinds of cases seem particularly appropriate for scientists in a particular discipline, the factual issues before the court do not respect disciplinary boundaries, and it is crucial that the expert not be limited by them either. For example, the political scientist who does not know the sociological literature on the relationship between race and voting behavior can look pretty silly if opposed by a sociologist who does. The attorney or plaintiff should look for a confident, competent, resourceful methodologist, well grounded in statistics, whose substantive training is reasonably related to the issues at hand, and who already knows or is willing to learn thoroughly the literature on these issues, even when it crosses disciplinary lines.

An example will clarify. Suppose I am an attorney for a black plaintiff who is challenging promotion procedures in a state agricultural extension service in which advancement hinges partly upon performance on an aptitude test. I might seek a social psychologist (who would have some background in tests and measurement), a sociologist (particularly if specialized in race relations), or a resource economist or agronomist (who could compare the overall qualifications of black and white employees and could also asses the extent to which the aptitude test was job related).

It follows that one expert often will not suffice. I have participated in cases with as many as nine expert witnesses on one side, forming an effective team with a division of labor. Each witness focused on the area he or she knew best. The attorney then coordinated exhibits and testimony so that they complemented and built a striking overall factual structure that stayed in the court's mind and influenced the opinion.

If I could hire exactly two experts, I might couple a nationally known scientist who has testified in this area before with a local researcher who is testifying for the first time. That way I would have someone close at hand who could help me interface with my distant expert and supervise any local data gathering. In addition, the neophyte expert might bring fresh ideas and statistical techniques to the topic, particularly if from a different discipline than my national expert. Also, by employing a local person, I create a resource I can use next time, whose expertise in the next case will be more secure because it has been accepted by a previous court.

The most crucial difference, however, is between no experts and one. How to begin? How does one locate the appropriate expert for a given case? A sensible way to approach the involvement of an expert is to hire someone who has already testified in the same field. Often the attorney will learn of that person's existence and prior testimony while researching previous cases. However, that expert may be unavailable, too expensive, or a poor choice. A local social scientist will be the better alternative when awareness of local conditions is important, when the data are available only locally, when data collection must be done or coordinated by the expert, or when the expert must communicate extensively with the plaintiff(s).[18] Sometimes the unavailable nationally known expert can recommend someone else, national or local, as a good substitute. Sometimes the attorney or client simply must contact a local university with no prior leads, exploring qualifications and willingness in several academic departments.

If I were the lawyer or client in a case that I thought could benefit from an expert witness, and if I had little money to spend, I would begin locally, of course, for then transportation is no expense. Moreover, the neophyte expert can sometimes be engaged for free (although this can backfire, as the next chapter points out), and her students may be available without charge for data collection or analysis. This new expert would not have extensive courtroom experience, by definition, and might also not have extensive training in the exact area (say, market research or demography) called for by the nature of the case.

Although I earlier praised the statistical training of social scientists, I overgeneralized. It is quite possible to get through graduate school with the bare minimum, hastily learned and hastily forgotten, and if a social scientist has then not used or taught statistical techniques for ten years, her analytic tools may have rusted past repair. Many types of data-gathering methods are not even required at all, and if the social scientist has not used them in her own research, she has probably never learned them thoroughly. Hence the attorney should seek two specific qualifications in an expert: teaching familiarity with statistics and research familiarity with the methods to be employed. If the social scientist has taught statistics, particularly on an introductory level, then she can probably teach it to the court. Conversely, if, owing to too much or too little erudition, she cannot clarify statistical tests to the lawyer who would employ them, surely she cannot be clear in court either.

Methods skills do not atrophy as rapidly as statistical skills, but they are built up through doing rather than classroom learning. Accordingly, if a case involves a survey (interview or questionnaire), an expert who has constructed and administered surveys should be engaged. This experience need not be court related and can even be as minor as term-paper research, but there is no substitute for it.

I would look first within academia for several reasons. First, a college or university, even one with but a few hundred students, represents a talent pool of at least a dozen social scientists (including related areas such as education and business), perhaps several hundred. If the first person contacted is unavailable or does not have the right qualification, she can suggest others so that the lawyer or plaintiff no longer approaches people without introductions. Second, although the tradition of academic freedom has its limitations, unless the lawsuit is against the expert's own institution, an academic social scientist will probably feel no job threat and will be able to testify as the data dictate. Indeed, academicians' careers can be enhanced by their courtroom experience. The next chapter suggests ways attorneys can help this take place, thus building a mutually beneficial relationship between attorney and expert. Academicians also have a form of free time available. Unlike the applied social scientist who is working for government or business, the academician need not make every second count. The research required for the case may result in professional publication, involve students in ways that promote teaching and learning, or lead to examples useful for later lectures, so it is hardly time wasted for the faculty member. Participation can also make social scientists feel relevant. Many academicians would like to make more of an impact upon the world than their ivory-towered publications allow, and most of them would like that impact to be in the direction of broadening the opportunities available to all Americans, rather than increasing the privileges available to the already privileged.

The academic expert has a final advantage—namely, a number of colleagues to go to for advice in statistics or in a specialized area. An expert should be sought who is not threatened by such interaction. Some professors are so afraid to show a knowledge gap that they refrain from ever seeking advice, instead bluffing it on their own. One test to uncover such prima donnas is to suggest they look over this book. If they refuse, or read it so rapidly they miss this sentence, avoid them. The expert is a conduit for the attorney to the entire realm of social science. She should not be threatened by the possibility of a second expert but should be able candidly to discuss the pros and cons of such a move. A good social scientist should know other good social scientists through old graduate-school connections, present departmental peers, and correspondence with fellow researchers. She also should have connections in related social-science disciplines.

Other places to look include among retirees. Some retired social scientists have lived for years in the local community, building a familiarity that may be valuable. Others are nationally known and enjoy the flexibility of not having to work for a living. Local academic experts can point you to them, or you might phone the national office of the discipline (these are listed at the end of this chapter). Social scientists working for the government, private industry, foundations, or other organizations should not be overlooked, particularly if they have testified before. They will probably charge more for their own time and for any data gathering, computer processing, or other steps in the research process. They are accustomed to explaining social-science procedures and results to laypersons, however, and that is a major plus. Graduate students are another possibility, especially if testimony can be shared between the graduate student, who does the bulk of the work, and the professor, under whose aegis it was done.

Whether national or local, highly experienced or just beginning, the social scientist has been located. Now the expert and lawyer, with help from the plaintiff, must work together to build an effective factual presentation.

Notes

1. U.S. Constitution, Fourteenth Amendment.

2. In order to imply that both sexes can play important roles in litigation, throughout this book I call the attorney he, the expert, she. Of course, this is arbitrary and could be reversed. To make everyone masculine would not do, however; research has shown that sexist language does make an unfortunate difference. Recourse to plural pronouns or passive verbs weakens my prose. Perhaps my pronoun usage is as graceful a solution to the problem as I can invent; better, anyway, than *s/he* and *his/her.*

3. Republican National Committee, "1980 Official Republican Poll on U.S. Defense and Foreign Policy," item No. 4 (Washington: Republican National Committee, 1980), brought to my attention by M. Stickney and D. Wagner.

4. Psychological/psychiatric testimony about individuals is discussed in Melvin G. Goldzband, *Custody Cases and Expert Witnesses* (New York: Law and Business, 1980); and Michael J. Saks and Reid Hastie, *Social Psychology in Court* (New York: Van Nostrand, 1978), pp. 144-149.

5. This discussion relies in part on William L. Taylor, "A Lawyer Looks at Social Science in the Courts," *Clearinghouse for Civil Rights Research* 7, no. 3-4 (1979): 3.

6. White authorship of segregation laws was openly acknowledged by both parties and the Court in *Rice* v. *Gong Lum* (275 U.S. 78), one of the last *Plessy* decisions of the Supreme Court. See James W. Loewen, *The Mississippi Chinese* (Cambridge, Mass.: Harvard University Press, 1971), pp. 66-69.

7. Much of the desegregation literature is summarized in Nancy St. John, *School Desegration: Outcomes for Children* (New York: Wiley, 1975); Meyer Weinberg, *Minority Students, A Research Appraisal* (Washington, D.C.: National Institute of Education, 1977); Robert Crain and R. Mahard, *Desegregation and*

Black Achievement (Durham: Duke University Institute of Policy Sciences, 1978); and Ronald Henderson and Mary von Euler, "What Research and Experience Teach Us about Desegregating Large Cities," *Clearinghouse for Civil Rights Research* 7, no. 1 (1979): 2-14.

8. Christine H. Rossell, "Social Science Research in Educational Equity Cases," *Review of Research in Education* 8 (1980): 237-250.

9. William Graham Sumner, *Folkways* (New York: New American Library, 1960); and Gunnar Myrdal, *An American Dilemna* (New York: Harper, 1962). The debate is summarized through excerpts in Logan Wilson and William Kolb, *Sociological Analysis* (New York: Harcourt Brace, 1949).

10. For a recent debate about anthropologists' roles, see Lawrence Rosen, "The Anthropologist as Expert Witness," *American Anthropologist* 79 (1977): 555-578; Omer C. Stewart, "An Expert Witness Answers Rosen," *American Anthropologist* 81 (1979): 108-111 and Rosen, "Response to Stewart," *ibid.,* pp. 111-112.

11. Rawleigh H. Ralls describes how and why to locate an economist in "Injury and Wrongful Death Litigation: Time to Find an Economist," *Trial* 13 (1977): 47-48.

12. The initial baffled-but-adulatory reaction of many historians to the controversial quantitative study of slavery, *Time on the Cross,* showed their mathematical naiveté. The ensuring debate increased awareness in the profession of the need to be able to critique treatments of quantitative data.

13. *Keyes* v. *School District No. 1 (Denver),* 93 Sup. Ct. 2686.

14. Robert Moore, *Stereotypes, Distortions and Omissions in U.S. History Textbooks* (New York: Council on Interracial Books for Children, 1977); Lee H. Bowker, "Red and Black in Contemporary American History Texts: A Content Analysis," in *Native Americans Today,* edited by Howard Bahr et al. pp. 101-110 (New York: Harper, 1972); and Neil J. Kressel and James W. Loewen, "How Multicultural Educational Materials Affect Children, *Clearinghouse for Civil Rights Research* 8, no. 2 (1980): 2-5.

15. The node for psychologists as expert witnesses is Robert Buckhout's Center for Responsive Psychology at Brooklyn College and its newsletter, *Social Action and the Law,* although their focus is largely on experts in criminal cases. See also S.L. Brodsky and K.S. Miller, "Coercing Changes in Prisons and Mental Hospitals: The Social Scientist and the Class Action Suit," in *Prevention through Political Action and Social Change,* edited by J.M. Joffe and G.W. Albee, pp. 208-226 (Hanover, N.H.: University Press of New England, 1981); and K. Ellison and Buckhout, *Psychology and Criminal Justice* (New York: Harper, 1981).

16. Discussions of sociologists as experts include, among others, Marvin Wolfgang, "The Social Scientist in Court," *Journal of Criminal Law and Criminology* 65 (1974): 239-247; Peter Rossi, "Market Research Data in Deceptive Advertising Cases," in *The Use/Nonuse/Misuse of Applied Social Research in the Courts,* edited by Michael J. Saks and C.H. Baron, pp. 98-101 (Cambridge,

Mass.: Abt, 1980); and Karl Taeuber, "Sociological Practice in the Courts," *Wisconsin Sociologist* 16 (1979): 112–122.

17. I have not even included every possible social science, let alone all other relevant areas. For instance, James K. Mitchell, an applied geographer, has written "The Expert Witness: A Geographer's Perspective on Environmental Litigation," *Geographical Review* 68 (1978): 209–14.

18. Mark Chesler et al., report that school desegregation experts whom they surveyed felt their gravest shortcoming was "lack of knowledge about the local area" ["Interactions among Scientists, Attorneys and Judges in School Desegregation Litigation," Working Paper 239 (Ann Arbor: University of Michigan Center for Research on Social Organization, 1981) p. 21]. In voting-rights testimony, however, I have not usually found this lack to be grave. The need for thorough knowledge of local conditions and history varies according to the nature of the lawsuit, so the attorney's job is to engage the appropriate mix of local and national experts.

Additional Resources

After each chapter in this book, I supply annotated readings for lawyers or social scientists who want more information on subjects treated in that chapter. These "Further Reading" sections are sometimes followed by other aids. For example, a list of social-science organizations forms the second part of this chapter's additional resources.

Further Reading

In order to promote their use, I have deliberately kept these selections few in number. I call your attention to two other sources of additional readings relevant to this chapter: the chapter's footnotes and the "Further Reading" lists following chapters 2, 3, and 4.

Philip Meyer, *Precision Journalism* (Bloomington: Indiana University Press, 1973), is a sympathetic account of a journalist's encounter with social science and statistics and makes good reading for the attorney who needs to be able to use ideas from those fields but who has been put off by them in the past.

B. Underwood, "Law and the Crystal Ball: Predicting Behavior with Statistical Inference and Individualized Judgment," *Yale Law Journal* 88 (1979): 1408–1448, discusses how to challenge selection systems that are based on predictive criteria; and most selection systems are—for example, university admissions based on "standardized tests" and prior grade-point averages, parole based on systematized prison conduct and offense records, or credit risk evaluations by banks. Hence, this article is an introduction to the use of statistics in a wide range of litigation.

In Marcy Hallock, "The Numbers Game—The Use and Misuse of Statistics in Civil Rights Litigation," *Villanova Law Review* 23 (1977-1978): 5-34, two famous sentences about statistics are taken from judicial opinions:

> In the problem of racial discrimination, statistics often tell much, and Courts listen.

> We believe it evident that if the statistics in the instant matter represent less than a shout, they certainly constitute far more than a mere whisper.

Hallock goes on to treat some subjects that I introduce later, such as the concept of statistical significance, but her article is relevant at this point because it shows some of the ways that social-science data have been used to win class-action lawsuits.

An earlier treatment of "Statistics as Legal Evidence," by Hans Zeisel, *International Encyclopedia of Social Sciences,* Vol. 15 (New York: Macmillan, 1968), pp. 246-250, is well written but dated.

A few lawyers may be without access to a social scientist or may wish to do their own computer analysis of data in preparation for litigation. Statistical Package for the Social Sciences (SPSS) is the most widely used program library in the United States and will probably be available for use on nearby university computers or wherever the computer analysis is being done. N. Nie *et al., Statistical Package for the Social Sciences* (New York: McGraw-Hill, 1975), is the basic paperback manual supplying the computer program commands to calculate the statistics commonly used in social-science research.

Joel Handler, *Social Movements and the Legal System* (New York: Academic Press, 1978), puts class-action litigation into a broader context. He discusses alternatives to litigation and treats extralegal factors such as alliances that can have an impact upon the lawsuit. To some extent, particularly in chapter 4, he treats the relevance of social-science data to this change process.

S. Collins, a law student, summarized the better-known instances of social-science testimony through about 1974 in "The Use of Social Research in the Courts" [in *Knowledge and Policy,* edited by L. Lynn, pp. 145-183 (Washington, D.C.: National Academy of Sciences, 1978)]. Her work is a bit antique because she missed many important pre-1974 cases and of course all recent cases. She also makes errors such as calling psychology "a more-scientific discipline dealing with individual behavior" compared to sociology. Her article does offer value, however, for it introduces many cases and areas compactly.

Organizations of Social Scientists

The following organizations can supply names and addresses of social scientists, sometimes by area and subfield. Each prints a directory of its membership that can be consulted at university libraries or in the relevant department offices:

American Economic Association
1313 21st Avenue South
Nashville, TN 37212
(615) 322-2595

American Educational Research
Association
1230 17th Street NW
Washington, DC 20036
(202) 223-9485

American Historical Association
400 A Street SE
Washington, DC 20003
(202) 544-2422

American Political Science
Association
1527 New Hampshire Avenue NW
Washington, DC 20036
(202) 483-2512

American Psychological
Association
1200 17th Street NW
Washington, DC 20036
(202) 833-7600

American Sociological
Association
1772 N Street NW
Washington, DC 20036
(202) 833-3410

American Statistical
Association
806 15th Street NW, Suite 640
Washington, DC 20005
(202) 393-3253

Organization of American
Historians
112 North Bryan Street
Bloomington, IN 47401
(812) 337-7311

The Planners Network
P.O. 4671
Berkeley, CA 94704
[also 825 Delaware Avenue SW
Washington, DC 20024
(202) 628-1121]

2 How Social Scientists and Lawyers Can Work Together

The purpose of this book is to help lawyers and social-science experts work together to win class-action lawsuits. This chapter covers the process of their working together, from the first work conference, through supplying or generating the necessary data, and through the analysis and tests required and the kinds of courtroom exhibits that must be prepared before trial. The largest part of the chapter then presents a complete outline of testimony for an expert witness, helping attorneys learn what questions to ask and what to avoid and helping social scientists learn what to expect and how to prepare for the courtroom. Tips on behavior in the courtroom are included, and the chapter concludes with suggestions for interaction between attorney and expert after trial. In short, this chapter provides a complete run-through of the attorney-expert relationship.

Reaching an Initial Understanding

Lawyers and social scientists are professionals who face rather different situations and have different needs. Both the lawyer and the scientist want the expert testimony to flow smoothly and to be convincing, but ego or other problems can interfere with proper preparation. These problems can be mitigated if each party is aware of the needs of the other.

Most basic is the need each party has to be heard and respected by the other. Lawyers in particular can sometimes inadvertently convey to experts that the experts are hired hands, getting paid for their work and working for the lawyer, and hence beneath the lawyer. While the lawyer does have the responsibility of directing the case, this attitude will not work. Social scientists do not perceive themselves as employees but as consultants, a relationship of equality. Moreover, competent social scientists see their work as partly directed by the data, not the lawyer, so if they feel a factual situation deserves complex analysis, they will want to analyze the matter complexly, even if the results are counterproductive. Social-science experts must be able to defend their research before other social scientists, whether on the other side of the courtroom or later, in the form of a tenure-review committee or editorial-advisory board. The lawyer must have the patience to deal with this characteristic of the expert, who is a professional concerned about maintaining professional standards. Indeed, the lawyer should take time to seek out the expert's advice on the best data to obtain, the most powerful ways to do the analysis, and the best ways to present the results.

Some social scientists display their own form of occupational arrogance. It is easy for a political scientist or sociologist to feel superior in knowledge about the social world compared to a layperson, including an attorney or judge. Judges and attorneys have not read the scientific literature about the topic at issue, but they already have their own commonsense knowledge about it. There are problems with common sense, and many introductory sociology courses contain exercises that show when common sense is plainly wrong.[1] In the courtroom, these exercises and the put-down of laypersons that they demonstrate can be a hindrance to effective testimony. After all, just as common sense has limitations, so does scientific knowledge. As soon as two social scientists gather to discuss a topic outside their direct research—is there discrimination against women at their university, for instance, or should there be wider general education requirements in the freshman year—it becomes apparent that their common sense is little better than a judge's. Judges and attorneys have knowledge, too—commonsense, everyday knowledge—and it must be reckoned with.[2]

In practice, this means that the lawyer must mesh the exhibits and conclusions offered by the expert with the testimony of plaintiffs and other witnesses, following his conception of the law and the audience—judge or jury. Therefore, when it comes to the exhibits or testimony to be presented to the court, the expert needs to defer to the lawyer. The expert should remain involved intellectually, suggesting every stratagem, pointing out every potential weakness, and raising every objection that comes to mind. The lawyer is expert on trial procedures and strategy. The expert must tell the truth and must not distort the factual reality by errors or omissions; but within the confines of that rule, the expert should listen to the lawyer's conclusions as to what has to be included, what should be deleted. The expert should be true to the data but be responsive to the needs of the case, which needs are the lawyer's determination.

Once mutual respect and a working relationship have been established, the initial conference should deal with the nature of the case and of the expert's participation in it. The attorney should have available for the social scientist a copy of testimony by an expert in prior cases of the same type. If the other side is known to have employed an expert, her testimony in prior cases should be located and supplied. A copy of the complaint or brief should be given to the expert, along with suggestions as to which passages are particularly important. The legal aspects of the case should be explained clearly so that the expert knows the context and purpose of her testimony and exhibits. If the judge in the case has written an opinion in this particular area, it should be provided to the expert so she can form an understanding of his concerns and reasoning. Relevant appellant opinions should be excerpted for the expert. Do we expect to lose and appeal? If so, how might the expert impact upon the appeals court, secondhand? Through all this discussion of strategy, the expert's questions and suggestions should be encouraged. Finally, the factual side of the case, so far as it is known, should be presented by the attorney. Sometimes the data are all already available from discovery, the census, or other sources; sometimes data collection must fall entirely on the expert's shoulders, such as when a survey of community attitudes is required.

Agreement on a data base (the information upon which the expert will rely in her analysis and conclusions) is an important next step, so important that I devote the next section to it. Sometimes the data base can be established at the initial conference; sometimes research by the scientist or discovery by the lawyer is required before the subject can even be discussed intelligently. In the initial conference, the attorney has dominated thus far. The scientist has asked questions. Now the scientist should be asked how she would go about proving what needs to be proved in this case. Can it be done? What data does she require? What analysis would she do? What exhibits would she prepare to convince the court? Now it is the scientist's turn to explain, and the attorney must ask until clarity is reached.

The attorney should ask the expert if she feels comfortable and competent in the role assigned. Should a different expert be sought? If not, explore the expert's feelings as to whether an additional expert should be engaged for some part of the analysis and presentation. Often the lawyer must assist the expert witness to focus, helping her to avoid making the analysis overly complex. The following list provides a sampling of questions the expert and lawyer should ask each other at this point in the conference:

Questions to Ask the Expert
1. Are you qualified to do this job? (If research is involved: Have you done research of this type before?) (If statistics are involved: Have you used these statistical tests before? Can you describe them to me?)
2. Do you have the time for the job? How much lead time will you need? (This can be a problem when the best data are not immediately available or when court dates or dates of deposition change suddenly.) What is your courtroom availability?
3. What can I supply or suggest that will strengthen your testimony?

Questions to Ask the Attorney
1. Do you understand the kinds of conclusions I can probably attest to, if the data turn out as we expect? Will that be adequate? What additional work can I do or suggest that might be helpful to the case?
2. Are the data in final form (if attorney is supplying)? What kind of schedule do you require?
3. Do you understand the ethical constraints under which I must work? (These include protecting any persons interviewed or otherwise studied, obeying the canons of scientific work, and ensuring the morally acceptable use of my research.)

Once lawyer and social scientist are both satisfied with their respective roles, they should discuss and reach agreement on two important points: ethics and a schedule. Ethical handling of the research is required and can be complex, so I have devoted all of the next chapter to it. It must be discussed now because the way data are first collected may make it hard to protect individuals later on. The lawyer must follow the code of legal ethics regarding matters such as performance for the client, supplying necessary material to the court and other side, and so on; the social scientist follows quite a different code regarding anonymity of subjects, appropriate comparison groups, and so on. Now is the time to understand and accommodate each other's needs.

A schedule should also be agreed to now because attorneys and academics are both famous procrastinators. Without a schedule, the attorney is likely to delay getting important data or instructions to the expert until the analysis is already underway, while the social scientist is likely to postpose the analysis until the week before trial. Each form of procrastination leads to its own disaster. For example, the social scientist may spend days doing the analysis, only to learn it must all be done over in order to be precisely correct for court since the attorney neglected an important point or some data need correction; or, too late to do anything about it, the social scientist may find that the results are not as expected, or that some additional piece of information or research step is necessary. Discussion of a schedule should include discussion of interim work products like computer output, drafts of exhibits, and research instructions. The lawyer must tell the social scientist what to expect in the way of requests from the other side to see these work products.

Now is an appropriate time for the expert and client(s) to meet. They may be working together if the client is taking part in obtaining data. If not, the expert still may be curious to meet the person(s) for whom the work is being done, and the client may want to express thanks for the scientist's involvement. (It may be important that the expert work blind, without knowing the names of those parties who allege discrimination, for example; in that case, the attorney should pass on the data, such as personnel files, with names removed and code numbers substituted, and the expert should not meet the plaintiffs until after data analysis is completed.)

Before the end of the initial conference, the lawyer and social scientist should be clear as to the contractual responsibilities of both parties and the rate and method of payment. The lawyer should draft a letter of agreement for the sake of clarity and because otherwise the expert is going out on a limb in doing the work without guarantee of recompense, even of expenses. Also, the expert may need such a letter to demonstrate later that the consultation and testimony did take place. The letter should be drafted in such a way that it can be shown to the other side if requested; indeed, the entire agreement should be aboveboard.

How much should the expert be paid? Let me offer three specific suggestions and then discuss the pros and cons of each. I have charged each of the following rates, depending upon the situation. First, the social scientist can divide her annual salary (including any summer earnings) by 100 and charge that amount per day of preparation and courtroom testimony. A professor earning $35,000 would thus charge $350/day. Second, the scientist may take her basic university salary and divide it by the number of work days in the academic year, including some additional weeks for course preparation. Our professor earning $35,000 might receive $30,000 of this as basic salary; dividing by perhaps 175 work days would lead to a charge of perhaps $175/day. Finally, because the professor believes in the cause or is just starting out as an expert witness and wants the experience, she may elect to charge nothing at all, just expenses, or a nominal amount.

I take into account ability to pay. If I am testifying for the federal government or other large client, I charge the highest fee, based on 1/100 of earnings. This is also appropriate when it is likely that the case will succeed and where the opposing party will have to pay costs. When I am working for a legal-services firm, I might charge the intermediate fee, based on my actual salary per working day. When helping a client who has clearly been wronged and is truly without resources, I have worked free.

Even social scientists who charge based on 1/100 of earnings receive much less per hour than the attorneys who employ them. Expert witnesses may therefore chafe at their unequal pay for equal work. However, expenses are an additional consideration. Lawyers must maintain a secretary and office from their hourly fees. Social scientists who testify infrequently usually pocket their entire fees because their regular employers supply not only offices and secretaries, but also computer facilities, copier, phone, and postage. Accordingly, an expert paid at the 1/100 rate may decide not to charge additionally for small computer runs, xeroxing of a few courtroom exhibits, or other minor expenses, especially if her regular employer does not usually charge for such incidentals. But if a survey was involved, for instance, that required several hours of secretarial time to type, run off, and mail, then the institution should be reimbursed. Again, the initial conference should cover the matter of expenses, with its conclusions becoming part of the letter of agreement between attorney and expert.

Experienced lawyers know that contractual relations with experts can become an issue in court. If an expert works for nothing, presumably because she believes in the case, then that belief can imply bias. Ironically, getting paid by one side implies to the court less beholdenness to that side. Conversely, paying an expert a startlingly large fee may smack of bribery, implying that the expert's conclusions were for sale for a high enough price. A middle course implies that the expert is a professional, working for an appropriate professional fee. To be sure, this fee is paid by one side, but its payment is viewed by the court as inevitable and reasonable.

The expert whose employer may be troubled by her participation should avoid even the appearance of impropriety. For example, if the case challenges a state agency and the social scientist teaches at a state university, it would be wise to make sure that computer use is reimbursed, phone calls to the lawyer are made collect, and work for which the professor seeks reimbursement is done on weekends. That way no one can charge that the university inadvertently subsidized or participated in the testimony.

Data Base

The next step is to agree on the nature of the data that will be required to prove the factual or statistical side of the case. Will these be collected by the scientist, the attorney or plaintiff, a student under the scientist's control or a paralegal assistant to the attorney, or through discovery from the other side? Will a sample be involved? How large? What methods will be used? Why? The data base varies, depending upon what is available and the needs of the case. Some general pointers apply, however.

If other people gather the data for the expert—students, perhaps, or the plaintiff(s), or a secretary of the attorney—it is important that this work be done under the supervision and at the behest of the expert witness. Therefore, the social scientist should talk with the gatherers before they begin, telling them what to watch for, what to collect, and so forth. Then they become agents under her supervision; their interviewing techniques have been refined by her, and they benefit from her expertise. Otherwise the data-gathering process may lose credibility and data may even be inadmissible owing to hearsay. It is strongly recommended that the expert participate, even minimally, in every step of the data collection—that she do some interviews, for instance. It is also important that attorney and expert be clear at the outset as to the responsibilities, supervision, payment, and possible courtroom role of any assistants.

Similar care must be taken to ensure the admissibility of exhibits based on published data or archival sources. If census data will be used in a map or paragraph, prepare a xeroxed copy of the pages on which the data were found. Accompany tables of voting statistics with certified election returns. In short, prepare to submit the best available evidence to ensure the least effective challenge to it.

The need to show the origin of data must not lead to abusing people who supplied it. For ethical reasons, it is wrong to submit to the court (or opposing counsel) completed interview forms or questionnaires unless specific releases, allowing use of their names and opinions in court, were obtained from all respondents. However, names and addresses can be separated from the forms so the forms are submitted naked; then the other side can check the work without compromising confidentiality. Be sure the names and addresses cannot be subpoenaed; social scientists have gone to jail for refusing to turn over records they possessed, in order to maintain research ethics. Also be sure that persons cannot be identified from their replies, even if names have been deleted. Early consultation between lawyer and expert can establish procedures so that the social scientist's concern for informed consent is met while the attorney violates no rule regarding destroying evidence (see chapter 3).

Consultation is also required to make sure that the data the lawyer will provide the scientist (or that the scientist will generate) will be the best possible data, in final form. Nothing is more discouraging to the scientist than to complete an elaborate computer run, only to learn that some of the figures were preliminary. Because final figures must be used in any analysis to be presented to the court, the lawyer should make sure the expert knows this and delays analysis until they are available.

Data Analysis

Although this is the province of the social scientist, the lawyer needs to understand the statistical analysis. The expert must be able to make this analysis clear to the lawyer as a trial run toward making it clear to the judge. The lawyer, meanwhile, must take time to prepare this testimony so that he does not ask statistically inane questions. From the first conference on, the attorney should ask what the data indicate. What assumptions lie behind the statistical tests and techniques? (Chapter 4 introduces some of these assumptions.) Are they met? Attorneys also want to know which test to use and why. The more they understand in the beginning, the less likely they are to raise new questions at the last minute. Usually, if a question on direct examination requires the expert to do any computation on the stand, that signifies inadequate preparation on the attorney's part. Social-science testimony can flow smoothly and effectively but only if the lawyer as well as the expert is prepared.

Another reason why an attorney should understand some principles of data analysis is so he can quickly perform ministudies to see what conclusions the data might support. These small analyses can then help him initially to determine whether to pursue the case and what kind of expert to hire for it. The sign test (chapter 6) and overlapping-percentages analysis (chapter 14) are examples of these quick and easy techniques.

To explain research designs and data analyses clearly and understandably to the court—a lay audience—is an art. Since undergraduate students and the general public also constitute important lay audiences to whom social scientists must communicate, it is an art well worth cultivating. The expert will want to be economical. Methodological prowess can be demonstrated later in a journal article; tailor courtroom testimony to the requirements of the case and the legal situation. The expert should do an extensive and sophisticated analysis, if appropriate, to ensure that she is testifying honestly and to protect against unturned stones that might be flipped over by the other side in cross-examination. However, do not allow pressure from having done the analysis to force "publication" in the form of a complete presentation of the results to the court. Although the expert may have controlled for thirteen variables at once and developed a path analysis unprecedented in elegance, what is presented to the court may need to be a single three-by-two table.

To help the lawyer and social scientist discuss the data analysis, the expert should prepare a simple one-page exhibit for each statistical analysis undertaken, showing the formula, explaining how it works, providing a small example, and citing references in the literature. These exhibits will probably be useful in court later, and they can also help the attorney write the brief after trial.

Occasionally a problem arises when the other side wants to see the results of ongoing data analysis. Some early tests and reports may not have been intended for outside eyes. Usually the claim of privilege for a work product suffices to maintain confidentiality until a finished product is available; again, this is a topic worth some thought by the lawyer ahead of time.

Coping with Negative Results

What if the results of the preliminary data analysis come out wrong? What if the data do not seem to support the contentions made in the complaint? What course should the expert follow? This question has two aspects. First, what should the expert do to meet her obligations to the lawyer, client, and case? Second, what should she do to make sure she has "done her damnedest with the data," as Freud once put it?

Ethically, the expert must do the best she can for the case and client, within the framework of scientific standards of truth and data handling, and also within the constraints of the time and activities for which she is being recompensed. If, after taking the steps suggested in the rest of this section, the expert remains convinced that the facts simply do not support the lawsuit, she must be honest with the attorney and client. Perhaps there is not only no evidence of gender-based discrimination, for example, but even some evidence of favoritism on behalf of women at the company. The social scientist must tell the attorney and must further point out that, if put on the stand, she will have to tell the court. The scientist may therefore recommend that the suit be modified, settled, or simply withdrawn. Perhaps the company's treatment of the individual plaintiff warrants court action without regard for the class that she (in this case) represents.

Of course, the attorney and the client must make the decisions about modifying, settling, or dropping the case. The scientist can only recommend, based on her partial understanding of its factual basis. Even a client in a hopeless situation has the right to legal representation, and may have a right to expert consultation, particularly if she can pay for it. So the social scientist should not get upset if her advice is not followed regarding overall strategy. If the case continues along lines that the expert's testimony would only undermine, however, owing to the fact that the data came out wrong, then the expert should confer with the attorney and drop out of the case. The social scientist cannot then publish the research results without undermining the case or subsequent similar cases. Even though the canons of scientific ethics suggest that data should not be suppressed, and the social scientist's own career might be enhanced by an interesting article based on the findings of the case, role conflict is involved, and the resolution of the conflict must not undermine the expert's role as expert—that is, no data gathered for this lawsuit should be published ever, or without a long delay, if it contravenes the interests of the lawyer and client who provided the occasion for gathering it in the first place.[3]

If the data do not show discrimination against women, to continue our example, the social scientist must be careful to avoid inferring from them that they show absence of discrimination against women. Lack of proof of a finding in one direction is not proof of its opposite. A simple coin-flip example will illustrate: If we suspect a coin is biased, typically coming up heads, we might flip it 10 times, hoping to get a disproportion of heads in the series. If we obtain 5 heads, precisely what would be predicted by chance with an unbiased coin, that does not demonstrate that the coin is unbiased. We merely failed to find that it was biased. A biased coin that would come up heads 70 percent of the time in an infinite series could nevertheless occasionally come up heads only 50 percent of the time in a relatively small series of ten tosses. Indeed, it would do so, by chance alone, in 15 out of every 100 such series.

At this point the expert, attorney, and perhaps plaintiff should caucus to discuss what may have caused the unexpected finding of nondiscrimination. Sometimes there is a great deal of *noise in the system*—my term for the many vagaries of research, such as items on questionnaires that were misunderstood, migration of populations so that they no longer match census-tract figures, and so on. All possible points of such noise should be investigated and the research design tightened to eliminate them. The expert can follow that step by developing hypothetical examples, going so far as to invent some mock data, embodying the discrimination but with unusual additional characteristics. She can subject these examples to the same analysis used with the real data; if the discrimination is now masked, that may point to a problem in the statistical design.

A common and appropriate tactic in social science is called controlling, or partialling. Here the expert realizes that a relationship may be masked by another relationship, so the third factor is eliminated. For instance, I worked on a case in which the employer apparently discriminated against black men but not black women, so when all the cases were compared along racial lines, little discrimination was apparent. Partialling by sex—looking at the male part of the data separately—disclosed the true pattern. Chapter 15 deals with controlling for third variables and should be reread by attorney and expert when faced with this kind of situation. A session with attorney, expert, and plaintiff can suggest possible masking variables that may be at work. There are also some nonparametric statistical techniques that can help to explore situations with small Ns—small samples—and can sometimes be more powerful than their more-common parametric alternatives.

Data Presentation

Data presentation is the neglected third of methods/statistics courses (which include data collection, data analysis, and data presentation but which usually overconcentrate on analysis). Perhaps that is why even experienced social scientists sometimes make elementary errors in data presentation. Moreover, almost no social scientists have had coursework in graphics or design, so they are not skilled at presenting data to laypersons in a form that is inviting or convincing. Chapters 4 and 5 discuss these topics at some length. Several pointers need to be stressed here, however, because they are topics that the lawyer and expert should discuss as the work is continuing.

Be sure that the planned presentation will be clear, simple, and effective. A complex table should be broken down into two tables, or better yet, two barographs or two maps. Well before trial, and well before all data analysis is complete, at least one exhibit for trial can usually be prepared from census data if nothing else. This task should be completed early so lawyer and scientist can go over the exhibit, making sure the lawyer understands it and that it is clear and effective. Problems ironed out now will avoid much grief with later exhibits.

The expert has two audiences: the trial judge (and jury, if there is one) and the appellate court. The second is reachable only through the record, which should therefore contain well-done exhibits with conclusions built in. At the bottom of each figure or table, be sure to include a sentence of conclusion or interpretation. The trial court or an appellate court may review the exhibit without connecting it to the transcript of courtroom testimony. This approach may be new to the social scientist, who usually constructs rather stark tables that are then embedded in the prose of an article or book; but an expert's prose in court is verbal and may even be excluded by the trial judge. If testimony is excluded, then the lawyer must extemporaneously make a proffer of proof, summarizing for the record what the expert would have said. This is a demanding task, particularly since the attorney is not expert in statistics or social science. Exhibits incorporating conclusions become an essential element of the proffer, making a much more-effective record for appeal.

Small one-page exhibits should also be developed to present the methods and statistical analyses used by the expert. It is just as important for the trial judge to understand the methodology as it is to understand the data and conclusions from the data. The lawyer may also wish to have his expert do a report for introduction in evidence at trial, containing the methods, data, and conclusions in tables and narrative form. The report, resembling a social-science article or paper, can help the attorney see any potential problems with the witness's testimony in advance. It also aids the trial judge, who can read the report at his leisure, even before the trial testimony is transcribed. Again, if the expert's testimony is excluded in court, the report itself constitutes the proffer.

Pretrial Conference

A day or two before trial, the attorney and expert will usually meet to go over the outline of testimony in order to tell each other what to expect in court. They might begin by discussing what the expert is to bring to court. Most important are several copies of all her exhibits, in order, including the expert's vita, for these exhibits will guide attorney and scientist through the testimony. Other items in a basic courtroom survival kit include

An electronic calculator;

A pellucid elementary statistics handbook;

A detailed advanced statistics text with tables;

A one-page bibliography of the standard authorities (statistical, research methods, and substantive areas) whose approaches and concepts were relied upon;

Best sources for data (see the discussion earlier in the chapter);

Any books or articles that have quotations supporting your conclusions or contradicting the opposing social scientist or position;

Work products, including computer programs and questionnaires, providing there is nothing untoward within them, such as names of persons interviewed, that were not to be provided to the court. (The expert should assume that if an item is in the courtroom, the other side may ask for it. Accordingly, items that should not be seen by the other side should not be brought.)

The pretrial conference should also give the expert some idea as to what the judge will be like, what courtroom norms to observe, and what to expect from the opposing attorney during cross-examination. If the expert has never testified before, the attorney might suggest she sit in on some prior trial, perhaps in the same room and with the same judge she will face, so that the setting and procedures will be familiar to her. (We know that unfamiliarity and its concomitant nervousness can decrease "standardized" test scores; there is no reason to assume that social scientists are immune to such worries.) Also, if your side is putting on several witnesses, consider seeking agreement with opposing counsel to avoid the rule that requires that witnesses be sequestered before they testify. Then a new expert can grow accustomed to the courtroom setting and judge while watching other experts perform. (Of course, there are often tactical reasons to invoke the rule. For example, perhaps you do not want one expert to be questioned about another expert's conclusions, or you may want to sequester the other side's witnesses from yours and each other.) In any event, during the pretrial conference the attorney should tell the expert what he knows about the judge—Is he patient? Upset by statistics? Does he appreciate brevity? Humor?

Experts who have not testified before need to be told how to dress and behave. They may unwittingly violate courtroom norms if not briefed about them. For example, even in the public seating area, spectators are supposed to be attentive to proceedings. The expert who is waiting all day to testify may grow bored and want to read a newspaper. This is usually a forbidden act, and the judge or marshal who notices someone reading in court will retain no more positive feelings toward that person than the professor who observes a student reading in class.

In the pretrial conference the expert should be asked to role-play her behavior on the witness stand. The social scientist needs to get used to the idea of speaking rather loudly and slowly and spelling key words so the court reporter can get everything down correctly. The witness and attorney need to agree as to the expert's use of notes. Experts may want to have an outline of their testimony in front of them, as they would for a classroom lecture, but for two reasons this may not be advisable. First, the other side may have the right to obtain the notes, which means they will have to be prepared carefully to exhibit only front-stage behavior. Second, the expert may seem to rely on her notes and thus not to know her subject matter as securely as the term *expert* might imply. I would suggest that the expert bring notes, particularly as to formulas or other matters she may not have committed to memory, but to avoid relying on those notes during trial for an outline of testimony. Her testimony will already be outlined in two ways: (1) her organized list of exhibits and (2) the list of questions to be asked by the attorney. It would be excellent if the expert would bring to the pretrial conference a detailed outline of testimony in question-and-answer format. The attorney can then take her outline and develop from it his own list of questions to put to her in court.

Other tips on courtroom behavior are sprinkled throughout the next section. The expert and attorney might go over that section during the pretrial conference. If some suggestions within it seem inappropriate, they should be discarded, while the remaining points can become a guide as to what will happen.

Cross-examination may particularly worry the neophyte expert. The attorney, too, has reason to worry, lest his expert become argumentative, defensive, or noncommittal in response to hostile questioning. Hostility is built into the adversarial system and rarely implies interpersonal hostility on the part of the questioner; the expert must avoid letting feelings of hostility creep into her replies. The expert should be cautioned to be brief on cross-examination, not to volunteer a lot, and not to allow harassment. For instance, if opposing counsel interrupts answers, the witness should know that she is as much in charge of the conversation as the lawyer; therefore, an appropriate response is to say deferentially, "Sir, you have interrupted my answer to the previous question you asked," and then to continue courteously with what was being said. The witness should also be advised to pause a moment before answering, to gather thoughts and to allow counsel to object to the question if appropriate.

The expert needs to have a sense of proportion as to what was essential in her testimony and what was unimportant detail. If her testimony is shaken on cross-examination as to some detail, she needs to concede to the strong points made by the other side, rather than to appear to be an unyielding fanatic, while at the same time demonstrating that the point is not crucial to the major generalizations of her direct testimony. She should not be argumentative, but at the same time, she should not allow herself to be limited to yes/no answers that will be built by opposing counsel into an argument quite different than what the expert meant to convey.

I would like to highlight three positive traits in the expert's response to cross-examination shown in figure 2-1. First, the expert did not go out on a limb regarding Wisconsin data she knew nothing about. At the same time, she did not use her ignorance to appear argumentative. Literacy levels in Wisconsin are probably high, given its relative absence of recent immigrants and massive poverty. Admitting as much does not damage one's factual case regarding some other locale and population.

Second, our expert did not argue every point. She was concise and simply replied "yes" when asked if 20 percent illiteracy represents a crisis, for example. On direct examination, she had said that 20 percent illiteracy and semiliteracy was what she was talking about but that it could be assumed that the opposing lawyer was merely using *illiteracy* as shorthand for the longer term and hence did not require correction. She held her temper, and she was willing to be pinned down regarding the partly arbitrary character of her definition.

Third, however, she quietly indicated objection to the "yes" answer she had been forced to supply. Probably the attorney will not let her introduce reasons for her choice since he has his own goals in mind for her cross-examination, but her lawyer has been alerted and can ask for her reasons after cross-examination ends, during what is called redirect. He will want to eliminate from the court's mind any taint from the word *arbitrary*. Lawyers cringe at experts' use of this word because they fear that it connotes an indefensibly capricious cut-off or definition. An expert's cut-off or definition is not arbitrary in the sense of capricious, but is supported by good reasons, even though another cut-off point could be just as reasonable.

The following questions and answers supply examples of how to deal with hostile cross-examination questions without arguing or conceding. On direct examination, the expert has testified that, in her judgment, if 20 percent or more of a population is illiterate or semiliterate, that constitutes a crisis regarding adult educational needs.

Q: You say 20 percent represents a crisis level of illiteracy, is that right?

A: Yes, sir.

Q: What if I showed you a county in Wisconsin, say, with 19 percent of its adults illiterate?

A: That would be a problem.

Q: Pretty unusual, for Wisconsin, wouldn't you say?

A: I don't know Wisconsin data, but I imagine so.

Q: But not a crisis?

A: Well, it would be a matter of definition.

Q: So it's arbitrary, isn't it? Your definition of crisis.

A: There are good reasons for my selection of the 20 percent level. And in the literature . . .

Q (interrupting): Just yes or no. Isn't there an element of arbitrariness in your selection of a 20 percent cut-off?

A: Yes.

Q: So 30 percent could also be a reasonable definition for crisis? Some experts might even choose 50 percent?

A: I would like to explain the nonarbitrary reasons for my use of 20 percent. But yes, some experts might choose 30 percent.

Figure 2-1. Coping with Hostile Questions

Cross-examination also faces witnesses who are being deposed. A deposition is basically similar to courtroom testimony, including direct questions by the attorney, cross-examination by opposing counsel, submission of exhibits, and the like, conducted in the absence of the judge but in the presence of a court reporter. Depositions are of two types—discovery and trial. Ideally, each side should take the discovery deposition of the other side's expert before trial. Chapter 16 tells how to depose their expert. When our expert is to be deposed, the attorney and social scientist will want to have a predeposition conference, covering the same points as the pretrial conference. Depositions requested by the other side should be considered the same as cross-examination. In neither setting should the expert do a lot of volunteering. Her responses should be concise, to the point, and even dull. Depositions are usually requested by the other side in order to learn what the expert is going to say so her conclusions can be nailed down and a rebuttal prepared. This purpose must be accomodated. The witness must be responsive, but she should not try to win over the opposition by the brilliance of her work or words. This brilliance she should save for the judge. Bearing that caution in mind, then, an expert can treat a discovery deposition like cross-examination.

Trial depositions are different. Attorneys depose their own witnesses for two reasons. First, logistics of distance and conflicting schedules may make it easier to enter an expert's findings into the court record through deposition rather than courtroom appearance. Second, when dealing with a judge known to be hostile to the kind of arguments to be made and likely to bar them altogether, a deposition offers a surer way to get material into the record for appeal. Spontaneity and direct contact with the judge (and jury) are lost on deposition, and attorneys always fear that judges don't really read exhibits and depositions submitted on paper, so expert witnesses can usually expect to appear in the courtroom. Trial depositions, entered in lieu of courtroom appearance, should be treated like court itself. Even though the judge is not present, the expert is trying to reach him and convince him of the soundness of her work and conclusions.

Outline of Testimony

Testimony or deposition of an expert social scientist will usually follow the following outline:

Qualifications,

Explanation of the nature of the data base,

Nature of the statistical test(s) performed by the expert and discussion as to why they are the appropriate tests,

Presentation of the results and conclusions,

Discussion, even speculation, involving interpretations by the expert.

Each of these elements is discussed at greater length in the following sections.

Qualifications

Move from the general to the particular. Begin with education, highlighting coursework in research methods, statistics, and relevant substantive areas. Moving through teaching and research experience, highlight areas using the statistical techniques or touching the substantive questions related to this research. Discuss relevant consultation, publication, and other activities. By the conclusion of this section, the court should perceive the witness as a well-qualified social scientist who has particular familiarity with the literature and research methods related to the topic at hand. A thoughtful, even artful, up-to-date vita buttresses this section. This vita should be modified to relate effectively to this court appearance.

Explanation of the Nature of the Data Base

Now that the expert's credentials and competencies have been told, the particular basis that legitimates her testimony in this case must be established. Prior witnesses or discovery may have generated the data with which the social scientist worked, in which case all that is needed is a reference to the appropriate exhibits and testimony. An earlier section described the care needed to ensure the admissibility of the data. If the expert gathered the data personally, she should describe at this point how this was done, in considerable detail. This is the methods section so essential to the persuasive power of social science, as portrayed in the first chapter, and as such it should not be dry as journal articles typically are. A series of tangible problems were solved as the expert took a sample (if one was involved), developed an observation form, or chose a census indicator for poverty across sections of the city. These problems should be presented suspensefully, and their solutions portrayed as the best compromises that could be found, so the judge empathizes with the work that has been done and the data that has been gathered as a result.

Statistical Analysis and Tests

Omit this step and move directly to the results when no elaborate statistical analysis was performed on the data. For example, if census bloc statistics were used to develop a map of poverty in the city, after describing the source of data and the methods used in combining the figures and determining shading categories, the expert can introduce the map and tell what it shows. Then she will move back to the description of the data base to introduce the evidence on which the next exhibit or conclusions were grounded. When significance tests, statistics of association, or other techniques have been used that are not in the everyday vocabulary of laypeople, then the expert and attorney should plan to explain them at some length. Suggestions for making this explanation clear have already been provided.

    In the presentation of testimony based upon these techniques, it is important to build in the court's mind the (correct) impression that statistics is a science and that the computed probabilities result from exact mathematical calculations, not opinion.[4] The terms *calculation* and *result* are recommended instead of *estimate*. Estimate has wide currency in statistics and social science; we use the mean (average) income of a sample of undergraduates, for instance, to form an estimate of the mean family income of an entire student body. In common parlance and in courtrooms unused to expert witnesses, however, estimate has a meaning that verges upon "guess." To use the term in the courtroom may invite misinterpretation, therefore, since a statistical estimate is not a guess but a precise calculation that eventuates in a range or interval within which the true population income (to continue our example) is almost certain to lie. It is important, then, for the expert to state, "I computed the band of incomes within which the mean family income for the entire student body is almost certain to fall; that band is $29,600 to $34,500." Later, then, the degree of confidence can be added (see chapter 4) after that concept has been explained to the court.

Presenting the Results in Court

If the suggestions regarding data presentation found earlier in this chapter have been followed, as well as those in chapters 4 and 5, then presenting the results in court will be a manageable task. The expert and lawyer will each have copies of the exhibits, which they have discussed and which contain the major conclusions at the bottom of each chart or table. The attorney helps the expert move from the bare results to the statistical analysis of them to the interpretation of their meaning and discussion of their importance. At this point, it can be helpful for the attorney to ask, "Is this your opinion, doctor, or would any competent social scientist or statistician have come up with this same conclusion?" The witness can then reply that virtually anyone would have used the same basic statistical test she did and would have come out with identical calculations and conclusions. Then the attorney and expert move on to the next part of the investigation and the next exhibit, and the cycle begins again.

Discussion

This section needs to be carefully reviewed so that witness and attorney know what to expect. At this point, the data and conclusions have been presented; what is needed is to make the facts sing, as an attorney once explained to me. Carefully controlled speculation, based on logical and accepted social-science postulates, is called for. If the expert has determined that the white elected officials in a county have been elected by a white bloc vote, for instance, while blacks have strongly voted for someone else, it also follows that those officials will likely be more responsive to the needs and interests of the white population than to their black constituents. After all, it is an accepted principle of political science that those who elect someone have more influence with him or her afterwards than those who did not. Citations are legion. Speculation to that point is hardly speculation but is based on the literature.

In order to avoid the charge of speculation, the attorney and witness must carefully restrain the scope of their questions and answers. The lawyer cannot put words into the mouth of the social scientist. Also, an expert who is expert on everything is expert on nothing. There need to be areas in which the expert does not claim expertise. She cannot claim to be knowledgeable in all areas of social science, as they touch upon questions involved in the lawsuit, without destroying her credibility as a true expert in her area of specialization. The lawyer and expert should discuss this point carefully, particularly regarding cross-examination questions. No statement should be risked that the expert does not know to be true. Useful is the phrase, "In have no direct knowledge of that from my own studies, although I do have an opinion," or, weaker, "This is outside the field of my particular expertise, but as an informed social scientist I can speculate as to what most of my colleagues in that area would conclude," followed by a pause. If the judge then asks the expert to go ahead, any objection from the other side has been headed off; if the judge calls a halt, then he is in the position of appreciating the honesty of the witness and implying that the rest of her testimony has been expert. In sum, the phrase "I don't know" can be a signal of strength, not of weakness.

Conclusions

In the discussion and interpretation of the data, the expert has her best chance to say something stirring to make an impact that the judge will remember, to emphasize the most important conclusions of her entire day in court. The previous paragraphs stressed a need for caution and control, but that emphasis should not be allowed to lead to dull testimony, especially in this last part of the work. The audience is tired, the expert and attorney may be tired, and the subject matter of research methods and statistical analyses is hardly one to rouse everyone to a frenzy. Now is the time for the attorney to appear interested and the expert to be personable and engaging.

Academic social scientists are trained to be cautious, to qualify their every statement. We learn in graduate school that epistemology (the study of how we know things) is full of pitfalls, that we can never know things for certain, that probablistic knowledge is all we can hope to attain, and that even the most established scientific theories are mere paradigms, open to possible revision. In everyday life, it is equally true that we have no certain knowledge that the sun will rise tomorrow morning, but we structure our lives in anticipation of it.

Overstressing caution in reporting research itself is a bias that leads to incorrect conclusions.[5] The scientist who is reluctant to conclude she has proved that women were discriminated against in pay simply because of their sex, when her data strongly indicate that they were, may think she has made some important statement about epistemological caution, but the court may just treat her reluctance to be definite as a sign of weakness from a wishy-washy expert.

A special prerogative of expert witnesses is the right to draw conclusions based on the evidence. That right should not be overused, but it is wholly vitiated by experts who cannot bear to say, "I know this to be true. . . ." I believe that proof in science means what it does in law—beyond a reasonable doubt—so I have no trouble saying that the data prove that race accounts for almost all of the variance in election outcomes in a Southern county, for instance. I will go further and assert that the outcome is caused by race or by factors themselves highly correlated with race. The social scientist who does have trouble with such statements should consider how to present probabilistic statements to a judge. A heuristic example can be presented, early in the testimony, to educate the court to the uncertainty of scientific conclusions while at the same time showing that the expression of uncertainty is merely a way of being careful about what is being said. Some social scientists may be loath to draw conclusions on matters that need study for another decade. Yet best judgments are often desperately needed by the court, especially when definitive conclusions are not yet available.

Another problem on the stand is keeping the judge's (and jury's) attention. The attorney can help the expert to communicate by asking short questions. After a long answer, the attorney can ask the expert to restate its main point. The attorney can also make repeated references to the judge through such phrases as, "Dr. Smith, would you tell the court what your research shows regarding . . . ." Ahead of time, the expert should be asked to address some remarks to the judge, saying "Your Honor, my research does show . . .", and maintaining eye contact with him, even though the questions are coming from a third person, the attorney. In short, the attorney and social scientist need to present themselves effectively, strategically, sometimes even theatrically. Again, this seems to violate an alleged tradition of diffidence in science, of letting the data speak for themselves, so scientists may be weak performers.[6] A related problem is the fact that very few social scientists have had even a single course in teaching methods so that many of them do not know how to impart information effectively. All that can be imparted here on the subject is this suggestion: Attorney and expert should consider at some length how to teach the sometimes complex statistical points to the judge and jury. Getting the research and analysis right is not the whole job; communicating it effectively is also required.

At any break in testimony, it is important for expert and lawyer to provide positive feedback to each other, even if it must be forced. The attorney should be particularly sure to compliment the witness, who will be anxious to know how she is doing. Suggestions can then be made in a context of mutual support. However, coaching the witness during breaks must be avoided.

After Trial

After trial, remarks can be more candid, although they should still be construct-ive and supportive of both attorney and expert. While the experience is still fresh, the lawyer and witness should debrief each other. This can be done over a beer after trial or over the phone the next day. The lawyer might begin by asking the witness if the trial went as she expected. The attorney might then ask about his own performance, particularly if asking questions about social-science re-search that was new to him. The expert should ask to have her performance critiqued, in turn.

Immediately after testifying, the expert may be accosted by members of the press. It is always appropriate to share exhibits with them and to repeat or clarify one's testimony. However, most questions by the press will probe beyond one's expertise or raise issues the attorney or plaintiff should handle. For ex-ample:

Don't you feel this problem afflicts *every* city?

What do you think should be the result of this case?

How much were you paid to come here to testify today?

In some situations, effective replies by the expert may become part of a hard-hitting and useful article or television interview, helpful to public opinion and hence to the plaintiff's case. In other situations, remarks by the expert may irritate a judge or otherwise provoke matters adversely. If the expert and attor-ney discuss this issue ahead of time, the expert will know what kinds of ques-tions to handle and what areas should be referred to the attorney for comment.

Several tidying-up tasks confront the lawyer. He should be sure to send the expert a letter of thanks for participation in the case, which may later prove helpful to the social scientist's career. The lawyer might also encourage the ex-pert to publish in a social-science journal an article based on the data and analy-sis, which might then be useful in future cases, either as an exhibit or to bolster the credentials of its author. The lawyer can invite the expert to share a draft for prepublication comment, which will aid the author and can also help ensure that the article avoids unwittingly counterproductive statements or errors. The lawyer must also remember to share with the expert a copy of trial testimony, seeking review and correction of any errors, and a copy of the decision or out-come.

This chapter has described the actual flow of interaction between lawyer and social scientist as they work together seeking victory in a class-action suit. Later chapters do not deal so directly with the process of interfacing. The central chapters, 6 through 14, describe specific research techniques or statistical tests of proved courtroom usefulness. Each technique or test is linked with a substantive area, but this is merely for the purpose of example; the methods are of much wider utility. Chapters 5 and 15 discuss the use of census and other existing data in court and how to control for extraneous variables. The presentations in all of these chapters are not technical and can be understood by the attorney with no statistical background. Reading them provides him with many suggestions to make to his witness and helps him understand what the expert is talking about. The chapters can spur the social scientist to consider many ideas she might otherwise have overlooked. The scientist and lawyer can modify these techniques to deal with a wide range of issues likely to be encountered in class-action litigation.

Chapters 3, 4, and 16 are more general and relate to any case. The ethical imperatives under which social scientists must work are so strict as to rule out some kinds of research of courtroom value; conversely, social scientists need to understand the principles that guide lawyers as they help flesh-and-blood clients in life-and-death settings. Chapter 3 covers these considerations. The next chapter is particularly oriented toward lawyers, teaching them many of the terms they will need in order to use social-science experts effectively. Chapter 16 is for expert and attorney alike and covers how to deal with the other side— how to cross-examine or depose their expert.

Notes

1. See, among others, Ian Robertson, *Sociology* (New York: Worth, 1979), p. 9. See also J. Loewen, "Introductory Sociology for the Privileged: Four Classroom Exercises," *Teaching Sociology* 6 (1979): 222–228.

2. C. Lindblom and D. Cohen, *Usable Knowledge* (New Haven: Yale University Press, 1979). See also comments by a judge, R.J. Hallisey, in *The Use/ Nonuse/Misuse of Applied Social Research in the Courts,* edited by M.J. Saks and C. Baron, pp. 135–140 (Cambridge, Mass.: Abt, 1980).

3. No doubt no hard-and-fast rule can presume to cover all cases, so there are probably exceptions to this one. Chapter 3 offers additional related pointers.

4. *Science* is here used imprecisely, since mathematics is not a science (just as grammar is not a form of literature).

5. Gunnar Myrdal, "Prologue," *Asian Drama* (New York: Pantheon, 1968).

6. Scientists do not really follow this norm, as any student of science knows. For a lively tale of how scientists really promote themselves and their findings, see J. Watson, *The Double Helix* (New York: Atheneum, 1968).

Additional Resources

Further Reading on Research Methods

The lawyer who wants an introduction to research methods might consult H. Smith, *Strategies of Social Research* (Englewood Cliffs, N.J.: Prentice-Hall, 1975). In short, readable chapters, this book explains each part of the research process from ethics to interpretation. It is written for social scientists, but the lawyer or other nonscientist will not find the language difficult, only unfamiliar.

Even simpler is J. Wiseman and M. Aron, *Field Projects for Sociology Students* (Cambridge, Mass.: Schenkman, 1970), which provides five-page summaries of eighteen research techniques. Ignore the student exercises.

Social-science experts should not immediately strike out on their own when facing an assignment but should see what other researchers facing similar situations have done. A good starting point is D. Miller, *Handbook of Research Design and Social Measurement* (New York: McKay, 1977), a compendium of books, scales, and other aspects of research design, helpfully arranged and annotated.

If data must be collected, see J. Fiedler, *Field Research* (San Francisco: Jossey-Bass, 1978). Many (although by no means all) social-science investigations of potential discrimination must be on-site; this book suggests ways of managing field research, particularly if the project must be large scale.

E. Webb et al., *Unobtrusive Measures* (Chicago: Rand McNally, 1966) suggests ways of collecting data other than through asking people questions. The first chapter is marred by sociological jargon, but later chapters can spur the imaginative mind to develop sources of data that are particularly authoritative because they are physical rather than created through opinions voiced in interviews or questionnaires. A practical guide to content analysis is included at the end of K. Krippendorff, *Content Analysis: An Introduction to its Methodology* (Beverly Hills: Sage, 1980).

References to other sources on specific social-science methods are found at the end of later chapters in this book, mostly on an introductory level, understandable by the lawyer as well as the social scientist. Most are standard resources in the field and are not to be disparaged merely because they are clear. In addition to those works, three publisher's series are of particular importance regarding applications of methodology and statistics. Many of the works in these series are on the cutting edge of their discipline, and some are written so as to be unintelligible to the average social scientist, let alone the average nonscientist, which restricts their usefulness. Nonetheless, potential social-science experts should be aware of them:

Quantitative Applications in the Social Sciences (series), Beverly Hills: Sage. See also other Sage books in evaluation research, methodology, and statistics.

Sociological Methodology (annual), San Francisco: Jossey-Bass. See also other Jossey-Bass books in methodology and statistics.

Various Wiley (New York) books in methodology and statistics.

Further Reading on Lawyer-Expert Relations

Morgan P. Ames, "Preparation of the Expert Witness," *Trial* 13 (August 1977): 20–28, offers fifteen "fundamental principles in the science (or art) of preparing an expert to take the stand." I disagree with some of his points, but most are well written and well taken. For example, Ames discusses the problems created by the expert who, from excessive modesty, states on the stand that she is no expert or implies that her findings are merely speculative. He also supplies specific suggestions for the lawyer and witness to go over before trial.

Mark Chesler et al., "Interactions among Scientists, Attorneys, and Judges in School Desegregation Litigation," Working Paper no. 230 (Ann Arbor: University of Michigan Center for Research on Social Organization, 1981), although an executive summary of a longer forthcoming report, contains useful quotations from social scientists, lawyers, and judges. These quotes were not intended to teach lawyers and prospective witnesses how to work with each other, but some sections—"The Conduct of Cross-Examination," "Preparation for Testimony," and "What Is a Good Witness?"—have that effect.

W.P. Finfrock and B.C. Spradlin, "How to Organize and Present Statistical Evidence," *Practical Lawyer* 24 (June 1978): 67–76, is an elementary presentation of how to use an expert witness in a case. It covers many points and is a useful introduction.

A. Konopka tells why social-science experts are allowed to testify and have little problem with the hearsay rule in *The Use/Nonuse/Misuse of Applied Social Research in the Courts,* edited by M.J. Saks and C. Baron (Cambridge, Mass.: Abt, 1980). See also "Statistical Evidence and the Hearsay Rule," in *Sources and Uses of Social and Economic Data: A Manual for Lawyers,* edited by L. Goodman, chapter 1 (Washington, D.C.: Bureau of Social Science Research, 1973). Since the bureau is a branch of the Legal Services Program, local legal-services lawyers are likely to have a copy of Goodman's book.

Harry M. Philo and L.M. Atkinson, "Products Liability: The Expert Witness", *Trial* 14 (November 1978): 37–41, supplies pointers regarding witness-lawyer interactions that apply generally, making this a useful small article.

David Sive offers pointers about the nature of cross-examination in "Scientists in the Courtroom," in *Scientists in the Legal System,* edited by W. Thomas, pp. 103–107 (Ann Arbor: Ann Arbor Science Publishers, 1974).

Karl Taeuber and Thomas Pettigrew had an interesting debate in 1979 regarding the payoffs and pains resulting from appearing as an expert witness in school desegregation cases. Pettigrew's comments are published as chapter 2 of Jack Greenberg et al., *Schools and the Courts* (Eugene: University of Oregon ERIC Clearinghouse on Educational Management, 1979). Taeuber's comments, "Social Science Evidence and Adversary Proceedings," are available as a "Note" from the University of Wisconsin Institute for Research on Poverty (Madison: 1979). Both references implicitly suggest steps that lawyers and witnesses can take to make their interactions more fruitful. However, their greater value is to sensitize social scientists to the differences between the court setting and a classroom or social-science-convention session. Taeuber points out effectively that the adversarial process of determining truth in the courtroom is not necessarily inferior to the scientific review process in academia.

Another paper by Taeuber, "Sociological Practice in the Courts," *Wisconsin Sociologist* 16 (1979): 112–123, is more specific in its suggestions for handling depositions, cross-examination, and other steps of the litigation process. Since Taeuber writes with humor, he is also enjoyable to read.

Marvin Wolfgang, "The Social Scientist in Court," *Journal of Criminal Law and Criminology* 65 (1974): 239–247, gives experts some idea of one style of cross-examination they may face.

3

Ethical Imperatives

Social-science researchers are supposed to obey several ethical considerations; almost every text on research methods discusses ethics.[1] One set of rules applies to treatment of the people directly encountered by the researcher—the subjects of the research. We call these rules microethics. A second set of considerations relates to the probable use of the research when finished—its implications for the group studied, for the social-science discipline, and for society as a whole. These wider issues we designate macroethics. Attorneys need to understand both levels of concern so they can obtain the social-science help they need without asking the researcher to violate a principle. They can address ethical questions raised by the researcher more effectively if they understand the principles underlying those questions. Social scientists who do research related to a legal case need to learn about the standards of ethical conduct that have grown up in the practice of law over the past three centuries. This chapter begins with a discussion of legal ethics as they affect the work of an expert witness. Then it discusses microethics and macroethics, particularly as they apply to research related to courtroom use. This organization reflects the fact that the lawyer and expert, as a team, will begin by obeying legal ethics but will also follow the additional cautions required for ethical social science.

Legal Ethics

Attorneys get more discussion of ethical issues in law school than social scientists get in graduate school. They need it. The issues they confront daily require them to affect the lives and fortunes of others, in situations where their own benefit is directly at stake. The social scientist lecturing in the classroom, or even researching in the factory, rarely faces such direct conflicts of interest. One result of this is that the code of ethics of the American Bar Association (ABA) is many times longer than that adopted by any social-science organization. Following is a summary of points in the ABA code that bear directly on the work of an expert witness:

EC 7-1: The duty of a lawyer, both to his client and to the legal system, is to represent his client zealously within the bounds of the law.

EC 7-10: [This duty] . . . does not militate against his concurrent obligation to treat with consideration all persons involved in the legal process and to avoid the infliction of needless harm.

EC 7-20: [There must be] . . . competent, adverse presentation of evidence and issues. . . .

EC 7-26: The law and Disciplinary Rules prohibit the use of fraudulent, false, or perjured testimony or evidence.

EC 7-27: Because it interferes with the proper administration of justice, a lawyer should not suppress evidence that he or his client has a legal obligation to reveal or produce.

EC 7-28: Witnesses should always testify truthfully and should be free from any financial inducements that might tempt them to do otherwise. . . . A lawyer may pay or agree to pay an expert witness a reasonable fee for his services as an expert. But in no event should a lawyer pay or agree to pay a contingent fee to any witness.[2]

No intrinsic conflict exists between most of these rules and the ethical canons of science in general, or social science in particular. The major apparent conflict relates to the adversary system. Although there are adversary relationships within social science, such as when one researcher tries, with new data, to rebut the findings or interpretations of another, according to the ideals of science both parties seek nothing at the expense of the other but seek as a common goal the more-correct understanding of the issue. Each scientist is supposed to include in her presentation a substantial treatment of interpretations that differ from her own so that her readers will have a context from which to judge her own new claims. In the courtroom, however, the lawyer will not want to elicit from his own witness a presentation of facts and theories that argue against the interpretation of the situation that he and his witness seek to establish.

In practice, this difference is more apparent than real. The treatment of alternative viewpoints in most scientific articles really amounts to nothing more than the old debater's trick of admitting the negative only in order to counter it or neutralize it by placing it in a strategic location within one's argument. In some situations, social scientists will become uncomfortable with the exaggeration or one-sided use of their findings by the attorneys who employed them. In such cases, a full, frank discussion should be instigated by the expert; if she is being asked to state more than she knows, there may be cross-examination troubles as well as a moral issue. If the data do not allow the expert to say what the attorney thinks the case demands, then either the expert's role should be more narrowly limited or she should withdraw entirely from the proceedings. Only the expert can decide this, but she should not suppress her discomfort in hopes that the situation will improve because it will not, unless discussed directly.

If the data really do lie on one side, the expert should not feel guilty about testifying one sidedly. Gunnar Myrdal has pointed out that our allegedly scientific emphasis on moderate evenhanded statements is itself a bias, a bias particularly inappropriate in the courtroom.[3] The adversary process at least guarantees that one's work will not be ignored or unthinkingly boosted, but will be scrutinized by a lawyer and perhaps an expert whose interest lies in destroying it. Hence the scientist need not feel forced to do the other side's job for them by indicating the most telling case that could be made against her findings. As Karl Taeuber has put it, tell the truth and nothing but the truth, but do not feel compelled to tell the whole truth, at least not if this means presenting all the findings and interpretations counter to the researcher's own findings and convictions.[4]

Occasionally an enthusiastic or unscrupulous lawyer will encourage an expert to reach conclusions that are not justifiable by the data or to state generalizations that are simply far too general. The social scientist will refuse and can cite as justification the prohibition of fraudulent testimony contained in the ABA code. Occasionally, too, an enthusiastic or unscrupulous social scientist will invent data or reach conclusions not supported by those data, in or out of court. The lawyer must reject such work and caution the expert that such so-called research can get both the expert and lawyer into hot water.[5]

Although legal proceedings are a serious game engaged in by real adversaries, as in other games, rules are involved to ensure fair play. Cases are not supposed to be won because of tricks, deception, or incompetent preparation and representation. To the expert witness, this means she should not conceal her findings during the process of discovery and deposition in order to surprise the other side in trial. The social scientist should be open and forthright as to her methods and major results. Specific suggestions as to dealing with the other side are contained in chapter 16. Usually there is no need to do their work for them, and the expert should avoid trying to win over the other side's expert or attorney by revealing as much as possible or being as persuasive as possible. At the same time, the ethical and legal theory underlying the opposition of two experts in court is that they should joust fairly, each side fully aware of the intentions and research of the other. If each side does its well-prepared best to present its own case and poke holes in the research of the other side, then those in the middle—the judge and jury—are in an ideal position to decide which side has been persuasive. If one side is disadvantaged by last-minute surprises sprung by the other, then the process cannot work ideally and a miscarriage of justice may result.

An additional implication of this principle is that an expert should not generate files or reports that she is not willing to let the other side see. This canon of legal ethics must be followed while also coping with its major implication regarding subject identifiability, a large item in the group of issues called microethics. Microethics are also implied by the ABA code requirement obliging lawyers "to treat with consideration" all persons involved in the legal process.

Microethics

Anonymity of those we study is a first principle of microethics, but anonymity has been hard enough to maintain in social-science research outside the courtroom. John Dollard disguised the name of Indianola, Mississippi, in *Caste and Class in a Southern Town,* but everyone there knew what town was involved as soon as his book came out, and they could also guess the identities of several of his key informants, although their names were also disguised. When research is used in litigation, the problem multiplies. The other side may imply that the alleged respondents never existed or were misquoted and may demand the right to see the original interview protocols to ensure that words were not taken out of context. Coding questionnaires is plagued with reliability errors, so it is scientifically defensible for the other side to claim that they should be able to double-check the process. Otherwise, sentences from white respondents could be coded to indicate satisfaction with municipal services, for instance, while the same type of sentence from black respondents could be coded to indicate dissatisfaction.

At the same time, the need for anonymity in research done for the courtroom is particularly great. Suppose a political scientist interviewed 100 randomly selected residents regarding municipal services and compiled the data for a lawsuit claiming unconstitutionally inferior services in black neighborhoods. One interviewee might be a black schoolteacher. If, to legitimate the exhibit, our expert filed with the court the original interview protocols, and if our teacher were the source of some particularly outspoken quotes, noted on the stand by the expert to make more vivid the extent of the discrimination shown statistically, the city might retaliate against the teacher at contract time. Obviously the teacher did not bargain for such pain when she answered questions at her doorstep some months earlier. It follows that anonymity must be guaranteed to any respondent in a survey.[6]

How is anonymity to be maintained while also maintaining the legitimacy and defensibility of data sources? One way is to remove the names and addresses from all questionnaires and interview schedules and to destroy them, even before the data are compiled. If the attorney fears that the other side will try to bar the denuded interview forms, this can be headed off beforehand: the full interview schedules, names attached, can be shown to a third party—a social scientist or other citizen—who can then state that names did exist and were attached to each form. Most surveys do not require this elaborate precaution. Indeed, judges have recently held that surveys can be more credible when they are anonymous, recognizing that the response rate will be enhanced and answers may be more open and complete. Usually only a blank form and the summary of responses is all that must be introduced into evidence.

Even if we have guaranteed respondents anonymity, we are still subjecting them to bother and perhaps to worry. If a famous murder trial looms and a social scientist responds by conducting a telephone poll of the community regarding a possible change-of-venue motion, the pollees are likely to feel they have been singled out, perhaps for jury duty or perhaps through some other unknown process. The fact that their names or numbers were drawn randomly, though true, may hardly seem believable to them, and reassurances from a telephone voice won't help much. What gives us the right to bother people?

This is a sticky subject in social science. The courtroom dimension can make it stickier still. I teach my students to consider three r's of research: role, relationships, and reciprocity. First, the researcher must develop a role that will not threaten or bother people. Her role must be clear to herself. Usually, it must be a true role; incognito research may be appropriate for infiltrating the Ku Klux Klan but involves implicit deception and should be avoided whenever an alternative is available. Second, the researcher must see even a brief interview as a relationship in which both parties have something at stake. She must treat her subjects as people with dignity and desires, and she must be aware that the wish of most people to be polite to her can lead to real impositions. Third, she must address the question of what is in it for them. Should she pay for each interview? Should she promise a copy of a final report? If she leaves nothing, she is behaving like a colonialist miner, extracting data from the community but leaving nothing behind.[7]

One of the hidden costs of ignoring any of the three r's is the bad name given social science. Persons or communities who have been lied to by a social scientist who was gathering data for a lawsuit but who did not want to say so are unlikely to welcome the next social scientist, even if her purpose is wholly benign and aboveboard. This is one reason why most social science national organizations have promulgated ethical codes. Like the ABA code, these codes tend to avoid the hard issues, but they do exist, and scientists and attorneys need to be aware of them. Following are excerpts from the *Preamble and Code of Ethics of the American Sociological Association:*

I-E-1: Research subjects are entitled to rights of privacy and dignity of treatment.

I-E-2: Research must not expose subjects to substantial risk or personal harm in the research process. Where risk or harm is anticipated, full informed consent must be obtained.

I-E-3: To the extent possible in a given study, researchers should anticipate potential threats to confidentiality. Such means as the removal of identifiers, the use of randomized responses, and other statistical solutions to problems of privacy should be used where appropriate.

I-A-3: Sociologists . . . must present their findings honestly and without distortion. There must be no omission of data from a research report which must significantly modify the interpretations of findings.

I-A-5: Sociologists must honor any commitments made to persons or groups in order to gain research access.[8]

One way to avoid microethical problems completely is to do no data collection, or at least none from individuals. Survey research is vastly overused in social science. Often other methods exist that could supply much better data. Rather than asking a sample of householders if they have had any problems with city services, city services can be directly observed. Street width, paving, guttering, sidewalks, and even less-physical services like garbage collection, police protection, and library-book availability can all be assessed on-site and from city records. Then there is no need to put a school teacher into a dilemma as to whether her job will be endangered by her candor or her honor will be endangered by her caution. As an alternative to phoning a large sample of residents regarding bias in the community toward the race or alleged criminality of a defendant, consider content analysis of newspaper and television coverage. As a way of learning something, asking people is cumbersome, imperfect, and to be avoided where possible.[9]

Until recently, social scientists seeking to do research for the courtroom often ran afoul of university review boards set up to evaluate all research proposals and to assure the government that any subject of social science or biomedical research give consent after being informed fully of all possible risks. This procedure was warranted in biomedical research, where terrible abuses such as the Tuskegee syphilis experiment clearly wrought harm, particularly on subjects without much social status or income. The regulations did not easily apply to some forms of social research. For example, suppose a sociologist plans to sit in medical waiting rooms, observing whether black and white patients are given similar waiting periods, nouns of address, and courtesy. Her aim is to compile data that might be used against some of the facilities in a lawsuit charging racism. Like many others in social science, this study requires that its subjects be unaware that it is in progress, or at least unaware of its specific aim. The researcher can hardly explain fully to the physicians the risk they run in letting her sit there. Few physicians would sign a statement indicating willingness to participate, and those who did would be sure to operate their waiting rooms in an exemplary manner while the sociologist was sitting in them, thus making the research trivial.

Probably the government never meant to rule out such research, even though it could harm offending physicians.[10] In 1981, the Department of Health and Human Services (DHHS) put out new guidelines explicitly exempting many kinds of research, including most participant observation, from the requirement of informed consent. The old guidelines, when enforced rigidly and unthinkingly, as some university committees did, ruled out almost all studies that might threaten the status quo, including almost all data gathering for the courtroom. Ironically, the group thus protected was precisely those members of society who already had disproportionate power and status. Overly rigid application of rules designed to promote microethics was having negative macroethical results.

Some social scientists and university research committees may be unaware of the differences made by the new regulations. Information at the end of the chapter can help avoid confrontations with such committees. However, even the researcher who has no difficulty with a committee should be familiar with the regulations, for they contain many important principles that should be followed to protect human subjects from needless bother and worry. The new regulations do not give a carte blanche to participant observers, for instance, to operate as they please. Moreover, some of the implications of the three r's described earlier go beyond any inference from the new or old government regulations. It is not easy to respect subjects' rights in doing social research, especially research for the courtroom, but it must be done.

Macroethics

Micro- and macroethics are often related: a study that treats members of a group cavalierly in the research process is unlikely to respect their world view in its finished product. The levels are separable, however, and one can easily imagine a marketing study, for instance, that scrupulously maintains confidentiality, minimizes the burden on respondents, and even recompenses their time with gifts of free products—all the while gathering data to help merchandise a dangerous new tampon.

Even a study with no firsthand data collection still involves ethical issues. Ethical social scientists must be concerned with the uses to which the information they generate will be put, as well as with the ways in which it was gathered. In the late 1960s, when "Black Power" was more frequently heard than now, social scientists had to confront this issue. Some ghettoes, particularly those in the vicinity of large universities, were studied over and over again, and the communities grew restive, asking whether the purpose of this seemingly endless research was community betterment, career enhancement, or perhaps more-effective forms of community control. Now things are calmer, and as a result the issue is less often discussed in social-science circles, but it refuses to disappear. The application of social science to legal disputes only sharpens the issue.

First of all, there are the macrolevel concerns of the disciplines themselves. If social scientists appear on each side of the aisle in lawsuits, this raises the image of science for hire and threatens to undermine their claim to scientific knowledge. Perhaps because they deal with the social/political world, the social sciences are particularly vulnerable to attack. Southern sociologists in the late

1950s remember the negative image from which that field suffered in the minds of legislators and journalists as a result of the footnote to Gunnar Myrdal's *An American Dilemma* in the 1954 Supreme Court desegregation decision. I have never met a sociologist who would unwrite Myrdal and only a few who would undo *Brown,* but the concern for maintaining public acceptance of social science is real and well founded. However, this concern cannot dictate ethical conduct. Ultimately it reduces to a paradox—namely, that free speech can be maintained in social science only so long as it is not really exercised.

Some social scientists believe that their discipline is intrinsically amoral and should be for sale to the highest bidder. This is simplistic. We have a basic value consensus in the United States. Our shared beliefs are pointed to by our Constitution and by the shared ideology of meritocracy. Only a few extremists would openly state that a job should not go to the best qualified applicant if that applicant is nonwhite. We all know that these principles are flouted as often as followed, but not openly, not as a matter of principle, at least not often. Even in the white-supremacy days of 1962, the University of Mississippi, when challenged by black James Meredith, shied away from telling him he could not attend because of his race. Instead, officials claimed the school had no racial policy and was only coincidentally segregated; Meredith, they argued, had not met all the qualifications. More recently, racist psychologists like Jensen and Herrnstein don't claim that people should be given fewer opportunities because they are black but that most blacks are genetically less intelligent than most whites. Their arguments for discrimination thus claim to rest on the same values regarding meritocracy as most of our laws.

Our public policies, particularly those we enact into law, are especially likely to reflect our value consensus regarding meritocracy. Thus, most class-action litigation regarding equal opportunity involves means-ends statements. To these, social science clearly applies.

When social science clearly applies, it usually applies in only one direction. In such cases, there is no excuse for social scientists to sit on both sides of the courtroom aisle. In two voting-rights cases, I faced experts across the aisle who argued that the data did not show overwhelming white bloc voting—when they did. In a school desegregation case, I have read testimony by a social scientist who excerpted the hundreds of research studies on school desegregation to claim that the process usually has bad consequences for children. Besides the fact that such testimony is irrelevant, it grossly misstates the preponderance of the evidence.[11]

These distortions trouble me. In rights cases, in order to testify for the side that opposes greater opportunity for the disprivileged, one usually must distort. That is a bold assertion, and some readers will conclude it merely exposes my own ideological bent. If true, however, then experts such as the three I described in the foregoing paragraph violate two norms at once. They misuse and misanalyze data; sometimes deliberately, sometimes not. They also produce exhibits and testimony that cannot be defended on macroethical grounds. Their work has the potential for causing misery in other jurisdictions many miles away; it also can smear the reputation of social science, not only among disprivileged groups but even among the cynical attorneys who employ them.

I call these users of social science cynical because they do not believe what their own experts claim, but rather they parade the claim and the experts before the court in order to confuse the issues. The Southern attorneys who hired experts to doubt that whites bloc voted knew exactly how whites voted—98 percent white. They merely wanted to obfuscate the facts so the judge, if not quick enough to assess the methods and statistics of each side, would not know whom to believe. Perhaps they hoped the court would throw up its hands and say, "A plague on both your houses!"

To conclude, then, although the ABA code states that "every person in our society should have ready access to a lawyer,"[12] it does not necessarily follow that everyone should have ready access to a social scientist. Social scientists do not want to waste part of their lives arguing the social-science equivalent of "the earth is flat," and that is just what the wrong side of some cases amounts to. Moreover, the presentation of social-science data is usually needed more by those arguing for social change. The conservative, arguing for the status quo, need not invoke data and methods but can merely cite precedent.[13] Social scientists make choices, then, when they accept or refuse cases and in the way they research them. Those choices are either macroethical or not. Social scientists, who are paid to think about people and society, make these decisions consciously. They cannot claim to be mere technicians, selling their analytic skills to the highest bidder. They know, too, that law is an instrument of social power, typically used to preserve the status quo. The ethical question for social scientists in court, then, is whether their work helps to open the court's eyes to the true factual situation or whether it further beclouds the issue.

Notes

1. See, for example, Norman K. Denzin, *The Research Act* (Chicago: Aldine, 1970), chapter 13; and John B. Williamson et al., *The Research Craft* (Boston: Little, Brown, 1977), chapter 4. For more-extended treatments of ethical issues in social science, see Gideon Sjoberg, ed., *Ethics, Politics, and Social Research* (Cambridge, Mass.: Schenkman, 1967); and Arthur J. Vidich et al., *Reflections on Community Studies* (New York: Wiley, 1964).

2. American Bar Association, *Code of Professional Responsibility* (Washington, D.C., 1977). Notwithstanding its length, this code still exhibits substantial lacunae and points of vagueness.

3. Gunnar Myrdal, *Asian Drama* (New York: Pantheon, 1968), pp. 20--24.

4. Karl Taeuber, "Sociological Practice in the Courts," *Wisconsin Sociologist* 16 (1979): 112–123.

5. See an account of fraudulent research in the courtroom in Arthur St. George and Patrick H. McNamara, "'Filthy Pictures' or the Case of the Fraudulent Social Scientist," *American Sociologist* 14 (1979): 142–149; and James W. Loewen, "Comment," *American Sociologist* 15 (1980): 116–117. Note also the fraudulent IQ data manufactured by Cyril Burt and exposed in Leon Kamin, *The Science and Politics of IQ* (New York: Wiley, 1974).

6. See Paul Nejelski and Lerman, "A Researcher-Subject Testimonial Privilege: What To Do before the Subpoena Arrives," *Wisconsin Law Review,* 1971, p. 1085.

7. Reciprocity, role, and relationships are discussed at length in Myron Glazer, *The Research Adventure* (New York: Random House, 1972).

8. Revised, Proposed, 1980, in American Sociological Association, *ASA Footnotes* Washington, DC, August 1980, p. 12.

9. Ways to avoid surveys are supplied by E.J. Webb et al., *Unobtrusive Measures* (Chicago: Rand McNally, 1966). Irwin Deutscher supplies a deep analysis of the differences between survey responses and behavior in *What We Say/What We Do* (Glenview, Ill.: Scott, Foresman, 1973).

10. This unexpected result of overly rigid application of the guidelines conflicted with other ethical considerations. Indeed, the government itself participated in and funded research of the kind seemingly ruled out. Government agencies required that principal investigators sign an assurance form, consistent with the requirement of the law, but never required that each subject of social research sign an informed-consent statement. The National Science Foundation funded a proposal of mine, for example, that involved interviewing school superintendents and observing classes in a dozen school districts, the purpose of which was to compare well-desegregated and poorly desegregated systems. I could not guarantee anonymity, since it would be easy to identify some of the districts from their unique character or the fact of my visit. Moreover, key phrases in the guidelines were "the ordinary risks of daily life" and the risks "inherent in a chosen occupation of field of service." Such risks obviously include the possibility of talking with people, of answering Gallup pollsters, of being observed as one serves patients.

11. See chapter 1, notes 5–8.

12. ABA *Code of Professional Responsibility,* section EC 1-1.

13. Michael J. Saks and C.H. Baron, eds.; *The Use/Nonuse/Misuse of Applied Social Research in the Courts* (Cambridge, Mass.: ABT, 1980), pp. 10–11.

Additional Resources

Excerpts from "Final Regulations Amending Basic Health and Human Services Policy for the Protection of Human Research Subjects," *Federal Register,* 26 January 1981, pp. 8366–8392:

p. 8367: The regulations contain broad exemptions for educational, behavioral, and social-science research which involves little or no risk to research subjects. These exemptions constitute a major deregulation from rules in force at the present time. They exclude most social science research projects from the jurisdiction of the regulations.

pp. 8386–8387, section 46.101(b): Research activities [that] are exempt from these regulations . . .:

1. Research activities conducted in educational settings . . . .
2; Research involving the use of educational tests . . . .
3. Research involving survey or interview procedures, except where all of the following conditions exist: (i) Responses are recorded in such a manner that the human subjects can be identified, directly or through identifiers linked to the subject; (ii) the subject's responses, if they became known outside the research, could reasonably place the subject at risk of criminal or civil liability or be damaging to the subject's financial standing or employability; and (iii) the research deals with sensitive aspects of the subject's own behavior, such as illegal conduct, drug use, sexual behavior, or use of alcohol. All research involving survey or interview procedures is exempt, without exception, when the respondents are elected or appointed public officials or candidates for public office.
4. Research involving the observation (including observation by participants) of public behavior, except where all of the following conditions exist: (i) Observations are recorded in such a manner that the human subjects can be identified, directly or through identifiers linked to the subjects; (ii) the observations recorded about the individual, if they became known outside the research, could reasonably place the subject at risk of criminal or civil liability or be damaging to the subject's financial standing or employability; and (iii) the research deals with sensitive aspects of the subject's own behavior . . . .
5. Research involving the collection or study of existing data, . . . if these sources are publicly available or if the information is recorded by the investigator in such a manner that subjects cannot be identified, directly or through identifiers linked to the subjects.

p. 8390, section 46.116: [For most other studies,] legally effective informed consent of the subject [is required.]

pp. 8390–8391, section 46.117: An Institutional Review Board may waive the requirement for the investigator to obtain a signed consent form for some or all subjects if it finds . . . that the research presents no more than minimal risk of harm to subjects and involves no procedures for which written consent is normally required outside of the research context.

4

The Nature of Statistics and Research as Used in the Courtroom

Statistics used in the courtroom do not differ intrinsically from statistics in other applications; neither do research methods. This chapter cannot be an introduction to those entire fields. General introductions are already available, usually at book length, and at the end of this chapter I recommend several that are especially lucid. This chapter provides a basic understanding of some aspects of statistics and methods to the attorney who plans to use an expert social scientist so he can ask the right questions of his witness, before and during court. If the chapter is successful, the lay reader should come away demystified and with a grasp of the basic process of research and data analysis, particularly as used in the courtroom. The social scientist may glean some ways to present statistics clearly to lay audiences.

Constructing a social-science argument for the courtroom typically involves five steps:

1. Gathering the data;
2. Summarizing the data using descriptive statistics;
3. Identifying relationships between two variables (or making comparisons between two groups, which amounts to finding a relationship between two variables), using statistics of association, and subjecting relationships that seem important to further controls to see if they hold up;
4. Testing important relationships for statistical significance;
5. Presenting the data effectively.

The first four steps form the organizing principle for this chapter. Data presentation is the subject of chapter 5.

Data Gathering

Social scientists have developed many different ways to obtain data on people and institutions. A list of them is useful at this point, coupled with brief descriptions and evaluations of their weaknesses and strengths.

1. *Content analysis* is the systematic examination of printed material (or speeches, photographs, songs, and so on). The analyst can search for every reference to a woman, for instance, compared to every reference to a man, and can code each citation along a continuum, such as active/passive or major/minor.

Typically this is all done by computer and can be very elegant; it also can be done by hand and be very simple, yet equally effective.

A simple form of content analysis is merely to count the number of persons in history texts, by race and sex, to see if a major group has been included far less than its numbers and historical importance would warrant. In a case of mine, simply counting index entries in an adopted state-history textbook revealed overwhelming reference to white names, even though the state was Mississippi and many important black leaders and artists existed. To take a more-complex example, in 1968 a border-state school district passed a bond issue to build a new school serving an emerging white suburb. The nearest older school was toward the center of the city and was black. An obvious reason for building this school within the white neighborhood, rather than locating it on a racial boundary or assigning its students to the older school, was to avoid making whites attend a black school. No one in 1958, four years after *Brown,* would say so, but proponents of the bond issue used such phrases as "neighborhood schools," "quality education," and "more-homogeneous student body, easier to teach." If content analysis of speeches, newspaper editorials, and school board minutes can establish that these phrases were used repetitively, and if to a student of the area's political history they have a tie to segregationist ideology, then they may help prove intent. (It would be telling to analyze earlier utterances of known segregationists and find the same code phrases.)

Occasionally, content analysis provides the backbone of a lawsuit, such as a suit charging plagiarism, or alleging bias in curricular materials. More often, it can provide an effective but minor component of the overall portrait of an institution that is being painted for the court. For example, if I were trying a case alleging sexual discrimination in employment, I would obtain copies of the firm's promotional brochures, training manuals, and other publications. A social scientist could analyze the persons in photographs, and individuals treated in the text, taking care to separate roles such as producer from consumer, supervisor from clerical. If the results showed male predominance, the printed material could be serving as both a cause and a result of limited opportunity for women in the company.

Other than its typically minor importance to the case, content analysis suffers from no particular weakness as a research method defensible in court. It is public and replicable. Its results are statistically impressive and clear. It is cheap. Also, since no interviewing or observing of people are involved, content analysis usually bothers no one and raises no microethical issues.

2. *Surveys* include questionnaires and interviews. Ranging from Gallup polls to the census to sociograms to market research, surveys are the most ubiquitous method in social science. However, they are often inferior to creative structured observation. Some social scientists and users of social science think all too quickly of surveys when something must be established. Surveys do create data, it is true, but those data typically are not about topic X, but about how people

think regarding topic X. Thus, a survey of householders about municipal services does not reveal much about city services but rather about images and evaluations of those services.

Surveys do have the advantage of being open and public. Unless the survey was done through diffuse informal interviews, the court can see every question in context. Sampling methods are equally public and defensible. Response rate is a problem with pencil-and-paper questionnaires, so structured interviews are commonly employed. These pose a potential for bothering people and raising microethical issues, but most surveys are bland and short and the public well aware of the method in general so that no insurmountable ethical issues are involved.

3. *Structured observation* includes most of what have sometimes been called unobtrusive methods. Rather than ask householders about city services, it makes more sense to observe, for example, street paving, lighting, and garbage collection directly, in an organized defensible way, using a random sample to make the task manageable.[1] Again, firsthand observation of differential use of courtesy terms by race in a hospital waiting room is more telling than interviews with receptionists and interns who have no reason to admit to prejudice.

Social psychologists and sociologists know many structured ways to observe, each yielding defensible quantitative data. Since space and place often relate powerfully to position in social structure, mapping can be a powerful tool, whether of patterns of industry and residency by social class or of office location in a building. R.F. Bales's Interaction Process Analysis suggests many modifications for observing group interaction systematically,[2] while W.L. Warner's Index of Status Characteristics suggests ways to measure social class without ever asking a question of anyone.[3]

A strength of structured observation is that its methods are clear and public. As with surveys, large numbers of observations are involved so the process is defensible. Usually one is observing the phenomenon more directly than the secondhand data created by asking people questions in surveys. Like surveys, though, structured observation is typically tedious, labor intensive, and costly. An additional drawback is the possibility of what could be called coding bias. Observers are recording the data and grouping them into categories such as upper/lower or polite/rude. Their discretion is involved, and the procedure must be routinized to minimize that discretion and make the entire investigation as standardized and defensible as possible.

4. *Participant observation* is a time-honored method in sociology and anthropology. The social scientist participates in the group or institution she is studying, sometimes incognito but more often being truthful about her research purpose. In the process she can make telling observations about the group, its formal operation, and its informal workings. However, for courtroom use such data often seem subjective and anecdotal, similar to the incidents related by non-expert witnesses rather that clothed in the garb of scientific reputability.

5. *Experiments,* the major method of the physical sciences, play a restricted role in social science because it is ethically and legally hard to subject persons and groups to controlled conditions and then watch for effects resulting from one experimental variable. Social scientists approximate controlled experimental results through statistical manipulations, holding other factors constant analytically. They also make controlled comparisons: prison records, with sex of prisoner removed, can be compared, and if the men's records do not differ from the women's, then any parole differential by gender can presumably be charged to sexism. In small-group research, controlled experiments can be important and can have legal implications, such as Strodtbeck et al.'s work on juries.[4] However, original experiments are rarely done for courtroom presentation because they are elaborate, time consuming, and usually involve an element of artificiality that renders them easy targets for cross-examination.

6. *Natural experiments,* or *historical comparisons,* are more often useful in court. For example, if it is claimed that the at-large election of city officials results in more-efficient government than ward elections, pairs of similar cities can be examined, one of which adopted commission or city-manager government, the other retaining ward-based council members.

7. *Secondary data analysis,* a major method of social science, does not generate or gather new data, but brings existing data to bear on the issue. Census figures, voting statistics, payroll information, tax rolls, jury lists, and a huge array of other data have been collected by every imaginable public and private office. City planning departments, regional economic-development boards, school systems, marketing firms, and other bureaucracies maintain files of potentially useful material. In chapter 5, this material is called archival data. Much of this information is public; much of the rest can be obtained by a social scientist or through discovery. Other data are just lying around, waiting to be created by being picked up. In a lawsuit charging racially discriminatory disciplining in a high school, for example, it might be relevant to show black alienation in the school by demonstrating that blacks are being excluded from major extracurricular activities. Why bother to devise a questionnaire, select a sample, and ask students if they feel blacks are participating equally—merely examine old yearbook photos.

In short, often data need not be created at all; often they already exist. Before deciding that data must be created, the lawyer and scientist should always brainstorm all sources of data that already exist. In this way vast sums of time and money are saved. No respondents are bothered anew, and because the information in files or published material was collected far before this new use of it was ever imagined, it is implausible to suggest that the method by which it was gathered was biased from its inception.

Lurking behind my evaluations of the methods just listed were two considerations, reliability and validity, that require some direct treatment. To be reliable, a study must come out the same way when replicated. In practice, studies are not often directly replicated, and research for the courtroom is particularly unlikely to be replicated by the other side in the few weeks before trial, so what reliability boils down to is the requirement that the methods look like they could be replicated. In short, this is the familiar requirement that methods be public and explicit and seem to have little or no chance for bias. In the courtroom this means that possibly subjective methods such as participant observation are suspect. On what basis did a participant observer conclude that a school, for instance, was racist? After all, the other side can hire its own expert to wander about the corridors and conclude that they have no aura of racial discrimination, and we would be back to the situation of one expert versus another, with the court's having little reason to believe one over the other. As soon as we move to buttress pure participant observation with more-organized evidence, we move back into the realm of statistical evidence, which again explains why there must be an emphasis on statistics in social-science testimony in the court and in this book.

A study is valid if it really measures what it purports to measure. Again, allow me to discuss this concept through example. Imagine a lawsuit charging that rural school districts were underfunded and provided less than equal educational opportunities to their students compared to suburban and urban districts. Suppose our measure of school quality included some easily measurable items like number of books per student in the school library, presence or absence of a chemistry lab, and the like. If we also included in it whether or not the school had a cafeteria, we would be contaminating our research design because cafeterias have nothing intrinsically to do with the intellectual quality of schools. Indeed, many of our finest suburban schools have no cafeterias, owing to the social structure and wishes of their communities. Accordingly, the presence or absence of a cafeteria, though easy to measure reliably, is not valid and has no place in a composite index of educational quality.

The term *operational definition* provides a way to summarize this matter of validity. We begin with concepts that have theoretical definitions—concepts that are important to the lawsuit or to social science or both. Educational quality might be such a concept. We must then measure it to decide if a school does or does not exemplify the concept. (Of course, usually an either/or determination is too crude and we wish to see to what degree the concept is exemplified.) Eventually we settle upon a measure—perhaps a ten-item scale with different items weighted according to their importance. That becomes our operational definition of educational quality. To have validity, our operational definitions must reasonably match our theoretical definitions. Again, public methods are a key, so that judges, juries, and others can scrutinize the study until they feel confident that its procedures do assess what they claim to assess—that it has validity.

Good research demands more than reliability and validity. It demands a mix of the methods listed here. Even a single conclusion, if important, should not rest on a single method or finding. Sometimes more than one study may be required by the nature of a case. To support a change-of-venue motion on behalf of a black defendant charged with murder of a white person, for instance, all of the following might be appropriate:

A sophisticated survey of white attitudes toward white and black criminals, asking in-depth but standardized questions of a random sample of white registered voters;

A comparison of arrest statistics, conviction rates, and sentencing data by race in the county over the past decade;

A study of the proportion of blacks on recent juries and venires compared to the voting-age population.

A content analysis of the treatment of black/white murder compared to white/white murder in the local newspaper.

It follows that more than one expert may be advisable to carry out these various researches. Relevant studies in the literature should also be invoked by the expert(s), even though these may be of distant communities, when they reinforce local findings or help to interpret them. No matter from what sources the data come, however, they must be summarized to be presented effectively to the court.

Descriptive Statistics

For our purposes, the field of statistics can be divded into three parts: descriptive statistics, measures of association, and inferential statistics. Descriptive statistics summarize an otherwise unwieldy body of information. If we are examining 950 male employees, for instance, we cannot hold in our minds even so simple a characteristic as their ages without using descriptive statistics. The data must be condensed: an age pyramid, table, mean (average), or median (midpoint) might be appropriate. Only then can a second variable be added, such as a comparison to female employees or employees at a different firm. Descriptive statistics comprise the basic information that will be presented to the court and will usually be the most important single part of the expert testimony.

Data are usually summarized with a frequency distribution or with a measure of central tendency and a measure of spread or dispersion. A frequency distribution presents all the data grouped or portrayed in some compact way. Measures of central tendency tell the reader where the center of the distribution lies. They provide a single number that roughly summarizes the entire distribution and allows for easy comparison to another distribution, summarized by its measure of central tendency. Three measures are common: the mean, median, and mode. Measures of dispersion tell how spread out the data are—whether most incomes are fairly close to the mean, for example, or whether they vary widely, making the mean a rather poor way to characterize them all. Three measures of spread are common: the range, variance, and standard deviation.

Which measures of dispersion and central tendency to use and which way to show the frequency distribution depend partly upon what kind of data we are dealing with—parametric or nonparametric. These often used terms will be in any expert witness's vocabulary and need to be in the lawyer's. A *parametric variable* is one that varies over a continuous range with a meaningful zero point. Income, for instance, varies over a continuous range, so that one could earn $10,931 as well as $11,000; $0 is also meaningful. Therefore incomes can be added or multiplied. A family with $36,000 has twice the income of one earning $18,000. *Nonparametric variables* vary over a range without a meaningful zero point or a range that is not continuous at all. Religion is an example: the values of religion as a variable might include Protestant, Catholic, Jew, none, and other. Is a Catholic more than a Protestant but less than a Jew? Obviously this scale is arbitrary, and we cannot add or multiply its scale divisions. Therefore, we must keep its categories separate. The most appropriate frequency distribution for nonparametric data is a bar graph, which graphically keeps separate its discrete categories, as in figure 4–1.

Parametric data can be grouped and then shown as a bar graph or left ungrouped and shown as a smooth continuous curve such as in figure 4–2. Because parametric data can be added, multiplied, and divided, we can also represent them by parameters—most importantly, the mean and standard deviation. The

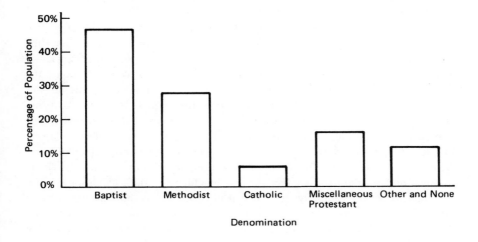

Figure 4–1. Religious Membership in Shale County, Arkansas

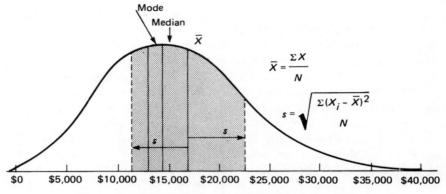

Figure 4–2. Family Income in Shale County, Arkansas

mean, $\bar{X}$, sometimes called arithmetic average, is found by adding all the items together and dividing by the number of items. The standard deviation, s, measures the spread or width of the distribution. Roughly 2/3 of all the cases, in this instance 2/3 of the family incomes, lie within one s above and below the mean when the data lie in a normal or bell curve.

If we represented figure 4-2 by its mean, about $17,000, and its standard deviation, about $5,000, we would be guilty of mild distortion. First, the mean is not precisely near the area of greatest concentration of families, the center of the distribution, which looks to be less than $15,000. Second, 2/3 of the distribution does not lie between $X - s$ and $X + s$. I have shaded that area, and by inspection it looks to be about 60 percent of the total area under the curve, not 66 2/3 percent. What is wrong?

The mean has been pulled up by a few extremely large incomes. If we had a society of ten sharecroppers, each earning $5,000, and one planter, netting $1,000,000, the mean income would be close to $100,000 for each family, but that mean would describe no family accurately. For many distributions, the mean is a good shorthand summary telling where the variable is centered, but when the distribution extends far out in one direction, as in income distributions, the median is the measure of choice to represent central tendency. The median is the midpoint found by listing all the cases from smallest to largest and selecting the middle number. The median income is not affected if the richest family makes $100,000 or $10,000,000, so for our example of sharecroppers and planters the median income would be $5,000, much more accurate than the mean. Similarly, the median in figure 4-2 is more accurate, more truthful to the distribution as a whole, than the mean. For parametric data, then, either the mean or median can be computed. The mean is more useful in statistical tests, as we shall see later, but the median is sometimes more accurate, a better measure of the center of a distribution.

For nonparametric data—data that do not come on a smooth scale with numerical values—there is no choice. No mean can be computed. The median can be computed when the data lie in a clear order. For example, grouping college students into freshman, sophomore, junior, senior, master's, and doctorate levels, we could compare the median category of students assigned to female professors to that assigned male professors, which could be worth doing if it was charged that women were told to teach freshmen while graduate research direction was always reserved for men. When no clear order exists, such as the religious denominations of figure 4-1, the only measure of central tendency that can be found is the mode, or modal category—Baptist in this instance. The entire frequency distribution would be a much better choice to show the religious membership of the county.

The spread of a distribution is almost as important as its center. If we know that whites are getting $0.13 more per hour than blacks, we cannot claim that anything actionable is happening; we need more information to evaluate whether $0.13 is a lot or a little. At one hospital I know, launderers earned from $2.78 to $2.94 per hour in 1977. Obviously, if black launderers made $0.13 less than white launderers, almost every black would earn less than almost every white. However, if hourly pay in management positions varies from $8 to $22, $0.13 is not very meaningful. The range, which we have been using in this paragraph to describe spread, is the largest number minus the smallest one. It is not really a good measure because it is drastically increased by a single extreme value. The range would be enormous in figure 4-2, for instance, especially if there were one million-dollar income in Shale County. Much better is the variance, found by calculating the difference between each income (or other item) and the mean, squaring each difference (multiplying it by itself), adding them all together, and dividing by the number of items. Because of all the squaring that has been done, this variance is usually a very large number, and although it is useful in formulas, it is unwieldy and has no obvious intuitive meaning. Therefore, statisticians take its square root to get s, the standard deviation, a number that has the handy characteristic of enclosing 2/3 of a distribution when added and subtracted from the mean of a normal curve, as mentioned earlier. Like the variance, the standard deviation is superior to the range as a measure of spread because it cannot be grossly distorted by a single very large or very small value.

Although rich families have inflated the mean in figure 4-2, it is still not very far from the center of the distribution, and thus any distribution that looks reasonably like a bell curve or normal curve, including figure 4-2, can be summarized reasonably well by its mean and standard deviation (or variance). Therefore, a number of statistical tests exist that compare two distributions by comparing their parameters—their means and standard deviations. Other tests exist for nonparametric distributions; among these are the chi-square and the sign test. In practice, once the two parameters—mean and standard deviation—are mastered, little mystery is involved in the dichotomy between parametric and nonparametric statistics. Indeed, any variable or relationship that is describable in parametric terms is also describable in nonparametric terms (the reverse, however, is not true). Income, for instance, can be dichotomized into high and low and treated like Baptist or Catholic. Sometimes nonparametric tests are more powerful than tests based on parametric assumptions, and sometimes they are not; often nonparametric tests are easier to understand. These considerations should dictate the appropriate test for a given set of parametric data.

The basic ideas behind statistical tests are presented in the section on inferential statistics, while specific statistical tests are suggested in chapters 6 through 12. Statistical testing is not usually as important in court as the clear presentation of the basic data, however, which is why this section has been devoted to descriptive statistics and why the next chapter expands on the topic of data presentation.

Statistics of Association

Usually the expert is not simply presenting data on one group but is making a comparison. We were already dealing with two groups when we discussed mean incomes that differed by $0.13. A comparison was also involved in the example with which we began this book, the grievance Mrs. Rephan felt toward her city for not providing wide, well-paved streets in black neighborhoods. Indeed, in isolation a statistic often has little meaning. If we are examining bank-loan data for evidence of possible redlining and we find a 60 percent rejection rate in a black neighborhood, does that show discrimination? It does not without more data, of course, which would probably include comparisons to white neighborhoods.

As soon as we compare two groups, we begin to engage in what are called statistics of association. We are trying to ascertain whether one variable affects another. In our redlining example, we would be seeing if race affects treatment of loan applications. The simplest form of statistics of association is merely to present descriptive statistics twice. Instead of one bar graph showing the distribution of a variable, two bar graphs can be paired to show the distribution of two variables or of one variable over two groups. Figure 4–3 shows income by race in Mississippi, for instance, and makes considerable graphic impact. Equally simple and often equally effective is the comparison of two measures of central tendency, such as the median incomes and educations of blacks and whites in a state or city. Obviously education lags somewhat, and income a lot, for blacks in our nation's capital (table 4–1).

A third common way to show if an association exists between two variables is a contingency table. In it, the independent variable, the factor that comes first in time and may influence the other variable under study, is shown across the top, or horizontally. The dependent variable, which may have been affected by

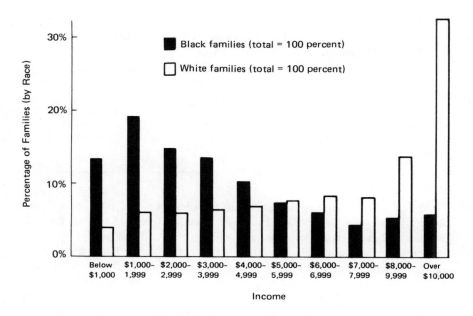

Figure 4–3. Family Income, by Race, Mississippi, 1970

the independent variable, is shown on the lefthand side, or vertically. In table 4-3, race is the independent variable, for race could have some effect on whether or not a family is in poverty, whereas being poor does not cause a family to change their race. Table 4-2 is the simplest contingency table possible, a two-by-two table, for in it each variable is divided into just two values. Similar in conception to the two-by-two table is the scattergram, shown and discussed in chapter 14.

Table 4–1

Median Family Income and Median Education in the Adult Population, by Race, Washington, D.C., 1970

Variable	Black	White
Median family income	$8,497	$14,940
Median education, adults age 25 and older	11.4 years	13.2 years

Source: 1970 Census.

Table 4–2
Number and Percentage of Families below the Poverty Line, Tunica County, Mississippi, by Race, 1970 Census

| | Black | | White | |
	N	Percentage	N	Percentage
Above poverty line	344	23.3%	781	83.6%
Below poverty line	1,132	76.7	153	16.4
Totals	1,476	100%	934	100%

Table 4-2 has shown an association between race and income in Tunica County—whites are richer. Two questions must then be asked about this relationship: What is its importance, and what is its statistical significance? The *importance* of a relationship is a difficult concept to define because it depends upon the setting. The difference between 51 percent and 49 percent is crucial in politics, for instance, but probably trivial when comparing the proportion of whites and blacks admitted to dental school. Importance is answered by the seat of one's pants, by common sense, by social theory, by statistical measures of association between two variables in contrast to measures between other variable pairs, and by the expert in the light of the social-science literature or other court cases. In the case of Tunica County incomes, elegant considerations might be brought to bear, such as minimum budget requirements for a family of four or reference-group theory regarding the probable effect on the self-concept of individuals drastically below the common U.S. standard of decency in expenditure, but almost any approach, common sense as well, tells us that the difference between 77 percent and 16 percent referring to proportion below the poverty line, is important. Often importance is just as mundane as that; it simply requires that an expert state that the difference is quite important.

Significance is a statistical term of rather precise meaning. It means that something is not likely to have occurred owing to chance. If we tossed the 2,420 Tunica County incomes up in a hat, for example, what is the likelihood that a selection of 934 of them would come up as different from the rest as has occurred among the white families in this county? This is a statistical question to be answered by inferential statistics as discussed in the next section. (The answer, for this example, is that it is very unlikely.)

Many social scientists blur the distinction between importance and significance. The chi-square test, for instance, often applied in court to complex tables, measures significance, not importance. Scientists who find their results significant may conclude they have an important finding, while if they do not find significance they conclude that no important difference between the two groups exists. These conclusions can be wrong. On one hand, if a sample is large, consisting of perhaps several thousand persons in each group, then a small differ-ence, say 3 percent, can be statistically significant. However, statistical signific-ance does not automatically confer importance, and a significant 3 percent difference is still just a 3 percent difference. On the other hand, with a small sample, the scientist may find, for example, that two of six women, 33 percent, were promoted within the past year, while seven of twelve similarly qualified men, 58 percent, were promoted. The difference in proportion promoted by sex, about 25 percent, is surely important, but because of the small samples, it is not statistically significant—that is, it could occur by chance. It would be wrong to stop analysis at this point, wronger still to conclude that there is no discrimina-tion at the firm. No evidence of nondiscrimination has been found. Indeed, some evidence of discrimination has been found, but since the samples were so small, nothing definite can be said about the matter. Effective testimony thus requires importance *and* significance.

Measures of significance are discussed in the next section. There are some measures of importance, however, to be mentioned here. The most common is *r,* the correlation coefficient, which is applied to scattergrams and is described in detail in chapter 13. Correlation coefficients vary in magnitude from 0 to 1. A coefficient of 0 between the percentage of blacks in neighborhoods of the city and the percentage of loans denied, for instance, indicates no relationship, while an *r* of 1 denotes a perfect relationship, so that knowing one variable (race) would enable us to predict the other (proportion of denials) with no error what-soever. In sociology and political science, which usually operate at the level of groups (precincts, neighborhoods, and the like), an *r* of .5 is considered strong, while *r*s of .3 and .4 warrant further research. In psychology, *r*s of .3 or .4 are sometimes considered strong, while .2 or even .15 are considered worthy of further study.

If we square *r,* the result, r^2, is a very important statistic. Recall the vari-ance, the measure of spread not drastically distorted by extreme values. The de-pendent variable (loan denial in the case imagined in the last paragraph) has a variance. In some neighborhoods, 90 percent of loan applications may be denied; in others, perhaps only 5 percent. r^2 tells the proportion of the variance in the dependent variable that is related to the independent variable. If we found *r* = .5 between percentage of nonwhite and percentage of loans denied, then we know that r^2, or 25 percent of all the variance in loan denials, by neighborhood, is associated with race. Thus, r^2 is a measure of importance. We can also see that an *r* = .3, with a corresponding r^2 of .09, is not very important, regardless of how many cases it is built upon, and regardless of how significant it may be, for the independent variable only "explains" 9 percent of the variance of the de-pendent variable, which is not a great feat.

The correlation coefficient is the most commonly accepted measure among social scientists to see if two parametric or continuous variables are related. Parametric variables, to review for a moment, are statistics that vary continuously and have a zero point, such as percentage of white, which can vary from 0 percent to 100 percent. So, for example, if we wanted to see whether public schools with smaller proportions of white students also had smaller school libraries, we could correlate the percentage of nonwhite with number of library books per student, both parametric variables. We could portray the relationship as a scattergram (see figure 14-1) or for graphic purposes, we could make discrete categories out of percentage of white, trichotomizing into predominantly white, desegregated, and predominently black schools. Then we could make a bar graph from the mean number of books per student of schools in each category, like figure 4-4. Even though our bar graph uses grouped data, we could still present to the court the r based on continuous data.

Sometimes data are grouped and cannot be treated as continuous, such as average salary of male and female employees. Salary is continuous, but sex or gender comes in two discrete categories. We could portray the data with a bar graph or a two-by-two table and could show its importance simply by talking about the differences in means, as we suggested earlier. We could also assign dummy values to sex, making each woman a 0 and each man a 1, for instance.[5] Then we could compute a correlation coefficient as before. This procedure, though common, is slightly illegitimate because merely assigning numbers to sex does not convert sex into a continuous or parametric variable.

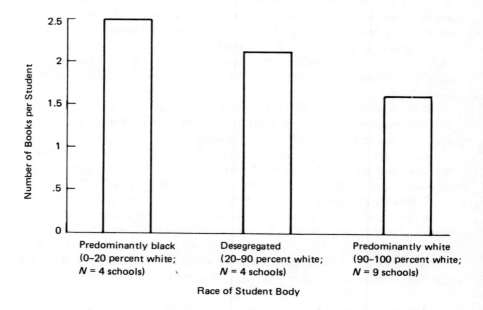

Figure 4-4. Average (Mean) Number of Library Books per Student in Junior High Schools Across the District, Grouped by Race of Student Body

When both variables are discrete, rather than continuous, correlation coefficients are never computed; instead two other measures, both of which also range from 0 to 1 in size, can be calculated: gamma and lambda. Neither is as widely accepted as *r*, however. At the same time, the difference between two percentages in a table or bar graph is easier to interpret directly, without the aid of a summary statistic of association, than a scattergram. In court, therefore, for nonparametric data it is more common to discuss the association between two variables and its importance by comparing the percentages rather than by these somewhat arcane statistics.

Before leaving the subject of statistics of association, I must speak to the cliché that is most likely to be bandied about in the courtroom when some perfectly obvious strong finding has been announced—that is, association is not the same as causation. If two variables have been shown to be associated, that does not prove that one causes the other, it will be said. Surely a correlation exists between *bleu*-cheese consumption and score on the Scholastic Aptitude Test. Yet eating *bleu* cheese does not *cause* better test performance. Correlation does not always mean causation. The point is true, and on occasion the caution is well taken. It can also be misleading. We know, for example, that the rise of the sun in early morning is associated with an increase in temperature, so we can predict a noontime temperature of perhaps 25°C if it was 20° when we arose. This association is seen over and over again but is not perfect, for on some days sunrise is followed by a plunge of the thermometer. Do we conclude that it is merely an association, that sunrise does not cause the temperature increase but is merely associated with it? I think not.

My point is this: All we ever have, in the social world, the world of physical science, or the realm of common sense, is association. We can never see causation directly. To infer that one variable causes another, we need a strong association that is not due to some third variable lurking behind the scenes. And we need theory, we need some ideas, usually based on commonly accepted principles of social behavior, that link the first and second variables.

Most important is the association. If the association is strong enough, then it creates what could be called a prima facie relationship between the independent and dependent variables that has to be explained or explained away by the other side. I have found *r*s of .9 and even higher between percentage white in voting precincts and the percentage of votes cast for white candidates. Such *r*s do not prove that race of voter causes the outcome, but if some other cause is alleged, such as poverty, then we must insist that it too correlate roughly .9 with race. In other words, the following statement can be made in court about a strong correlation: I have found that race explains 80 percent of the variance in voting results.[6] It may be that something other than race is at work causing this association, but if so, that variable must itself be so strongly tied to race as to amount to something we might term a racial characteristic. My inference is that race itself is at work, that whites form one community of rhetoric, addressed by one set of candidates, while blacks form another.

An r of .9 is not required. An r of .5 is also quite telling, as is a difference of the magnitude reported in figure 4–4, dealing with race and library books. To be sure, some third variable may be at work. This is a subject for chapter 14. For now, let us conclude that if a relationship between two variables looks important, as shown by a table, graph, scattergram, or summary statistic such as r, the other side is in some difficulty, providing the association is based on enough cases to achieve statistical significance.

Inferential Statistics

Significance, the statistical concept that means unlikely to occur due to chance, is the question posed and answered by inferential statistics. It is usually introduced using coin flips as the vehicle. Let us add some substance to the example. Consider two professors, one of each sex, having identical ranks (associate, tenured, for instance). Probably they are not identical in actual qualifications. One is surely more qualified than the other, perhaps considerably more so. Like a single coin flip, either the male or the female professor has to be more qualified, and hence underranked, although if the difference is small, the underranking would not amount to a full difference in position and could justifiably be disregarded by the college. If the woman in our example happened to be more qualified, hence underranked, no one would assume institutional bias, just as no one would assume a coin to be biased if a single toss came up heads.

If nine out of ten flips came up heads, no reasonable person would doubt that the coin was biased. This is the basic principle of inferential statistics, and it parallels common sense, for the likelihood of nine heads in ten flips is a mere .011 or 1.1 percent—if we engaged in 100 series of ten flips with an unbiased coin and an unbiased flipping procedure, only one of those series would come out with nine or more heads. Far more likely would be five heads or four, or six or even seven.

Statisticians and social scientists use this kind of analysis, inferential statistics or statistical inference, to rule out change as a likely cause of the result they have observed. Thus, if we amassed ten pairs of vitas (resumés), each pair consisting of a woman and a man of equal rank, we could reasonably expect by chance that in about half of those pairs the woman would in fact have superior qualifications and that in half the man would be superior. If the woman's qualifications were superior in nine or ten out of ten pairs, then to conclude that this happened by chance would be wrong, for it would occur by chance only 1.1 times in 100. If an outcome is unlikely due to chance, then some bias, some cause, is involved.

Obviously, sample size plays a big role. If we flip a coin ten times and get nine heads, we are almost sure our coin or our flipping procedure is biased. If we get seven heads, we can come to no sure conclusion. However, if out of 100 tosses we get 70 heads, even though the proportion is the same, now we can safely conclude that some bias is involved, for it is not likely to deviate so far from 50, our expected unbiased outcome, by chance. To get from a small sample the same level of significance, the same confidence that chance was not at work, a greater difference between the groups is required.

Two levels of significance are common in social science and in court. Researchers usually like to have at least the .05 level of significance, meaning a result that would occur fewer than 5 times in 100 by chance. Our example of nine heads in ten flips meets this criterion and almost meets the more-rigorous .01 level of significance, the other benchmark in social science.

If we conclude that something is going on, that chance is not involved, then we reject the null hypothesis, which as its name implies, states that nothing is going on, that chance alone produced the disparity. If we mistakenly reject the null hypothesis, then we mistakenly assume that a finding results from discrimination or some other social process, when in fact the outcome was one of those rare cases produced by chance. This happens, but it usually results from searching for the hypothesis after the face. For example, a professor wants to explain her grade distribution in a class of 100 students. She looks at the men compared to the women. No significant difference appears. She compares the upperclassmen to the underclassmen—no difference. Height seems irrelevant too. Finally she notes that the students in the first half of her grade book, listed by last names, had lower grades than in the last half. This result is significant at the .05 level. She thus develops a quick theory, perhaps about Swedes whose names are Amundsen and Anderson, to account for the "finding" and rushes to tell her colleagues. The problem is that she searched for her hypothesis. In any given batch of data, some grouping by some independent variable will result in .05 significance. To avoid this, use the .01 significance level wherever possible, and state your hypothesis before beginning analysis.

The opposite error is more common: accepting the null hypothesis when in fact some discrimination was going on. To return to our ten female college professors for a final time, suppose only seven of them had been more qualified than their male equivalents. In that case, rather than a significance level of .011, we would have .172, not significant. Then we could not reject the null hypothesis and could not conclude that our findings were due to discrimination. Such a lack of statistical significance will sometimes be used by the other side to rebut a finding against it. This is a misuse of statistical inference. It would be wrong for us to accept the null hypothesis and affirm that our results were due to chance. Absence of proof of discrimination is not proof of the absence of discrimination. What should be done, obviously, is to expand the sample size and test again.

We can also place what are called confidence limits around our finding. Based on our ten pairs of professors, we have found that in 70 percent of the cases, the woman was better qualified, hence underranked. We cannot be sure that exactly 70 percent of all such matched pairs would show this result. We can state, at the .01 level of confidence (similar to that level of significance), that the number of women who would be more qualified than their equivalent men, in all matched pairs, would be somewhere between about 30 percent and 100 percent. These confidence limits are so wide because the sample is so small. Confidence limits based on 40 matched pairs would be 51 percent to 88 percent. In that case, the researcher could state she is 99 percent sure that the true population proportion—the percentage of all matched pairs in which the woman was better qualified—lies between 51 percent and 88 percent. Now, based on the larger sample size, she can conclude that women are significantly overqualified. If the proportion of all cases in which the woman were overqualified is really 50 percent, as would be expected by chance, without discrimination, then our 70 percent outcome could almost never have occurred. The confidence limits, which our researcher is 99 percent sure enclose the true proportion of all cases, do not include 50 percent. Something other than chance caused her outcome.

If, after a larger sample, statistical significance still cannot be shown, then the case is in trouble. In order to go to court with a finding (or in order to persuade another social scientist of it), importance and significance must both be shown. Then an effective presentation of the data and conclusions can be made.

Notes

1. E. Webb et al., *Unobstrusive Measures* (Chicago: Rand McNally, 1966); see also D. Miller, *Handbook of Research Design and Social Measurement* (New York: McKay, 1977).

2. R.F. Bales, "A Set of Categories for the Analysis of Small Group Interaction," *American Sociological Review* 15 (1950): 257-263.

3. W.L. Warner, *Social Class in America* (New York: Harper, 1960).

4. F. Strodtbeck et al., "Social Status in Jury Deliberations," *American Sociological Review* 22 (1957): 713-719.

5. There is a reason why women get the zero—namely, we believe men will have higher pay. Therefore we assign men the higher number so that if we are right, our r will be positive. (If r were negative, say $r = -.6$, no harm would be done, and r^2 would still show the proportion of variance explained by sex, but some people are uneasy with negative numbers.)

6. In this discussion I commit the econological fallacy, but it does not vitiate my conclusions. Chapter 13 describes this fallacy.

Additional Resources

Further Reading on Statistics

Each book is listed for a distinct reason. If I were a lawyer, about to purchase an introduction to statistics, I would buy two: a basic statistics primer (Anderson and Zelditch or Loether and McTavish) and Siegel's guide to nonparametric statistical tests.

T. Anderson and M. Zelditch, *A Basic Course in Statistics* (New York: Holt, 1968), contains concise, clear chapters.

M. Finkelstein, *Quantitative Methods in Law* (New York: Free Press, 1978), discusses, in the first chapter, the increasing use of statistics in legal cases. Other useful chapters cover jury discrimination, voting (regarding one man/one vote reapportionment), and regression models in administrative proceedings.

D. Freedman et al., *Statistics* (New York: Norton, 1978), is a massive, thorough reference work with clear discussions of which test to use for which purpose.

M. Hallock, "The Numbers Game—The Use and Misuse of Statistics in Civil Rights Litigation," *Villanova Law Review* 23 (1977): 5–34, includes a good discussion of inferential statistics and levels of significance, statistically and judicially considered. It treats jury and employment discrimination, demographic data, regression, and chi square.

D. Koosis, *Statistics* (New York: Wiley, 1972), offers excellent step-by-step exercises to teach the use of some statistical techniques, including frequency distributions, sampling, and difference between two means.

E. Lehmann, *Nonparametrics* (San Francisco: Holden-Day, 1975), is an update of Siegel and is thorough and useful but does not have Siegel's unique clarity and utility for the neophyte.

H. Loether and D. McTavish, *Descriptive Statistics for Sociologists* and *Inferential Statistics for Sociologists* (Boston: Allyn and Bacon, 1974), are a little more difficult than Anderson and Zelditch but are more complete. *Descriptive Statistics* includes a useful how-to section on graphic presentation. The delineation between descriptive and inferential statistics helps avoid confusion.

H.T. Reynolds, *Analysis of Nominal Data* (Beverly Hills: Sage, 1977), is a sophisticated but compact presentation of chi square and other ways to analyze nonparametric variables. Many analyses, including chi square, which are usually though of as measures of association, really amount to significance tests and hence are part of inferential statistics. This book suggests some useful but unfortunately uncommon true measures of association as alternatives.

S. Siegel, *Nonparametric Statistics* (New York: McGraw-Hill, 1956), is the classic source for many simple yet powerful statistical tests, including the sign test, chi square, runs test, Wilcoxon signed-ranks test, and Spearman correlation coefficient. It is clearly written, and each section concludes with a crystalline summary of procedure.

M. Zelditch, *A Basic Course in Sociological Statistics* (New York: Holt, 1959), is even simpler and clearer than Anderson and Zelditch, its successor.

5

Organizing Data for Courtroom Use

Tables of census data are often long and complex. Even for a single town or county, they may run more than a page, and they contain a great deal more data than are relevant to a given court case or a single factual issue within that case. The information within a single table needs condensing and organizing to be effective in court; often information must be excerpted from two or more tables into a single courtroom exhibit. Data from noncensus sources such as the social scientist's own research or files of local government agencies are even less organized and concise. This chapter suggests to lawyers and prospective expert witnesses ways to present data to maximum effect. Because graduate training in social science often overemphasizes data analysis (the controlling and inferential statistics that can often become quite elaborate), prospective witnesses are often weak at data presentation. Pointers in this chapter may help the lawyer suggest more-effective graphics to his witness, therefore. Even though the information will not be new to the social scientist, the review may be helpful.

Condensing Data into Tables and Graphs

Table 5-1 is a page from the 1970 census for Hinds County, Mississippi, showing employment statistics. No black/white comparison can be made without some calculations referring to the same data for blacks alone, which I also obtained from the census. Although the information is extensive, it is also a bit forbidding. Table 5-2 shows a courtroom exhibit I made from these data. It is organized to highlight the vast gap between white and black populations in the country. I used it to buttress my claim that the black community had strikingly different needs and interests from the white community. The table was also relevant to my assertion that it was easier for whites to register, support political campaigns, and vote, helping to explain the fact that although blacks made up 34.2 percent of the voting-age population in the county, they comprised only 28.7 percent of the turnout at the polls in a recent election.

Minor decisions must be made in creating an exhibit like table 5-2, and they are more defensible when made by an expert. To find the number of whites in each occupational category, for instance, the black figure is subtracted from the total figure. What about "others"? Their treatment depends upon the situation. For example, if others are a handful of Asian-Americans intermixed occupationally and residentially with whites, then they should be included with that

Table 5-1
Occupation and Earnings for Hinds County, Mississippi, 1970 Census

Occupation	Number of Workers
Total employed, 16 years and over	81,833
Professional, technical, and kindred workers	14,026
Engineers	947
Physicians, dentists, and related practitioners	869
Health workers, except practitioners	1,672
Teachers, elementary and secondary schools	3,109
Technicians, except health	786
Other professional workers	6,643
Managers and administrators, except farm	8,218
Salaried: Manufacturing	735
Retail trade	1,468
Other industries	4,665
Self-employed: Retail trade	629
Other industries	721
Sales workers	6,998
Retail trade	3,104
Other than retail trade	3,894
Clerical and kindred workers	15,910
Craftsmen, foremen, and kindred workers	8,781
Automobile mechanics, including body repairmen	837
Mechanics and repairmen, except automobile	1,173
Metal craftsmen, except mechanics	468
Construction craftsmen	2,570
Other craftsmen	3,733
Operatives, except transport	7,126
Durable-goods manufacturing	2,548
Nondurable-goods manufacturing	1,712
Nonmanufacturing industries	2,866
Transport-equipment operatives	3,100
Laborers, except farm	3,469
Construction laborers	931
Freight, stock, and material handlers	1,285
Other laborers, except farm	1,253
Farmers and farm managers	445
Farm laborers and farm foremen	750
Service workers, except private household[a]	9,582
Cleaning-service workers	2,216
Food-service workers	2,649
Health-service workers	1,466
Personal-service workers	1,479
Protective-service workers	1,079
Private household workers	3,428
Female employed, 16 years old and over	34,725
Professional, technical, and kindred workers	6,365
Nurses	1,076
Health workers, except nurses	493
Teachers, elementary and secondary schools	2,497
Technicians, except health	139
Other professional workers	2,160
Managers and administrators, except farm	1,325
Sales workers	2,100
Retail trade	1,698
Other than retail trade	402

Table 5-1 continued

Occupation	Number of Workers
Clerical and kindred workers	11,963
Bookkeepers	1,431
Secretaries, stenographers, and typists	4,762
Other clerical workers	5,770
Craftsmen, foremen, and kindred workers	463
Operatives, except transport	2,768
Durable-goods manufacturing	798
Nondurable-goods manufacturing	919
Nonmanufacturing industries	1,051
Transport-equipment operatives	169
Laborers, except farm	266
Farmers and farm managers	19
Farm laborers and farm foremen	72
Service workers, except private household[a]	5,890
Cleaning-service workers	1,001
Food-service workers	2,084
Health-service workers	1,216
Personal-service workers	1,051
Protective-service workers	95
Private household workers	3,325
Male employed, 14 and 15 years old	377
White-collar workers	164
Blue-collar workers	166
Farm workers	10
Service workers, including private household	37
Female employed, 14 and 15 years old	129
White-collar workers	53
Blue-collar workers	7
Farm workers	4
Service workers, except private household	47
Private household workers	18
Median Earnings in 1969 of persons in experienced civilian labor force for selected occupation groups	
Male, 16 years old and over with earnings	$6,554
Professional, managerial, and kindred workers	10,447
Craftsmen, foremen, and kindred workers	6,365
Operatives, including transport	4,573
Laborers, except farm	3,274
Farmers and farm managers	2,867
Farm laborers, except unpaid, and farm foremen	2,194
Female, 16 years old and over with earnings	$3,366
Clerical and kindred workers	4,142
Operatives, including transport	3,005

[a]Includes allocated cases, not shown separately.

Source: U.S. Census, 1970.

Table 5-2

Proportion of White-Collar and Blue-Collar Workers, by Race, Hinds County, Mississippi, 1970 Census

Occupation	White		Black	
	N	Percentage	N	Percentage
White collar (professional, technical, managerial, sales, clerical, farm owners and managers)	40,262	71.0%	5,335	21.3%
Blue collar (craftsmen, operatives, transport workers laborers, farm labor, service workers, domestic workers)	16,475	29.0	19,761	78.7
Totals	56,737	100%	25,096	100%

Notes: Only employed persons are included. White totals include a few nonblack, nonwhite others.

Conclusion: These two work categories are very important in the literature; the difference between the populations is dramatic, with whites' being overwhelmingly white collar, blacks' overwhelmingly blue collar.

population. If they constitute a sizable community of Native Americans then the table should show all three groups. If the county contains a few nonwhite, non-black farm workers, similar in status and income to black farm workers, then blacks and other races should be combined. Decisions to group occupations as white collar or years of education as illiterate and semiliterate, although common in the literature, are again more defensible if made by a social scientist with a doctorate.

The expert can also make projections and interpolations required to make the data apply to a given area or year. For example, to calculate the proportion of whites and blacks who voted in a given precinct, we need the voting-age population by race. If the precinct lines match census enumeration district lines, we can obtain the population by race but not by age. Census data for minor civil subdivisions will give us age breakdowns for that part of the county including our precinct, but not by race. Calculations using the age-by-race data for the county as a whole, corrected for the age breakdown of the minor subdivision and applied to the population by race from the enumeration districts, will yield a good estimate of the voting-age population by race. These calculations should be done in a routine and straightforward way, defensible in court, by or under the direction of an expert.

Be careful to avoid errors. Double-check all calculations, even simple addition. Conceptual errors are possible, too. For example, if the black median income is $4,277 and the total median income is $8,272, the white median cannot be found by any subtraction or balancing procedure. The number of white families in each income category ($0–1,000, $1,000–1,999, and so on) must be calculated; then the white median can be found from those new figures.[1]

The final error to avoid is mispercentaged tables. Like bridge bidding rules, and like the other admonitions in this book, the following rule is not absolute. but a first principle regarding tables is to put the independent variable across the top and percentage the table vertically. Table 5-2 is percentaged in that manner, with race being the independent variable that may or may not affect occupational distribution. Occasionally, social scientists percentage tables so that the entire table adds to 100 percent, rather than each column. Table 5-3 demonstrates this layout for the data in table 5-2, but table 5-3 is not clear. It does answer the question, "What proportion of the entire employed population is white *and* white collar?" For some purposes we might want to know that. However, it obscures the relationship between race and employment by contaminating its percentages with the proportion each race is in the population.

Table 5-4 demonstrates another way tables are sometimes laid out. Now each row adds to 100 percent rather than each column. Table 5-4 answers the question, "What proportion of all blue-collar workers are black?" If we wanted to examine a single trucking firm, for instance, we could use this proportion as a baseline and compare the proportion of its drivers who are black. As an overall description of the population, however, table 5-4 is not clear. It, too, obscures the relationship between race and employment because its percentages are influenced by the proportion each race is in the population. Thus, in a heavily white but egalitarian county, a statistician could present the appearance of discrimination by emphasizing the fact that whites hold almost all of the white-collar jobs.

Table 5-3
Percentage of All Workers Who Are of a Given Race and Employment Category, Hinds County, Mississippi, 1970 Census

	White		Black	
Occupation	N	*Percentage*	N	*Percentage*
White collar (professional, technical, managerial, sales, clerical, farm owners and managers)	40,262	49.2%	5,335	6.5%
Blue collar (craftsmen, operatives, transport workers, laborers, farm labor, service workers, domestic workers)	16,475	20.1%	19,761	24.1%

Note: This table partially obscures the relationship between race and employment and is contaminated by the proportion each race is in the population. It is inferior to table 5-2.

Table 5-4
Percentage of Each Race in White-Collar and Blue-Collar Categories, Hinds County, Mississippi, 1970 Census

Occupation	White		Black		Total	
	N	Percentage	N	Percentage	N	Percentage
White collar (professional, technical, managerial, sales, clerical, farm owners and managers)	40,262	88.3%	5,335	11.7%	45,597	100%
Blue collar (craftsmen, operatives, transport workers, laborers, farm labor, service workers, domestic workers)	16,475	45.5%	19,761	54.5%	32,326	100%

Note: This table partially obscures the relationship between race and employment and is contaminated by the proportion each race is in the population. It is inferior to table 5-2.

Table 5-2 is the correct way to ascertain whether race influences jobs held. In table 5-2, I percentaged to find the proportion of blacks in white-collar jobs in order to compare it to the proportion of whites in white-collar jobs. The proportions of blacks in white- and blue-collar jobs must add up to all employed blacks, or 100 percent. Each percentage is found by dividing the cell value (5,335 for white-collar blacks) by the column total, 25,096.

When the social scientist has gathered the data herself, or when a noncensus agency has compiled them, still more organization and condensation may be necessary for courtroom presentation. A common failing, made even by experts, is to present the data in the order in which it was collected, without a logical organizing prinicple. If the work forces in seven area manufacturing firms were surveyed regarding proportion of women, for instance, these firms should probably be listed in order of increasing percentage of women. If twenty firms were surveyed, they would probably not be listed at all but grouped by industry, with only the industry totals put into the body of the table. Details can always be provided in an appendix. "Don't knows" or "unknowns" can usually be eliminated from the body of a table and handled in a footnote, making the table much less cluttered.

A bar graph is usually more effective than a table. Figure 5-1 is a bar graph made from the data of table 5-2. Shaded plastic ribbons, for sale at office-supply houses, make bar graphs easy to construct. Chapter 4 points out that bar graphs are more appropriate than other ways of representing frequency distributions for nonparametric data. Even for parametric or continuous data such as incomes, bar graphs often make the greatest visual impact (figure 4-4 offers an example).

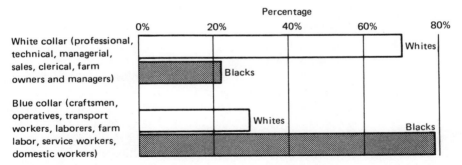

Note: Only employed persons are included. White totals include a few nonblack, nonwhite others.

Conclusion: These two work categories are very important in the literature: the difference between the populations is dramatic, with whites being overwhelmingly white collar, blacks' overwhelmingly blue collar.

Figure 5-1. Percentage of White-Collar and Blue-Collar Workers, by Race, Hinds County, Mississippi 1970 Census

There is one type of data for which bar graphs are mildly inferior—namely, data over time. Here a trend line is easier and usually shows the trend more clearly than discontinuous bars. Figure 5-2 shows a trend line for the proportion of voting-age blacks who were registered to vote in Shell County, Arkansas, over ten years. Again, this graph is superior in impact to a table of numbers. If a photo is occasionally worth a thousand words, then a graph can replace a thousand digits.

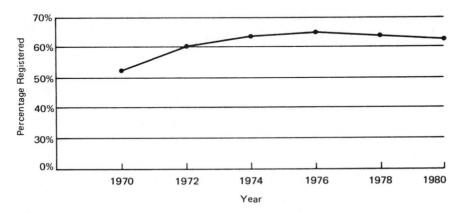

Figure 5-2. Percentage of Voting-Age Blacks Who Were Registered to Vote, Shell County, Arkansas, 1970-1980

Mapping

A pair of shaded maps offers a riveting way to show the court the relationship between two variables. Students under my direction once shaded the census-tract map of Jackson, Mississippi, according to proportion of residential land that was zoned nonresidentially—homes unprotected against commercial or industrial invasion. They shaded black all tracts where this problem was pervasive, left white all tracts where it did not occur, and used greys for intermediate proportions. The map then overlapped almost perfectly with a similarly shaded map showing proportion black in the population. The resulting exhibit was more effective than a correlation coefficient between percentage black and percentage miszoned could ever have been.

No more than five shading categories should be used in any map; they should progress systematically from light to dark. Colors do not reproduce well and should be avoided; grey shadings on plastic film are available from any office-supply store.

Usually, but not always, the same number of tracts should be shaded in each shade. If there are forty census tracts, it would make sense to set limits on the variable, proportion black, for instance, such that about ten tracts are shaded to indicate heavily black, ten fairly black, ten fairly white, and ten heavily white. The next map, showing the variable believed to correlate with race, can then be shaded with the same four categories, each with about ten tracts, so that if the maps overlap, then the relationship is apparent. Figures 5-3 and 5-4 show such a relationship that made a strong impact in the courtroom. They indicate that supporters of the national Democratic presidential nominee in 1968 were unlikely to be white.

Even experienced social scientists sometimes blunder while shading maps. They use nonintuitive shading—colors or shading patterns that do not get darker as the areas have more and more of a variable. Sometimes they do not use equal-N shading, either. For example, some analysts would be reluctant to set the limits for the "high in Humphrey vote" county as low as 35 percent. They might object that high must imply at least 50 percent, perhaps 60 percent, leaving figure 5-4 almost entirely devoid of black-shaded counties. If they picked an arbitrary definition of high, rather than the equal-N definition used in figure 5-3, they would then have to reset it for the presidential election of 1964, in which Goldwater captured 87 percent of the votes. For this election, equal-N shading yields a definition of 94-100 percent for high. Retaining the arbitrary 60 percent mark would mean shading the entire state black.

If arbitrary (but often well-meant) definitions for high and other shade categories are allowed, two errors can occur. The obvious mistake is that a relationship can be obfuscated in the paired maps, even though in fact it is strong. This always occurs when a map is overwhelmingly shaded with just one shading; it can also happen in some other circumstances. The less-obvious error is that the

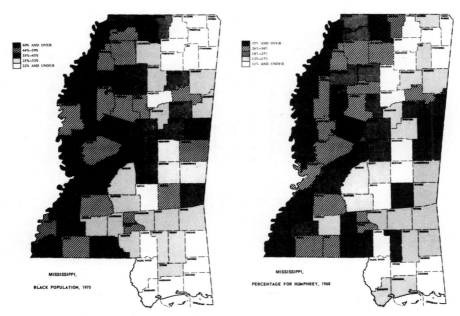

Figure 5-3. Black Population, Mississip- **Figure 5-4.** Percentage of Votes for
pi, 1970 Census   Humphrey, Mississippi,
                                                                   1968

maps can sometimes be shaded to imply a relationship when only a weak correlation exists. Equal-N shading offers the best chance for two maps to look alike
if in fact there is a relationship between them. At the same time, because it is
standardized, it prevents the shader from searching for arbitrary categories that
might imply a relationship falsely.

Demographic Techniques

The best way to show age and sex data is through a population pyramid. Often
set by five-year intervals, such a pyramid shows graphically some processes that
can be inferred only laboriously from tables. Figure 5-5 shows much outmigration from Hinds County, particularly amoung blacks, for usually there would be
only a gradual tapering from broad base to old age. The drastic shortening of the
bars beginning at age twenty, amounting to a wasp waist, can only have been
caused by death, migration, or dramatically lower birth rates twenty to twenty-
five years ago contrasted to ten to fifteen years ago.

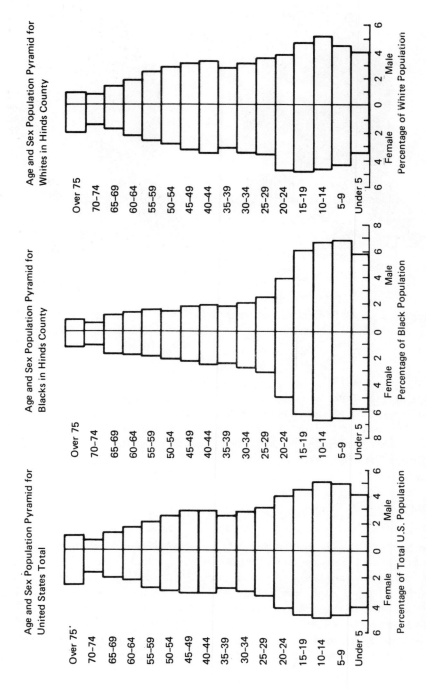

Figure 5-5. Age and Sex Population Pyramids for the United States and Hinds County, Mississippi, 1970 Census

The term *cohort* is basic in demography, the study of population. A cohort is the group of all people who entered a system at the same time. A birth cohort refers to everyone born in a given year. Other cohorts include college freshmen or everyone hired by the Los Angeles Police Department in 1982. By keeping cohorts separate, demographers can analyze various changes over time. They can also make accurate short-term projections into the future.

To demonstrate that the difference between the bars for 20-24 and 15-19 years in figure 5-5 shows outmigration, compare the actual number of 20-24-year olds in 1970 with the 10-14-year olds in 1960. In 1960, 8,589 persons decreased to only 7,326 in 1970. Death could never account for such a drop, not in such a young age bracket (and if it did, the analyst would seek to know why so many young blacks were dying). Similar comparisons can be made for other cohorts.

Although courts usually consider census data to be almost unchallengeable, social scientists know that they can grow fairly obsolete and inaccurate by, say, the sixth year after the census. Be wary of projections other than by your own expert. Census Bureau projections by race in a midpoint year (1975) were notoriously inaccurate. Local agencies often have an axe to grind, so they can produce even less-accurate work. Municipal governments want to maximize populations; sometimes they want to maximize whiteness; therefore they may ignore decreasing household size and concentrate on the new housing at the edge of town. My suggestion for most projections from the most recent census is to make them simple by using procedures that are demographically defensible yet easy to explain. Figure 5-6 is an example. The scientist should check her projections by using the most recent estimates from the census or other agencies. Unlike simple projections, intercensal estimates are based on new intercensal data, sometimes including births, deaths, auto registrations, or spot or sample surveys.

Census Data in the Courtroom: An Example

In many civil rights cases, whether relating to voting rights, school discipline, or employment tests, it is useful to show the disparity between whites and blacks in the community. We may have shown that blacks are underregistered compared to whites, or perhaps that they are less likely to take or pass a state civil service exam. At this point, socioeconomic data on the two or more groups can help explain why the association between the variables exists and can show how that association affects the overall situation of the disadvantaged group. Census data are the most readily available resource and include information on a wide range of potentially relevant topics from plumbing fixtures to illiteracy. Table 5-5 summarizes some of this information for a Southern county. It comprised an exhibit I presented in a voting-rights case. If I were making the exhibit

Following is an age table for black women in Shell County, Arkansas, for 1970 and 1980. We wish to construct an age table for 1984 because, perhaps, we are trying a lawsuit regarding voting rights or employment pools in that year.

Black Female Population, Shell County, Arkansas, 1970 and 1980

Age in 1970	Number in 1970	Age in 1980	Number in 1980	Age in 1984	Projected Number in 1984
—	—	—	—	Under 4	518
—	—	Under 5	647	4–8	
—	—	5–9	590	9–13	
Under 5	1,210	10–14	626	14–18	450
5–9	955	15–19	491	19–23	
10–14	791	20–24	235	24–28	
15–19	632	25–29	179	29–33	
20–24	336	30–34	136	34–38	
25–29	264	35–39	153	39–43	
30–34	277	40–44	158	44–48	
35–39	319	45–49	186	49–53	
40–44	305	50–54	159	54–58	
45–49	338	55–59	187	59–63	
50–54	282	60–64	191	64–68	
55–59	248	65–69	176	69–73	
60–64	241	70–74	129	74–78	
65–69	260		206		
70–74	142	Over 74	—	Over 78	
Over 74	156				

Twelve-year olds in 1970 were 22 by 1980. Obviously, everyone in the 10–14 age category in 1970 was still in the 20–24 age bloc in 1980 or had died or moved away. Whatever processes—immigration, outmigration, illness, and so on—were affecting adolescents in the 1970s have probably continued into the 1980s, or so we assume, having no basis to infer a change.

Accordingly, we summarize those processes by a ratio, 235/791—the end (1980, 20–24 age category) divided by the beginning (1970, 10–14 age category)—and we apply that ratio, .297, to the new batch of 10–14-year olds (1980, 10–14 age category). The result, (.297)(626) = 186, is the number of black women aged 20–24 we would expect to find in the county in 1990 if the 1980s behave like the 1970s. A total of 440 girls, aged 10–14 in 1980, would be gone by 1990.

Figure 5–6. How to Do a Simple Demographic Projection

Since we only wanted to project to 1984, not 1990, we do not actually subtract all of the 440 persons that our calculations suggest, but only 4/10 of them, since 1984 is 4/10 of the way to 1990. The result, 176, is subtracted from our 626 who begin in 1980 to yield 450, our projection (not estimate) for 14–18-year olds in 1984.[2] We do the same for all other age groups that existed in 1970. Newborns, aged 0–4 in 1984, pose a special problem. Changes in fertility between 1970 and 1980 have affected the number of infants in 1980, as well as changes wrought by migration and disease. Without more information, we cannot tell exactly what has happened to fertility alone, so we cannot predict 1984 infants. The simplest procedure, since these young children do not contribute to employment pools or voting-age populations anyway, is simply to repeat the 1980 figure for under 5, multiplied by 0.8 to take account of the four-year rather than five-year span, 1980–1984. Finally, we sum all the 1984 categories for the total number of black women in the county. Repeat the entire procedure for black men, white women, and white men.

Figure 5–6. *continued*

today, I would use bar graphs for all this information in order to make greater graphic impact. I would also add this conclusion to the bottom of the table: The black community faces a very different socioeconomic position and has very different needs than the white community.

The table shows that, in many communities, the median education for whites is much higher than for blacks. Most whites have at least some post-high-school education, but most blacks do not. Whites are more likely to be employed in white-collar jobs; this in turn affects their income level, which is more than twice as high in some communities. The physical circumstances of the black community are also inferior. Often most whites are homeowners while most blacks rent. As renters, blacks are less able to get their municipal governments to improve services because they lack the clout of direct taxpayers. These differences mean that blacks are likely to have different political goals. The black community is more likely to support public housing and rent subsidies, whereas fewer whites would be eligible for such benefits. Blacks, as renters, would be more interested in enforcement of inspection codes to deal with substandard housing than white landlords who would have to comply.

The lower socioeconomic status of blacks, in addition to shaping their goals, also affects their ability to attain those goals. Since blacks are more likely to be working class, they are usually less able to take time off to register and vote. The lower median income of the black community means less money available to buy all the things that help cause people to score well on standardized tests.[3] In our society, money helps one participate in everything from swimming to reading. Thus, the disparities pointed to by census data have wide implications for all sorts of class-election lawsuits.

Table 5-5

Comparison of Basic Socioeconomic Position, by Race, Shell County, Arkansas, 1970 Census

Item	Whites	Blacks
Education		
Median years of education among the adult population (25 and older)		
Men	10.4	7.0
Women	10.2	8.4
Illiteracy and semiliteracy among the adult population (25 and older, percentage with 0–4 years of education)	4.1%	27.3%
Number of college graduates among the adult population (25 and older)	2,009	313
Occupational Groupings		
Percentage of blue-collar and white-collar workers		
White collar (professional, technical, and kindred; managers, administrators; farm managers and owners; clerical; sales)	60.2%	18.0%
Blue collar (craftsmen, foremen, and kindred; operatives; transport; laborers and farm labor; service workers; domestic workers)	39.8%	82.0%
Total employed, civilian labor force	100%	100%
Unemployment		
Percentage of the civilian labor force unemployed	2.9%	7.2%
Income		
Median income (families and unrelated individuals)	$9,782	$3,794
Percentage below poverty line (families)	7.3%	49.0%
Housing		
Percentage of dwelling units lacking some or all plumbing	8.2%	44.1%
Percentage of dwellings with more than one person per room	6.6%	26.6%
Percentage of families occupying rental housing	24.8%	53.3%
Percentage of rental housing lacking some or all plumbing	6.3%	56.2%

Notes

1. These calculations can be condensed, but the basic procedure cannot be circumvented.

2. There is a shorter way to do these calculations, but the procedure suggested is basic and intuitively clear.

3. Loewen, "Breaking the Vicious Circle," *Clearinghouse for Civil Rights Research* 6 (1978): 24–35: and M.B. Goldfarb et al. "Recent Developments in IQ Research: What Policymakers Need to Know," ibid., pp. 3–19. These researchers document some of the ways that income helps purchase aptitude-test scores.

Additional Resources

Further Reading

G. Barclay, *Techniques of Population Analysis* (New York: Wiley, 1958), is a basic text in demography.

N. Glenn, *Cohort Analysis* (Beverly Hills: Sage, 1978), is a recent compact booklet aimed at the social scientist, not the lay reader.

L. Goodman, ed., *Sources and Uses of Social and Economic Data: A Manual for Lawyers* (Washington, D.C.: Bureau of Social Science Research, 1973), contains a chapter (chapter 5) with a clear discussion of how to collapse a census table for courtroom use. It also supplies four case studies in which statistics were used to aid lawsuits.

P. Hauser, ed., *Handbook for Social Research in Urban Areas* (Paris: UNESCO, 1964), provides a good introduction to doing research based on existing data from the census and other similar sources. It describes probable data sources and discusses the question of unit of analysis. Chapter 6 provides a compact introduction to demographic analysis. The book is a good starting reference for anyone involved with school desegregation, municipal-services discrimination, or other research or litigation involving urban areas.

N.B. Ryder, "The Cohort as a Concept in the Study of Social Change," *American Sociological Review* 30 (1965): 843–861, presents many ways to use cohort analysis. For example, the effects on a Southern birth cohort from school desegregation, which happened around 1969, will still be importantly felt in society in the year 2005, for then the children who underwent desegregation will be in their fifties and will be directing banks, running universities, and the like. Thus, one use of cohort analysis is to study the continuing effects of segregation, discrimination, or other events or practices.

H. Shryock and J. Fiegel, *The Methods and Materials of Demography* (Washington, D.C.: Government Printing Office (and Bureau of the Census), 1973), is a large, detailed text. Pages 236–240 present population pyramids clearly with examples.

Transaction/Society 18 (January/February 1981): 5–25, presents a symposium on the accuracy of the 1980 census that might be useful in court. It concludes that the 1980 count was much more accurate than the 1970 count.

    J. Weeks, *Population* (Belmont, Calif.: Wadsworth, 1978), provides a good
basic understanding of demography. Part II explains the three basic population
processes—fertility, mortality, and migration. Part III explains the age and sex
structure and the impact of the processes upon it. It is clearly organized, but
not a how-to book, and does not teach specific demographic methods.

6 The Sign Test in Employment Discrimination

This chapter is the first of several that have a dual nature. It treats a specific statistical or research technique, in this case the sign test, while focusing upon a specific social and legal context, in this case employment discrimination. To introduce the sign test without some context of applications for it would be artificial and unstimulating. At the same time, lawyers and social scientists need to realize that the uses of the sign test go far beyond employment discrimination, while many other statistical and research techniques might be applied to employment-discrimination cases besides the sign test.

It follows that this chapter should be read by any attorney who is trying an employment case but also by any attorney with a case in which the sign test, in particular, or inferential statistics in general, might be useful. Additional areas where the sign test might be useful include discrimination in municipal services; taxation or assessment cases; admission into college, professional school, or apprenticeship programs; textbook-discrimination cases; school discipline; and even trademark infringement and product comparisons. Moreover, I have deliberately placed this chapter first after use of archival data because the sign test provides the best possible introduction to the world of inferential statistics. That world and its principles are crucial to a huge variety of legal issues.

The chapter should also be read by any social scientist seeking an introduction to inferential statistics in the courtroom. It will help her present inferential statistics clearly to a lay audience, even if she elects to use other, more-complicated tests than the sign test. The chapter also provides the social scientist with an introduction to employment-discrimination cases.

The structure of the chapter is simple. It consists of two main sections: an introduction to employment discrimination and a presentation of the sign test. Several principles discussed in the employment-discrimination section are of general importance in class-action suits—the concept of a statistical prima facie case of discrimination, the need for a comparison population or control group, and the alternatives of an external comparison or an internal one within the company's work force. The principles discussed within the presentation of the sign test are even more general, including the .05 and .01 levels of significance, the nature of one-tailed and two-tailed tests and when to use each, and a review of the basic idea of inferential statistics in a context that is easy to understand. A concluding section points out the strengths of the technique and suggests ways to complement it in court.

Employment Discrimination

An entire cottage industry has grown up of social scientists testifying in employment-discrimination lawsuits. So has a considerable literature, and I list and annotate much of it for you in "Additional Recources" at the end of the chapter. In most cases, social-science statistics are used to make what is called a prima facie case of discrimination. If an employer hires or promotes in such a way as to treat one class of applicants or employees worse than another, whether intentionally or not, this disparate treatment can usually be shown statistically. For example, women may comprise 38 percent of the work force in a community, but only 14 percent of the labor force of a given temployer against whom some women have filed specific charges of sex-based discrimination. Establishing a prima facie case of discrimination usually means showing that the group in question is underrepresented or underpromoted in the defendant's labor force and that this underrepresentation or underpromotion results from the defendant's hiring and promotion policies and practices.[1]

In *Teamsters* v. *U.S.*, 431 U.S. 324 (1977), the Supreme Court made a distinction between disparate treatment in employment and disparate impact. On the one hand, *disparate treatment* means treating

> some people less favorably than others because of their race, color, re
> ligion, sex, or national origin. Proof of discriminatory motive is cri
> tical, although it can in some situations be inferred from the mere fact
> of difference in treatment.[2]

Disparate impact, on the other hand, involves

> employment practices that are facially neutral in their treatment of dif
> ferent groups but that in fact fall more harshly on one group than
> another and cannot be justified by business necessity.[3]

Under a disparate-impact theory, proof of discriminatory motive is not required. For example, an Alabama statute set minimum height and weight requirements for prison guards. Of course these excluded women disproportionately. In *Dothard* v. *Rawlinson,* the plaintiff never claimed that the Alabama legislature intended to keep women from being prison guards. Her prima facie case first showed that only 13 percent of Alabama's prison guards were women, while women made up 37 percent of Alabama's total labor force. Then she introduced census data to show that the height and weight criteria (5'2" and 120 lbs.) would exclude 33 percent of all women but only 1.3 percent of men. She prevailed in the Supreme Court.

Once a prima facie case has been established, the burden of proof shifts to the defendant. There are two main lines his defense may take. He may counter or impugn the plaintiff's statistical case by arguing that the comparison group was inappropriate or that the statistics do not really show discrimination or by presenting alternative statistics and alternative social science theory to account for them. He may also claim that the differential treatment is job related. For example, Alabama might have claimed in *Dothard* that physical size was a job-related requirement for the position of prison guard. (The state did so claim, but its reasoning and evidence on the point were not convincing.)

Employment-discrimination lawsuits may be brought under Title VII of the Civil Rights Act of 1964; under other laws, including some passed during Reconstruction; or as constitutional cases under the Fourteenth Amendment. Sometimes they are brought under more than one of these, but a majority are brought as alleged violations of Title VII (42 U.S.C. §2000e et seq. (1970 and Supp. V 1975)). In practice, the social scientist does about the same initial analysis regardless of which statute or section of the Constitution and which theory of the case are relied upon. Her first job is usually to see if there has been disparate impact—that is, have members of the minority (for example, blacks or women) been treated so as to exclude them disproportionately from hiring, promotion, or whatever other benefit is at issue?

Immediately a comparison is involved, but to whom? Consider a university charged with racial discrimination in hiring. If we are talking about excluding blacks from the buildings-and-grounds department, we might compare the proportion of black in the buildings-and-grounds work force with that in the entire labor force of the metropolitan area or county in which the university stands. A better comparison would be to the proportion of blacks in the kinds of jobs comparable to and including buildings-and-grounds work—the skilled and unskilled working class, excluding the professional and managerial classes who would not be competing for buildings-and-grounds jobs.

However, if we were talking about excluding women from full professorships, we would surely not look at the proportion of women in the metropolitan-area labor market. College faculty members are normally hired nationally, not locally, so the local comparison would be pointless. Moreover, doctorates are the minimal qualification in many fields for university professorships, and the proportion of Ph.D.s who are women is much smaller than the proportion of the population or the entire work force that is made up of women.

Comparisons can be grouped into two categories, external and internal. The examples in the previous paragraph are external: hiring at one firm is compared to some larger population. A first comparison might be with the proportion of blacks (or women and so on) in the entire area population, in the age groups from which hiring is done, and in the social class(es) from which applicants might be expected to come. Quite often, this is the relevant comparison. If a city is 42 percent black and Chicano, for instance, and if only 2.3 percent of the police force is from those two minority groups, that disparity alone provides some evidence of discrimination. Looking within age and social-class groups would be still more appropriate than taking the overall population figure of 42 percent. Then the difference-of-two-proportions test (chapter 8) can be used to see if the disproportion is statistically significant.

Comparing the firm's employees with a subset of the general population is reasonable for jobs requiring no special education or skills, but for skilled jobs, white collar or blue, employers will reply that they must hire only persons with certain qualifications and will claim that those qualifications are not widely present in the minority or among women. To modify the general population beyond gross age and social-class characteristics can become fruitless. If our social scientist tried to determine the number of women with doctorates in physics, for instance, then the employer might counter that many of those women were not mobile, chose not to apply for the job, and hence were not available.

Sometimes it can be useful to refer to statistics from other comparable firms, similarly situated, or from the industry as a whole. If our firm cannot seem to employ women, has only a 14 percent female labor force while the industry average is 38 percent and the average for firms in that metropolitan area is also 38 percent, then a prima facie case of discrimination may be demonstrable. The problem with this approach is simple: if the whole industry is discriminating, then no one firm will stand out. The sins of the group will legitimate the sins of each.

At some point, one side or the other may rely upon the pool of applicants. The applicant pool is manageable, and comparing it to hirees seems logical and can sometimes show disparate results regarding minorities or women. Using the applicant pool also has a major drawback, however. If the applicant pool contains few women or minorities, then the company can cite it as evidence that women or minorities do not want the jobs under investigation, or are not qualified for them, and hence do not even apply. Of course, there are many ways an employer can behave so as to receive few appliations from minorities or women. Most obviously, it can refuse to hire them, thus developing a reputation that certain jobs are for men or for whites only. After all, if a woman knew an assembly line hired only men, she would be silly to waste time applying. Other behaviors that can influence applications include plant location, hours and style of the personnel office, language and photographs in company publications, choice of vehicle for advertising the position, race and sex of recruiters and interviewers, amount of work required to complete the application, and a host of others. It follows, then, that if we find a substantially higher proportion of women or minorities in the applicant pool than in the pool of hirees, that is evidence of possible discrimination, but if we do not, if few applicants come from these groups, that is not yet evidence of the absence of discrimination.[4]

To look at applicants is to move from external comparisons based on census data, industrywide figures, or other information outside this employer's control to an internal comparison using data supplied by the defendant. There are advantages and drawbacks to relying on the defendant's data. The disadvantage for the plaintiff is that the data can be hard to obtain. Discovery and interrogatories are cumbersome, and the defendant can sometimes manipulate the data that are provided, provide only part of what is required, or claim not to have information on rejected applicants. Moreover, if the plaintiff wants to see all data on hired and rejected applicants, which certainly might be relevant, the defendant can reasonably object that compliance with such a request is a huge burden for the employer and also an invasion of privacy for the applicants, particularly for the rejected applicants. After all, job applicants fill out the forms thinking they will go to the personnel officer and nowhere else; they may volunteer or even falsify information that they would hate to see come out in court.

These problems can be overcome with the help of the social scientist. She can suggest sampling procedures to minimize the burden on the company (and on herself). She can also serve as a buffer, protecting the identity of each applicant while using the combined data from the accepted and rejected applications for her determination of possible hiring bias.

The advantage of internal comparisons for the plaintiff is that data from the defendant can hardly be said to be biased toward the plaintiff. Conversely, any study of its own data done by the defendant's expert is open to the charge that the data base itself was biased in some way, perhaps even in its collection.

In addition to applicants, internal comparison groups can also be found within the ranks of the firm's employees. For example, if a lawsuit challenges promotion practices, claiming that women are kept in bottom-rung positions, then comparisons can be made between female and male applicants for promotions. In the example that follows, an even simpler comparison is made—that is, between men and women who hold the same positions at a given point in time. This analysis uses data from many of the firm's employees, not just those who recently were considered for promotion or initial hiring, with the concurrent advantage of using data from persons not involved in the lawsuit, not identifiable by name, and not likely to be sensitive about the use of their files.

The Sign Test

Suppose the University of Northern Maryland (fictitious) has the proportions of female faculty members shown in table 6-1. Women obviously are underrepresented in the higher positions, but the university may claim that women are less qualified, have degrees of lesser quality, have published less, or that their seniority has been broken by pregnancies. In such circumstances, having a set of full professors that is 13 percent women may represent equal treatment or even affirmative action on behalf of women, the college may argue. How is the court to know?

The sign test can be used to test these countering claims.[5] This simple statistical procedure is economical in terms of time and resources, easy for judges

Table 6–1
Faculty Positions, by Gender

Position	Women	Men	Total
Full professor	13%	87	100%
Associate professors	17%	83	100%
Assistant professors	29%	71	100%
Instructors	35%	65	100%

or juries to understand, applicable to a wide variety of situations, and constitutes powerful evidence of the presence or absence of discrimination. It is a simple example of inferential statistics. Our discussion here will elaborate the example we used in chapter 4, in which we began with pairs of professors. Each pair included one professor of each sex, having identical ranks. Probably they were not identical in actual qualifications. If blind refereeing were to show that the woman's qualifications were superior in most of these pairs, then something would be going on. Women appear to be better qualified than men who hold similar positions. To put it another way, women appear to be underpromoted. Something besides chance is involved, and while we cannot say that outright sex discrimination has been proved, we can say that whatever factor is responsible correlates highly with sex. Thus the plaintiff has shown a statistical pattern of discrimination, shifting the burden to the defendant to establish that there is a nondiscriminatory explanation for the pattern.

What follows is a set of directions on how to do the complete analysis, from gathering the data through presenting the conclusions. Again, let me remind you that although the context of this example is employment discrimination, the same statistical test and principles of inferential statistics apply to cases of municipal-services discrimination, unequal taxation, and many other areas.

Through discovery or other means, obtain the vitas of all faculty employees. Xerox them, delete names and all references to sex, and rexerox. These documents can now be compared blind by referees who are obviously unbiased because they will not know the sex of the individuals whose vitas are being compared. Match each woman with a man of the same current employment rank within the department or area.

If more than one man is available, it is important to select your match randomly to preserve statistical independence. (Chapter 9 discusses random selection.) A layperson might envision pairing the best qualified woman with the best qualified man and so forth. However, if just one woman were underpromoted, hence dramatically overqualified, she would use up the most qualified man, so that the next best man might be overpowered by the next best woman, who would ordinarily be the best woman, and so on, down the line. The one underpromoted woman would bias the result of all other comparisons. Obviously that would not be fair.

Now give your randomly paired vitas to the expert, who should be familiar with college administration, perhaps a former dean or department chairperson. She is then to choose the more-outstanding vita of each pair. If there is no significant difference, a tie is reported and that pair is dropped, cutting the N.

Obvious refinements can be added. For instance, you could use multiple referees. Two persons could evaluate the entire sample, or someone with credentials in natural science could evaluate persons in that area, someone in the humanities could evaluate those teachers, and a social scientist could evaluate social scientists. You might be in a position to evaluate not just the vitas but the entire promotion/tenure files of each faculty member, including copies of publications, teaching evaluations, and other data. If you were dealing with an exceedingly large institution with many female professors, you might choose to cut your workload and N by using a random sample of them.

Each case is a pair of vitas, one man's, one woman's. The number of such cases that is enough is a tactical and strategic decision for lawyer and expert. By tactical I refer to the need for an N large enough that overwhelming differences in treatment are not required to show statistical significance. Table 6-2 shows some of the proportions required for different levels of significance with different sample sizes. By strategic I mean the need to be convincing to the judge and/or jury. Courts should be convinced by statistically significant results regardless of sample size, but sometimes they are not. So you may choose a larger sample than you need statistically, in order to be overly convincing.

Table 6-2 is based on the fact that the probability of getting various results in a 50/50, or chance, situation is known. For a sample of 10 cases, that probability is shown visually in figure 6-1. Figure 6-1 resembles the well-known normal curve, or bell curve, and if the sample size were increased beyond 10, the resemblance would grow ever closer; in figure 6-2, where $N = 100$, the two are so similar that the normal curve has been used to approximate the actual distribution. Figure 6-2 shows that the probability of getting, say, 60 or more heads, or favorable outcomes, is rare. Thus the probability of women coming

Table 6-2
Probability, or Significance Level, for Selected Results of the Sign Test

Result (Number of Positive Outcomes, or Heads	Trials (Number of Flips)	Probability of that Result or One More Extreme by Chance
6	10	.377
9	10	.011
60	100	.029
90	100	Less than .00001

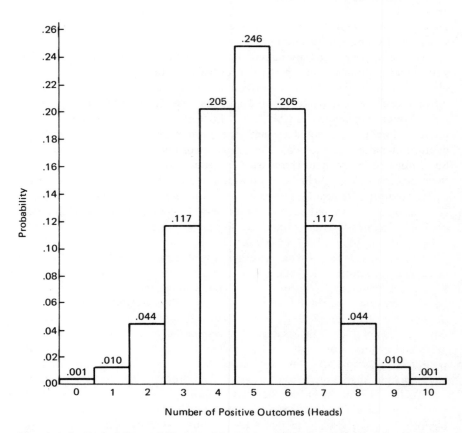

Figure 6–1. Probability of Various Numbers of Positive Outcomes out of Ten
Trials

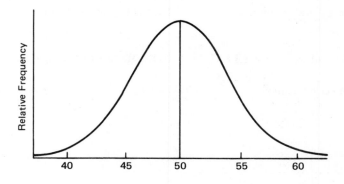

Figure 6–2. Normal Curve to Approximate the Probability of Various Numbers
of Positive Outcomes out of 100 Trials

out more qualified than men in 60 paired comparisons out of 100 is also rare—about .03.

Note that we do not inquire about the likelihood of obtaining precisely 60 heads, for we would surely not withdraw our hypothesis that women are over-qualified if we found 61 of them to be more qualified than their male counter-parts. We always seek the probability that 60 or more of the cases show female overqualification. Hence we are inquiring about the likelihood of all the out-comes from 60 to 100 in figure 6-2; this is the proportion of all the area under the curve that lies to the right of 60. We call this a tail of the distribution, and we always seek to know how large this tail is. If we had obtained female superior-ity in 90 of 100 cases, we could infer from figure 6-2 that the chances of that outcome, or a more-extreme one, are vanishingly small—table 6-2 shows them to be less than .00001.

Statistical tests can be done in a one-tailed or two-tailed direction. We have just described a one-tailed way of looking at the graph, hence a one-tailed read-int of table 6-2. There are times in social science when the investigator is simply interested in whether her two groups differed, and not in which direction. This does not happen in the courtroom. For example, if we found that, in our uni-versity, men were overqualified, if our blind expert ranked men higher in 70 or 55 or even 51 of the cases, we would withdraw the lawsuit or litigate it on a very different basis. Hence, in class-action cases statistical analyses should usually be done on a one-tailed basis.

Table 6-2 and figures 6-1 and 6-2 also imply that a decision must be made as to significance level. This is another topic introduced in chapter 4, and again this decision must be made jointly for it has tactical and strategic implications. As stated earlier, level of significance is the crucial concept of interential sta-tistics. It means the probability that a given outcome (or one even more ex-treme) could have occurred by chance. In our example, obtaining 60 cases of female overqualification (heads) out of 100 matched pairs (flips) would happen by chance 3 times in 100 attempts; the level of significance is .03 or 3 percent. In social science we usually like to have at least the .05 level of significance, meaning a result that would occur fewer than 5 times in 100 by chance; here we have met that criterion. Table 6-2 indicates that a larger sample makes signific-ance easier to obtain. This statistical or mathematical results is again parallel to common sense. Levels of significance are calculable from what is called the bi-nomial expansion, but there is no need to know what that is; statistics books have these tables built in.[6] I would always seek a .01 level of significance, bear-ing in mind that there are times when it is difficult or impossible to obtain.[7]

Advantages of the Sign Test and Internal Comparisons

If the sign test has resulted in a statistically significant difference, a very power-ful prima facie case has been made against the defendant for three reasons. First, as mentioned, the data originally came from the defendant, so there need be no long discussions as to whether our expert collected them in a biased manner. Second, the sign test is so simple, its analogy to coin flips so clear, that it is easy to grasp by the court. Finally, owing to the fact that the comparisons were blind, the expert has already anticipated most of the lines of rebuttal the defendant might use.

That last statement bears repetition and clarification. To return to our university example, the expert was not privy to the thoughts of the promotion-tenure committee or administration. Thus she cannot know whether sex was a factor inhibiting promotion for women, or if perhaps height (or some other sex-linked characteristic) was. Women often are shorter than men, and if the committee liked height, female shortness may have held women back. At any rate, something held them back, something that is female related and not job related, or at any rate that does not show up on the vitas or other documents.

Educational background, for instance, does show up on the vitas. The university might claim that women went to inferior colleges or did inferior graduate work, hence were passed over for promotion. However, if the blind expert(s) looking at anonymous vitas did not recognize this inferiority, then it probably does not exist. Not only does the expert's reputation as an expert increase the credibility of the judging but so does the blindness of the procedure. The vitas themselves, with names and genders removed, can become an exhibit if there is no danger that individuals will be sought out and identified from the easy clues (such as book titles) contained within them. Then the judge, having the data before him, can imagine making the test himself.

Since the vitas were compared blind, no factor contained within them could reasonably have escaped the expert's notice. There is no way the expert could have discounted the allegedly inferior colleges attended by the women, for instance, for she had no knowledge as to which professors were women when she compared the vitas. Perhaps the employer can claim that she did not read the vitas correctly—that she stressed factors that the employer did not stress—but that unlikely defense can be headed off by obtaining for the expert a copy of the university's published standards for promotion and tenure before she begins her work, with instructions to let those criteria guide her comparisons. With that safeguard, which amounts to nothing more than making sure the expert's standards of comparison are explainable and defensible, the use of blind referees thwarts any possible charge of bias on the part of the expert and makes the internal comparison and sign test difficult to defend against.

The sign test is economical of time and resources, easy for judges or juries to understand, and constitutes powerful evidence of the presence (or absence) of discrimination. Many other uses of it should suggest themselves. Obviously, initial hiring is amenable to the same treatment. It has been claimed that black department heads and principals were placed under less-qualified whites after court-ordered faculty desegregation in many public school systems; the sign test could easily be used to see if this was the case. In areas outside employment, the applications are equally wide; some of them are listed in the second paragraph of this chapter.

In any case of alleged discrimination, employment or not, if you can find a reasonable match for each person (or house, and so on) in the class of alleged victims, and if you cannot easily quantify the supposedly nondiscriminatory grounds on which the decisions were allegedly made but can only assess them comparatively and imprecisely, then the sign test is appropriate. Always the aspect that is hard to measure precisely is the aspect to be measured comparatively. Sex and rank are precise; qualifications are not. Hence you would pair persons of equal rank and opposite sexes and then compare their qualifications blindly. Housing assessment in the tax rolls is precise; actual value of the house (appraisal) is not. Hence you would pair houses of identical tax assessment but opposite race (if racial discrimination was at issue), then compare their actual values or appraisals.

It is hard to establish objective standards for comparing the many elements that constitute good qualifications for a faculty member or good performance as one. It is much easier and more defensible in court to claim that vita A was superior to vita B, vita D was better that C, and so forth, particularly with the added safeguard of blindness, so the expert could not have exercised bias even if she had wanted to. Applying the sign test in this way develops a prima facie case that is hard to rebut.

The sign test on an internal comparison can be augmented by an external comparison. If we were comparing black and white applicants for a police force using the sign test, for example, it would be useful to show in addition that the proportion black in the outside labor force, modified to include only positions of status comparable to police officer, was higher than the proportion black on the police force (see chapter 8). Additional icing on the cake would be an investigation into some of the mechanisms by which the discriminatory process works. For example, a survey of lower-level workers in an institution might disclose reasons why they fail to apply for higher positions and might show that they perceive those jobs to be white or for men (see chapter 10). Job descriptions, employee handbooks, company promotional materials, and other publications might be content analyzed for white-male bias (see chapter 4). Segregation of workers into different jobs and different areas of the plant, by race or sex, can affect promotion in several ways and can be examined with a segregation index (see chapter 11). The outside community, or a subset of it such as high-school seniors, might be surveyed for image of jobs at the firm, the point being to show that much of the white-male image of those jobs is not intrinsically job related, yet that it does chill applications for the positions from nonwhites and women, while the company has done nothing to counter the images and indeed maintains them inadvertently by its personnel practices themselves. If testing for hiring or promotion plays a role in chilling applications and restricting minority hiring or promotion, the test can be examined for possible bias in content or form (see chapter 13). If the employer is likely to claim that some quantifiable variable such as years of education largely determines employment, promotion, or pay, correlation and regression analysis can be used to assess this claim (see chapter 14).

The basic simplicity of the sign test is its ranking of one member of a pair as better, or more qualified than another; this can also be a weakness. Sometimes among many persons or items we can not only say that A is better than B but that A is much better. A refinement of the sign test takes this into account and is suggested in the next chapter, which also applies the technique to the field of discrimination in taxation.

Notes

1. Benjamin S. Wolf, "The Role of Statistical Evidence in Title XII Cases," *Boston College Law Review* 19 (1978): 884.

2. *Teamsters* v. *U.S.,* 431 U.S. 324 (1977), at 335-336, n. 15.

3. *Ibid.*

4. See D. Copus, "The Numbers Game Is the Only Game in Town," *Howard Law Journal* 20 (1977): 392-397.

5. S. Siegel, *Nonparametric Statistics* (New York: McGraw-Hill, 1956), pp. 68-75.

6. Ibid., p. 250. This table is the same as a binomial table where $p = .5$, or a chi-square table where df = 1.

7. For example, if only twelve women have been employed by the college, and if only ten men hold comparable appointments to those twelve (perhaps because some of the women are in home economics), then only ten comparisons can be made. However, there are often inventive ways of increasing the effective sample size. For example, if only ten women are on the faculty, that does not limit the possible pairs to ten. Comparisons can be made to each of the comparable male faculty members, using the women more than once. Thus, in a department with two female and three male assistant professors, six paired comparisons are possible across sex lines. Each is independent, an important characteristic defined in the next chapter, so the number of cases from this department would be six, not two.

Additional Resources

Further Reading

More has been written about employment discrimination and the role of statistics and social science in legal cases challenging it than any other field. Here I provide an annotated tour through some of the literature.

A good introduction to the legal principles involved in winning or defending against employment-discrimination suits is Benjamin S. Wolf, "The Role of Statistical Evidence in Title VII Cases," *Boston College Law Review* 19 (1978): 881–898. An older law-review article is N. Blumrosen, "Strangers in Paradise: *Griggs* v. *Duke Power Co.* and the Concept of Employment Discrimination," *Michigan Law Review* 71 (1972):59–93. Particularly valuable are D. Copus, "The Numbers Game Is the Only Game in Town," *Howard Law Journal* 20 (1977):374–418 and its copious footnotes.

An entire book has been written "intended primarily to guide lawyers and judges handling cases which employ statistical proofs" and focusing on employment discrimination: David C. Baldus and James W.L. Cole, *Statistical Proof of Discrimination* (Colorado Springs: Shepard's/McGraw-Hill, 1980). However, it is repetitive, marred by lugubrious prose and neologisms, and generally unclear. Do not read it before mastering this chapter and the Wolf article cited previously; thereafter, if you find it penetrable, you will be rewarded by an extended treatment, with many legal citations, of the issues introduced in this chapter. Additional overall treatments are Frank C. Morris, Jr., *Current Trends in the Use and Misuse of Statistics in Employment Discrimination Litigation* (Washington, D.C.: Equal Employment Advisory Council, 1980); *Equal Employment Opportunity Court Cases* (Washington, D.C.: U.S. Office of Personnel Management and Government Printing Office, 1979); and L. Modjeska, *Handling Employment Discrimination Cases* (Rochester, N.Y.: Lawyers Co-operative Publishing, 1981).

Social scientists will want to consult Rudolfo Alvarez et al., *Discrimination in Organizations* (San Francisco: Jossey-Bass, 1979), which presents many examples of researches by social scientists studying discrimination in promotion, recruitment, and decision making. Several sources treat sex discrimination specifically, including Francine D. Blau, *Equal Pay in the Office* (Lexington, Mass.: Lexington Books, D.C. Heath and Company, 1977); C. Beere, *Women and Women's Issues: A Handbook of Tests and Measures* (San Francisco: Jossey-Bass, 1979); and Esther E. Diamond, ed., *Issues of Sex Bias and Sex Fairness in Career Interest Measurement* (Washington, D.C.: National Institute of Education, 1975). Blau uses labor-marker analysis to examine segregation of men and women in firms and relates that segregation to pay differentials. Beere contains dozens of research instruments for measuring degree of work orientation, which jobs are perceived to be open to women, attitudes toward sex discrimination, male reactions to female competence, and many other topics and would be useful for the social scientist who needs to develop her own measures of any of these topics. Diamond's book focuses on an issue tangential but related to employment discrimination; of particular value are its bibliographies at the end of each article and the final article, "The Legal Implications of Sex Bias in Interest Inventories."

Some of the uses of expertise in employment case are so recent that news articles are important sources of information about them. Regarding two different experts, one on each side, and the resulting confusion for the court, see K. Arenson, "Flood of Data in Women's Suit Fills a Sea of Complexity," *The New York Times,* 16 November 1980. The issue in San Jose, California, was whether women are underpaid for jobs that are different from men's; see "Upping the Ante," *Time*, 20 July 1981, p. 61.

7

The Signed-Ranks Test in Tax-Assessment Discrimination

Often a social scientist (or layperson) can tell more about a pair of items or forms than merely which is better. Often at least a rough ranking can be developed. Such is the case when comparing houses, for instance. Hence a statistical technique that takes account of this additional ranking can be used, and since this technique, the Wilcoxon matched-pairs signed-ranks test, uses more information, it is more powerful.[1]

Suppose in a small town in Arizona, for example, Hispanic-Americans complain that the Anglo town government has overassessed their homes, making them pay a disproportionate share of the tax burden. We can select a Hispanic-owned home and compare it to an Anglo-owned home of identical assessed value. If the Anglo home is better, then it would appear that the Hispanic home is overassessed and that the minority family does pay too much. This is not because Hispanic homes are poorer. Probably they are, on the whole, but between two houses of equal assessments there should be no appreciable difference. Appreciable and systematic differences indicate discrimination, and minority-group membership is not the only possible cause. I know of one middle-sized city in which any resident active in politics enjoys a lower assessment than his quiescent neighbors. In other jurisdictions, Republicans might suffer at the hands of Democratic officials or vice versa.

This basic idea is identical to the sign test described in the previous chapter but contains an additional refinement. Like the sign test, the signed-ranks test is economical of time and resources and has wide applicability far beyond discrimination cases. The reader is urged to become familiar with chapter 6 before continuing here. Accordingly, this chapter does not repeat the basic principles of inferential statistics but consists of just two sections: a discussion of how to take the sample and prepare the information for the expert to analyze and an example of how to do the analysis.

Collecting the Data

The signed-ranks test is a natural for the employment of two experts: a social scientist (usually as economist, sociologist, or political scientist) and a real-estate appraiser or realtor. Both experts can be local persons because no great prior experience in other cases is required, and thus two experts need cost no more than one from whom more time is demanded. The expert who does the ratings cannot journey to the homes without compromising the blindness as to their ownership that is essential to the research. Hence the rating expert must work from documents. This method also has the advantage of being more objective because the documents can be presented to the court as supporting evidence. If resources are scarce, however, one expert can do the analysis; I will assume that only one expert is available in the procedures I suggest later.

The first step is for the social scientist to take a random sample of Hispanic-owned homes in the town. There are creative ways to obtain this sample. Perhaps the plaintiff(s) believe that a particular Hispanic area or subdivision is paying too much in taxes compared to a reasonably comparable Anglo subdivision. In that case, the expert or an assistant or student under her direction could number each house consecutively on a plat book for the Hispanic area, choose a defensibly large sample size, and use a random-numbers table to pick that many houses. Chapter 9 tells how to take such a sample and how large it should be. Then select Anglo houses randomly, keeping track of which house you chose first, which second, and so on, until at least twice as many Anglo homes are chosen as Hispanic homes.

The next step is to find the assessment of each home in your sample from the city tax records. List the Hispanic homes from richest to poorest. Now begin at the top of your Anglo list to match them. Suppose the richest Hispanic house in your sample was assessed at $25,000. Go down the Anglo list to the first home assessed at $25,000 and pair it with that Hispanic home. Do the same for the next Hispanic house, and so forth, until every Hispanic home has been matched.

You may have to select still more Anglo homes in order to obtain a match for Hispanic homes. Simply ignore all Anglo homes left over. You may also have to set up reasonable dollar intervals as to what constitutes a match. If assessments in your city are to odd dollars, you may conclude that anything between $25,000 and $26,999 constitutes a match. You may need to sample the entire city or you may not to able to identify Anglo and Hispanic homes by area; they may be intermixed. In that case, you could number each block in the city, as explained in chapter 9, select blocks randomly, sample two or three houses in each selected block, interview householders to determine race of ownership, at the same time filling out the forms described in the next paragraph, and then, knowing race, construct matched pairs of assessment.

Step three is to visit each home in your sample, fill out an appraisal form on the spot, and take a front and side instant photo of the building, making sure to include no people. (An appraisal form is supplied at the end of the chapter.) You are then ready to analyze the data.

Example of the Signed-Ranks Test

To give you an example of the process, I report here the results of a white/black study I conducted in a town in Mississippi. I had available to me a list of all homes by race of owner, generated by the plaintiff or other community experts. I excluded all rental housing because the race of a house owned by whites but lived in by blacks is ambiguous, as is the question of who pays the tax. I was left with about 300 black-owned and 300 white-owned homes. I chose 15 black homes randomly and selected white matches as explained previously. A student under my direction learned how to fill out appraisal forms (using homes in another community, matched against my efforts) and then developed a packet of 30 appraisal forms, each with photos attached. I did not know which homes were occupied and owned by blacks, nor which by whites. I then ranked the 30 homes in order, from best to worst, using the photos and appraisal-form information to guide me. Where I could determine no significant difference, I ranked two homes as tied.

Then I turned to my student's master list that indicated the race and the matched tax assessments of these homes. I examined the first pair of homes, one white, one black, with the highest (and identical) assessed valuation. One of them, the white-owned, was the second finest home in the entire sample; the other ranked 12. The difference, listing white-owned first, was 10 points. I did the same for all other homes. The results are shown in table 7-1. Note that I set up the table so that any positive number in the right-hand column would be contrary to my hypothesis and would indicate a white-owned home worth less than the comparably assessed black-owned home. Only two pairs came out that way. Moreover, their disparities in rank were small—2 and 1 1/2 points—while some enormous differences fell in the other direction. Table 7-1 shows, in other words, that in 13 of 15 pairs of equally assessed homes, the white-owned home was better and should be carrying a higher tax load.

Table 7-1
Tax Assessments and My Appraisals

Tax-Assessment Rank for This Pair	My Appraisal Rank		Difference (Signed)
	White-Owned Home	Black-Owned Home	
1	2	12	−10
2	15	13	2
3	3	19	−16
4	5	21	−16
5	1	23	−22
6	8.5	20	−11.5
7	6	24	−18
8	8.5	7	1.5
9	4	26	−22
10	10	25	−15
11	11	30	−19
12	14	29	−15
13	17	22	−5
14	16	28	−12
15	18	27	−9

All the positive differences are added (summing to 3.5), and the sum is then looked up in the appropriate table.[2] In this case the disparities in assessments could happen much less than 0.1 percent of the time due to chance—less than once in a thousand such studies. We can conclude that chance was not responsible, that something is biasing black assessments compared to white assessments.

I would not want my Mississippi example to leave you with the impression that unequal taxation is primarily a Southern problem. A study at the University of Illinois at Chicago Circle indicated widespread racial discrimination in taxation in Chicago.[3] Similar studies in other cities would probably reveal similar findings.

The next chapter continues our survey of inferential-statistics tests with proved courtroom utility.

Notes

1. S. Siegel, *Nonparametric Statistics* (New York: McGraw-Hill, 1956), pp. 75–83.

2. Ibid., p. 254.

3. E. McManus, "Blacks Demand Probe of High Property Tax." *Chicago Tribune,* 15 April 1979, p. 1.

Additional Resource

A standard form for residential appraisals is reproduced on the following page, courtesy of the Veterans Administration and the Department of Housing and Urban Development.

Form Approved
OMB No. 2900-0045

RESIDENTIAL APPRAISAL REPORT

HUD Section of Act	1. CASE NUMBER

2. PROPERTY ADDRESS (Include ZIP Code and county)	3. LEGAL DESCRIPTION	4. TITLE LIMITATIONS AND RESTRICTIVE COVENANTS
		1. ☐ CONDOMINIUM 2. ☐ PLANNED UNIT DEVELOPMENT

5. NAME AND ADDRESS OF FIRM OR PERSON MAKING REQUEST/APPLICATION (Include ZIP Code)	6. LOT DIMENSIONS:

1. ☐ IRREGULAR: SQ/FT 2. ☐ ACRES:

7. UTILITIES (√)		ELEC.	GAS	WATER	SAN. SEWER
1. PUBLIC					
2. COMMUNITY					
3. INDIVIDUAL					

EQUIP.	8.	1. ☐ RANGE/OVEN	4. ☐ CLOTHES WASHER	7. ☐ VENT FAN
		2. ☐ REFRIG.	5. ☐ DRYER	8. ☐ W/W CARPET
		3. ☐ DISH-WASHER	6. ☐ GARBAGE DISP.	9. ☐

9. BUILDING STATUS		10. BUILDING TYPE		11. FACTORY FABRICATED?	12. NUMBER OF UNITS	13A. STREET ACCESS	13B. STREET MAINT.
1. ☐ PROPOSED 3. ☐ UNDER CONSTR.		1. ☐ DETACHED 3. ☐ ROW				1. ☐ PRIVATE	1. ☐ PRIVATE
2. ☐ SUBSTANTIAL REHABILITATION 4. ☐ EXISTING		2. ☐ SEMI-DETACHED 4. ☐ APT. UNIT		1. ☐ YES 2. ☐ NO		2. ☐ PUBLIC	2. ☐ PUBLIC

14. STRUCTURE	15. DESCRIPTION (Complete only one item)	16. UNDERGROUND WIRE?	17. CONSTR. WARRANTY INCLUDED?
1. ☐ FRAME 2. ☐ MASONRY 3. ☐ CON-CRETE 7. ☐ SPLIT FOYER 8. ☐ BI-LEVEL 9. ☐ SPLIT LEVEL OTHER (Enter No. of Stories) ▶		1. ☐ YES 2. ☐ NO	1. ☐ YES 2. ☐ NO

	ITEM	DESCRIPTION	COND. (Observed)

	18. NEIGHBORHOOD DATA					19. FOUNDATION		
A. CHECK ONE	B. PRESENT LAND USE	D. BUILT-UP	%	H. TYPICAL RENT	I. TYP. BLDG. AGE	FOUNDATION		
1. ☐ URBAN		E. OWNED	%	$ /MO.	YEAR(S)	ROOF		
2. ☐ SUB-URBAN	C. ANTICIPATED LAND USE	F. RENTED	%	J. PRICE RANGE		EXT. WALLS		
3. ☐ RURAL		G. VACANT	%			INT. WALLS		

20. OFFSITE IMPROVEMENTS	21. STREET SURFACE	22A. FEDERAL FLOOD HAZARD MAP ISSUED?	22B. PROPERTY IN SPECIAL FLOOD HAZARD AREA?	FLOORS		
1. ☐ CURB 3. ☐ GUTTER				HTG. SYSTEM		
2. ☐ SIDE-WALK 4. ☐ STORM SEWER		1. ☐ YES 2. ☐ NO	1. ☐ YES 2. ☐ NO	PLUMBING		

23. EVIDENCE OF:	24. UNIT RATING (Check (√))	GOOD	AVG.	POOR	ELEC. (Amps)		
1. ☐ DRY ROT 3. ☐ SETTLEMENT	A. GENERAL CONDITION				INSULATION		
2. ☐ TERMITES 4. ☐ DAMPNESS 5. ☐ NO EVIDENCE	B. ROOM SIZES AND LAYOUT				1. ☐ % BSMT. 1. ☐ CENT. AIR COND. 1. ☐ FIREPLACE		
25. ESTIMATED REMAINING LIFE	C. ADEQUACY OF CLOSETS/STORAGE				2. ☐ SLAB 2. ☐ WALL AIR COND. 2. ☐ REC. ROOM		
▶ YEAR(S) 1. ☐ ECO-NOMIC 2. ☐ PHYSICAL	D. KITCHEN CABINETS/WORKSPACE				3. ☐ CRAWL SP. NO. OF UNITS: 3. ☐		

	ITEM	SUBJECT PROPERTY	COMPARABLE NO. 1	COMPARABLE NO. 2	COMPARABLE NO. 3
	ADDRESS				
	PROXIMITY TO SUBJ.				
	DATA SOURCE				
	TYPE OF FINANCING AND SALE PRICE		$	$	$

26.	ITEM	DESCRIPTION	DESCRIPTION	(+) (−) ADJ.	DESCRIPTION	(+) (−) ADJ.	DESCRIPTION	(+) (−) ADJ.
M A R K E T D A T A A N A L Y S I S	ROOM COUNT	TOTAL LIVING AREA (Square feet)	ROOMS BDRMS BATH TOTAL S.F.	ROOMS BDRMS BATH TOT.S.F.	$	ROOMS BDRMS BATH TOT. S.F.	$	ROOMS BDRMS BATH TOT. S. F.	$
	DATE OF SALE							
	LOCATION							
	SITE/VIEW							
	DESIGN AND APPEAL							
	CONSTR. QUALITY							
	AGE/CONDITION							
	BSMT./BSMT FIN. RMS.							
	FUNCTIONAL UTILITY							
	AIR CONDITIONING							
	ENERGY EFFIC. ITEMS							
	STORAGE							
	PARKING FACILITIES							
	COMMON ELEMENTS AND MONTHLY ASSESSMENT							
	OTHER (e.g. Fireplace, kitchen equipment, remodeling, etc.)							
	TOTAL NET ADJUSTMENT		ENTER (+) OR (−) $	ENTER (+) OR (−) $	ENTER (+) OR (−) $
	INDICATED VALUE		$	$	$

R E C O N C I L I A T I O N	27A. INDICATED VALUE BY MARKET DATA APPROACH ▶ $	28. ESTIMATED LAND VALUE $	29. LEASE DATA (Complete if applic.)	A. ANNUAL GROUND RENT $
	27B. INDICATED VALUE BY INCOME APPROACH (If applicable) ECON. MRKT. TIMES GROSS RENT MULTIPL. $ /MO. X ▶ $			CAP. AT % = $ B. VAL. OF LEASED FEE $ C. VAL. OF LEASEHOLD EST.
	27C. IND. VAL. BY COST APPROACH (If appl.) (Attach calculations.) ▶ $			
	30. DOES PROP. CONFORM TO APPLICABLE MINIMUM PROPERTY REQUIREMENTS?	31. APPRAISAL IS MADE:		33. FINAL RECONCILIATION/ESTIMATED VALUE
	1. ☐ YES 2. ☐ NO (If "No," explain in Item 32.)	1. ☐ AS IS 2. ☐ SUBJECT TO COMPLETION PER PLANS/SPECS. 3. ☐ SUBJECT TO REPAIRS, ALTERATIONS, ETC.		
	32. ADDITIONAL COMMENTS (Include repairs necessary to make property conform to applicable MPR's. Attach separate sheet if necessary.)			

NOTE: No determination of reasonable value may be made unless a completed appraisal report is received (38 U.S.C. 1810 (VA ONLY)).
I CERTIFY that (a) I have carefully viewed the property described in this report, INSIDE AND OUTSIDE, so far as it has been completed; that (b) it is the same property that is identified by description in my appraisal assignment; that (c) I HAVE NOT RECEIVED, HAVE NO AGREEMENT TO RECEIVE, NOR WILL I ACCEPT FROM ANY PARTY ANY GRATUITY OR PAYMENT OTHER THAN MY APPRAISAL FEE FOR MAKING THIS APPRAISAL (HUD/VA ONLY); that (d) I have no interest, prospective, in the applicant, seller, property, or mortgage; that (e) in arriving at the estimated value I have not been influenced in any manner whatsoever by the race, color, religion, national origin, or sex of any person residing in the property or in the neighborhood wherein it is located. I understand that, if I am a fee appraiser, violation of this certification can result in my removal from the fee appraiser's roster.

34A. SIGNATURE OF APPRAISER (Enter I.D. No. for HUD cases only)	34B. DATE	OFFICE USE ONLY (Reviewer's I.D. No. – HUD cases only)

VA FORM 26-1803, AUG 1980
HUD 92800-3 FmHA 1922-8

VA/HUD/FmHA FILE COPY 5

8

The *t* Test for the Difference of Two Proportions in Jury Discrimination

The most common statistical test for analyzing whether a sample proportion is significantly different from that of the population is the *t* test for the difference of two proportions. Conceptually this test is identical to the sign test presented in chapter 6. Like other inferential-statistics techniques, the *t* test allows the social scientist to see if a result was likely due to chance or possesses statistical significance and was probably not due to chance. Like the sign test, the normal curve that would result from chance events is used, and the actual result is compared with that curve to see how unlikely it was. The *t* test is the first parametric test to be presented. It has wide utility; a *t* test usually can be used whenever items can be counted or summed. The *t* test for the difference of two proportions can usually be applied wherever two classes of persons or cases are involved, such as blacks and whites, women and men, Hispanics and Anglos, families below the poverty line and those above it, products of one company and their failure rate compared to products of another company, and so on. The list is literally without end.

A common use for the *t* test is to compare a sample with an underlying population to see if the sample was drawn randomly from that population. A random sample is representative. It is like its parent population in every regard. Therefore, if a reasonably large ($N = 30$) sample is drawn randomly from the adult population of a community, it should approximate the average height of that population, its range of ideologies, incomes, and so on, in addition to its racial and sexual makeup. Many processes in the social world are forms of sample drawing, including hiring, jury selection, admissions to colleges and training programs, the military draft, and some kinds of purchasing. Suppose a police force is 32 percent black, while the total labor force of the community is 59 percent black. Or there may have been 130 infant deaths in the previous 12 months, of which 52 were minority babies, while minority babies made up only 15 percent of all births. In each case, a statistician can state that the disparity is too great to have occurred by change, that something else must be involved.

Often no one claims that the sampling procedure was random. A pipe company wants to hire the best welders who apply, for example, not a random sample of them. But no defendant wants to claim that the procedure was intrinsically and unnecessarily biased against the class of persons or items that is represented by the plaintiff. So if the *t* test for the difference of two proportions can establish that a group does not appear to be selected as often as would be allowed by chance, that something other than chance seems to be involved, then considerable burden has shifted to the defendants to show that their procedure was not biased but related to some necessary qualification.

Juries are supposed to be a random sample of the community, or at least their underlying venires are. Hence the operation of the t test is particularly clear and appropriate when considering jury characteristics by race, sex, age, or social class. This chapter contains a section on the substantive area, jury discrimination, followed by a presentation of the statistical test and an example of its use.

Jury Discrimination

Juries are to be composed of peers of the person on trial. This has not been construed to mean that left-handed Irish-American bartenders get to be judged by left-handed Irish-American bartenders but rather that juries should constitute a representative cross section of the adult members of a community. Such samples should not be biased by race, sex, age, social class, or any other salient social characteristic. If a defendant is to be judged by a jury whose composition is biased against him on one or more of those dimensions, the bias itself can constitute evidence of unfairness and thus provide grounds for appeal, retrial, jury dismissal and reselection, change of venue, or other legal action.

We have pointed out that a random sample is representative. Usually officials claim to have used a random procedure in selecting jury lists. Sometimes close examination of the results proves them to be so unlikely that the selection process could not have been random at all. For instance, the same persons may be drawn repeatedly to constitute at least some part of a jury. The probability of this happening randomly is vanishingly small. In at least one Southern county, this device has been used to bias juries against blacks, for although each jury looked racially balanced, the same blacks recurred, blacks who could be relied upon to follow the lead of the white foreman.

Frequently a random procedure may be in place, but the underlying population of names from which it selects may be biased, may not be a true listing of the adult population. If officials use a voter list that is two years out of date for their jury selection, all adults aged 18-20 are left out, and since young people are less likely to have registered, many persons aged 20-24 will also be omitted. Indeed, registered-voter lists typically are biased samples of the population, even if they are up to date, because persons of higher socioeconomic rank are more likely to keep their voter registration current. If a black defendant is on trial, political scientists or political sociologists could do a quick precinct-level analysis of registration patterns compared to voting-age population by race along the lines suggested in chapter 14 and then could testify that registration rolls are indeed biased in favor of whites as a source of jurors. Combined with evidence that past registration practices and socioeconomic discrimination made it difficult for blacks to register, compared to whites, such testimony might suffice to show jury bias.[1]

It would be more powerful if bias in selecting jury pools could be shown in addition to the bias in the original source. For instance, in some jurisdictions, persons with college addresses are routinely not picked for jury duty, again excluding young adults. In many victimless or life-style crimes, however, if a jury is composed mainly of older adults, with scant representation of what might be termed youthful points of view toward homosexuality, marijuana, and so forth, then the defendant faces bias and is not being judged by a jury of his peers, a representative selection of the adults in the community.

To remedy the situation, to attack the jury-selection system in order to ensure fairer trials, the lawyer and expert witness don't need to learn how the jury lists are drawn, even though that information would be helpful. Nor is it necessary to learn or challenge the source, the population list, though again that would be helpful. The results of the entire procedure are public knowledge. Names of persons called for jury duty are recorded. Sometimes information such as race, age, sex, and address (which can be a clue to social class) are also recorded, perhaps on voter-registration cards. Using the U.S. census as a base for comparison, these results can be tested against chance.

Often officials use five-tier procedure to select juries. The first step is to obtain some list of the population from the entire adult population. As we noted, voter-registration lists often are used, with no attempt to supplement them with lists of welfare recipients, telephone customers, automobile license-tag registrants, or other easily available sources of names. Therefore, this first step is usually biased, with young people, blacks, and less-affluent groups underrepresented.

The second step is to select a master jury list from the list of the entire voting-age population. Often this master list will be a small sample of the entire county, perhaps totalling 500 names from a county of 100,000. There is no excuse for it to be unrepresentative of the population list from which it derives, but often it is, perhaps owing to informal exclusion by officials of college students, people they believe cannot serve, addresses in public housing or on an airbase, and so forth.

For each session of court, a venire is selected from the master jury list in some jurisdictions. This venire might total fifty names, hopefully enough to constitute a jury for that session of court after some persons are excused owing to occupational responsibilities, possible bias, knowledge of the case, and other reasons. Again, the venire should be a random sample of the master jury list— but often it is not.

Finally, the list of actual jurors (and perhaps alternates) is a subset of the venire. Although juries are not intended to be radom samples since the excuses listed previously may particularly affect one race, age group, sex, or social class, nonetheless it would be important to show that the selection of jury after jury resulted in further decreases in the number of young persons, poor persons, blacks, or whatever class of persons is of your concern, compared to their proportions in the venires.

In the example to follow, we shall compare a master jury list to census statistics regarding the voting-age population. This comparison checks the results of two steps in the five-tier jury-selection process at once. Depending on your case and the data available to you, you might choose to conduct five different analyses or to make an overall input/output comparison of voting-age population to actual jurors. (The last approach is vulnerable to the claim that no discrimination by officials was involved, merely challenges and excuses that occurred in the courtroom and that were quite proper. I would not recommend it as the only analysis to be done.)

Example of a *t* Test in the Courtroom

We are defending a young male adult charged with a drug offense. Suppose in Robertshaw County (fictitious, but the census data are real), whose county seat is a college town, the 1980 adult population contains 8,949 people aged 18–24, 47 percent of the adult population, while the 1981 county master jury list included 108 young adults (18–24) and 432 older adults.

The first step would be to construct a table like table 8-1 for submission to the court and to note that on the face of it, young adults do not seem to be represented on juries as often as their presence in the voting-age population would indicate. The difference between the proportion of young people in the population and the master jury list, 27 percent, seems substantial. Common sense (or social theory) indicates that a jury composed of 47 percent young adults (perhaps 6 of 12) might behave differently from a jury about 20 percent young (2 or 3 of 12). Thus the difference seems important. What about statistical significance? Is the difference meaningful statistically, or could it easily occur by chance?

As with our coin flip examples in chapter 6, the answer depends upon sample size (N). A sample will not exactly mirror the population even if taken randomly. If the population is 47 percent young adult, a random sample of 10 might include 5 young adults, or 4 to 6, perhaps 8. A sample of 540 would

Table 8-1
Voting-Age Population and Master Jury List, Robertshaw County

Age Group	Voting-Age Population		Master Jury List	
	N	Percentage	N	Percentage
Young adults (18–24)	8,949	47%	108	20%
Older adults (25 and over)	10,126	53%	432	80%
Total	19,075	100%	540	100%

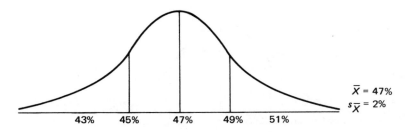

43%   45%   47%   49%   51%

$\bar{X} = 47\%$
$s_{\bar{X}} = 2\%$

Figure 8–1. Normal Curve for Sample of 540

include about 254 young adults, 47 percent, and although 48 percent or 51 percent might be young, to find 60 percent or 40 percent of young adults in a random sample that large would be rare. If you took repeated samples, their young-adult proportions would come out about 47 percent; we could create a distribution of those proportions that would look like figure 8-1. This is the famous bell-shaped, or normal, curve and it indicates, like common sense, that 47 percent is a likely outcome of a sample, 49 percent is fairly likely, and 20 percent (our observed outcome) is very unlikely.

Figure 8-1 is the curve that would result if we took many samples, each of 540 persons, from the voting-age population of Robertshaw County. It is a rather tight curve, as shown by its scale: about two-thirds of the samples, shown by two-thirds of the area under the total curve, would come in with between 45 percent and 49 percent young adults. This curve, like any other normal curve, has two key characteristics or parameters: its mean and standard deviation. Remember that we are talking about a curve of percentages—that is, figure 8-1 was created by taking repeated samples, size 540, and recording the proportion of young adults in each sample. Such a curve, made up of many samples, is always going to center about the population mean, and we know that in the voting-age population 47 percent are young adults.

The standard deviation of a proportion is computed by the formula,

$$ s = \sqrt{\frac{\left(\begin{array}{c}\text{Percentage young in}\\\text{voting-age population}\end{array}\right)\left(\begin{array}{c}\text{Percentage older in}\\\text{voting-age population}\end{array}\right)}{\text{Total number on master jury list}}} $$

Because sample size (here, the *N* of our master jury list) is in the denominator, the larger the sample, the smaller the *s*. Unlike the *X*, or mean, which is unaffected by sample size, the standard deviation of our curve of many samples will change, depending upon how large our samples are. Figure 8-2 shows a curve with mean of 47 percent but standard deviation of 20 percent. This curve would result from recording the proportion of young in many samples drawn from our

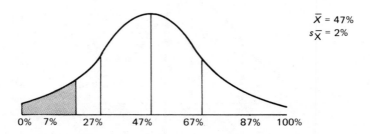

Figure 8-2. Normal Curve for Sample of 6

population if our sample size was a mere 6. The standard deviation tells how spread out the curve is; figure 8-2 shows a curve much broader than the previous curve. The shaded portion of the graph indicates the likelihood that our outcome of 20 percent young could have occurred by chance on this broader curve, and we see that likelihood, though small, is not inconsequential; perhaps 8 percent of the area is shaded. As we did in chapter 6, we have just examined the area under one tail of the curve and have concluded that, with a sample size of 6, it is unlikely to find only 20 percent of the sample being young, but not out of the question.

Figures 8-1 and 8-2 explain the t test intuitively. The t-test formula parallels this explanation mathematically:

$$t = \frac{\left(\begin{array}{c}\text{Percentage young in}\\\text{voting-age population}\end{array}\right) - \left(\begin{array}{c}\text{Percentage young on}\\\text{master jury list}\end{array}\right)}{\sqrt{\dfrac{\left(\begin{array}{c}\text{Percentage young in}\\\text{voting-age population}\end{array}\right)\left(\begin{array}{c}\text{Percentage older in}\\\text{voting-age population}\end{array}\right)}{\text{Total number on master jury list}}}}$$

All percentages are to be expressed as decimals. In our example,

$$t = \frac{0.47-0.20}{\sqrt{\dfrac{(0.47)(0.53)}{540}}} = \frac{0.27}{0.021} = 12.6.$$

The t table in the back of any statistics text explains what t values mean.[2] This t value means a master jury list containing 20 percent or fewer young adults would happen by chance far less than one time in 100,000.

Let us take time to understand this formula and example more fully, since it is basic to other related tests such as the t test for difference between two means. Note that the formula involves a difference divided by a number, the latter expressed in square-root form. All *t* tests share this characteristic. The difference is the population proportion (or mean) minus the observed sample proportion (or the observed sample mean). Subtracting 47 percent minus 20 percent leaves 27 percent or .27, but we do not immediately know if that difference is great or trivial.

The standard deviation of a proportion is shown by the denominator of the formula, so our *t* value actually tells how far out from the mean proportion is our observed proportion, in standard deviations. The *t* table then tells how likely such a result is, visually equivalent to the shaded area on figure 8-2. Because our sample was large, its standard deviation was about 2 percent, shown in figure 8-1, and the probability of obtaining a representation of young adults of 20 percent or less is vanishingly small so there is no shaded area on that figure. Any statistician should conclude that the selection was not random but was instead influenced by age or by some characteristic itself associated with age (such as having registered to vote several years earlier). Age bias has been shown. The master jury list could not have been drawn randomly from the population. Some process or factor that is biased against young adults had to be involved.

Of course, the analysis is not yet complete. We do not know what the biasing factor was, and we may never know, for it may be simply a capricious clerk who throws out all names with university addresses in our college town. We should check out some prime alternatives, however. It may be claimed that the names were drawn from the list of registered voters, for instance, and that since students are transient, perhaps maintaining registration and legal residence in their home towns, young adults do not register locally. Although that may not excuse the resulting jury bias, it is quite a different process from a capricious clerk. We thus obtain access to voter-registration cards to find birthdates and to calculate ages. We can do this for a random sample if it would be too arduous to skim all the cards; if we do select a sample, we must slightly alter the formula.[3] Suppose we check all cards and learn that of 11,440 total, 4,920 (43 percent) are young. A disparity remains between the master jury list and the roll of registered voters; calculating a new *t* indicates again that chance could not have accounted for the fact of a 20 percent young master jury list from a 43 percent young registration list.

Jury bias is widespread in the United States. As Michael Saks and Reid Hastie put it, "The United States Supreme Court has been ruling for nearly 100 years that jury pools must be representative. . . . Still, they are widely found to be unrepresentative."[4] These authors report that in Philadelphia, in 1970, white upper- and middle-income areas were overrepresented on juries and that black and lower-income areas were underrepresented. So it goes; but it is not legal. With assistance from social scientists, lawyers can wipe it out.

Notes

1. John B. McConahay et al., cite cases on both sides of this question in "The Uses of Social Science in Trials with Political and Racial Overtones: The Trial of Joan Little," *Law and Contemporary Problems* 41 (1977):207.

2. Consult, for example, H.J. Loether and D.G. McTavish, *Inferential Statistics for Sociologists* (Boston: Allyn and Bacon, 1974), pp. 163–168, 293–295.

3. Ibid., pp. 169-175.

4. Michael J. Saks and R. Hastie, *Social Psychology in Court* (New York: Van Nostrand, 1978), p. 51.

Additional Resources

Further Reading Regarding Jury Selection

Extensive social-science writings cover four main issues regarding juries: size of juries, the process of social interaction that takes place in juries, selection of persons to juries once they have been picked on a venire, and the overrepresentation of affluent majority-group members on juries and venires. The selections that follow cover all of those issues and are listed alphabetically.

G. Bermant et al., eds. *Psychology and the Law.* Lexington, Mass.: Lexington Books, D.C. Heath and Company, 1976.

K. Ellison and R. Buckhout, *Psychology and Criminal Justice.* New York: Harper, 1981.

A. Etzioni, "Creating an Imbalance," *Trial* 10 (November 1974):28–30.

M. Finkelstein, "The Application of Statistical Decision Theory to the Jury Discrimination Cases," *Harvard Law Review* 80 (1966):338–376.

J. McConahay et al., "The Uses of Social Science in Trials with Political and Racial Overtones: The Trial of Joan Little," *Law and Contemporary Problems* 41 (1977):207.

H. Moore, Jr., "Redressing the Balance," *Trial* 10 (November 1974):29, 31, 35.

Michael J. Saks, *Jury Verdicts: The Role of Group Size and Social Decision Rule.* Lexington, Mass.: Lexington Books, D.C. Heath and Company, 1977.

Fred Strodtbeck et al., "Social Status in Jury Deliberations," *American Sociological Review* 22 (1957):713–719.

H. Zeisel and S. Diamond, "Effect of Peremptory Challenges on Jury and Verdict," *Stanford Law Review* 30 (1978):491–531.

Question and Answer (Q and A) on Statistical Significance

Almost every social scientist who testifies in court in a class-action suit will at some point need to discuss the topic of statistical significance. Because the word *significance* is used in such a specific and crucial way in statistics, the lawyer and expert need to cooperate to make its meaning clear to the court. The following suggested questions and answers suggest a way to go about this. They are incomplete and are only a starting point for your own modification. For this discussion, assume the results from table 8-1 and figures 8-1 and 8-2, provided earlier in this chapter. In the voting-age population, 47 percent are young (18-24 years old), but only 20 percent of the persons on the master jury list are that young.

Q: Dr. Smith, have you subjected these results to any statistical tests or analysis?

A: Yes, I have.

Q: What test did you use?

A: I relied chiefly on what is called the *t* test—that is a small t, underlined—for the difference of two proportions. You see, your Honor, here we have two proportions, one in the voting-age population, another in the master jury list: 47% young adult in the voting-age population, but only 20% on the master jury list. The *t* test for the difference of two proportions is the standard significance test to apply to this problem.

Q: Would most social scientists use it?

A: Yes.

Q: Can you explain it to us?

A: Yes. As you know, your Honor, most of the time statisticians and social scientits work with samples, not with whole populations. The Gallup Poll, for instance, doesn't ask every American what he or she thinks of the president's performance but only a small sample. The same is true when a drug company monitors its quality—it pulls only a small sample of pills for analysis. So statisticians and social scientists have developed tests to tell how different a sample is likely to be from the underlying population from which it was drawn.

Now in this case, your Honor, the population is the list of all registered voters, and the sample is the master jury list, taken last year. Our problem is an easy one because we do have complete data on the population, at least with regard to race, age, and sex.

If the master jury list is a random sample, taken without regard to race, then it will be about the same as the population and not just in its racial composition. It will have about the same proportion of men and women as in the population as a whole. In fact, if the adult population has an average height of 5'7", then our sample, provided it's reasonably large, will also have a mean height of about 5'7".

Q: What is reasonably large?

A: Well, a sample needs to be 30 or larger to have really stable statistics. Beyond that, no set rule holds. Gallup projects U.S. opinion rather well with a sample of about 1,700 people, which is just .001% of the U.S. population.

Q: What about a sample of 540 for a population of 19,075?

A: That would be more than ample. You would expect a sample of that size to mirror the population quite closely.

Q: Did it?

A: No, at least not so far as age was concerned. As we have seen from exhibit 3 [table 8-1 in this chapter], almost half of the voting-age population is less than 25 years old, but only 20 percent or 1 in 5, of the sample, the master jury list, was under 25.

Q: Couldn't that happen by chance?

A: No, not likely. To return to the t test, exhibit 4 [Figure 8-1] shows the proportion of young adults we would obtain if we sampled Robertshaw County again and again, randomly, each time with a sample of $N = 540$. As you can see there, most of the samples include between 45 percent and 49 percent young adults; a few would have 43 percent or even 42 percent.

Q: What would be the likelihood of getting 20 percent?

A: The proper way to ask that question statistically is to ask "what is the probability of getting a master jury list that is 20 percent or less young adults?" On exhibit 4, that likelihood is shown by the little tail of the curve, on the left side, beginning at 20 percent and going to the left.

As your Honor can infer from the fact that 20 percent is not even on the graph, the likelihood of obtaining a master jury list with so few young adults as 20 percent is vanishingly small—that probability is less than .01 percent, or much less than once in a thousand.

Q: Do statisticians consider .01 percent a small probability?

A: Indeed. Social scientists use two benchmarks as guides to whether a result possesses what we call statistical significance. One is the 5 percent level. If an outcome is so unlikely that less than 5 percent of the time it would happen by chance, social scientists will usually reject the hypothesis that chance was responsible and accept the alternative hypothesis that the sample was not drawn from the population without bias. A second and more-rigorous threshold is the 1 percent level of significance. Our outcome, .01 percent, is a hundred times less likely than even this 1 percent level.

Q: What does a social scientist conclude from such a level of significance?

A: That this master jury list was not drawn randomly from the voting-age population. Something in the process was biased on the basis of age or something tied to age.

9

Selecting a Defensible Sample in Municipal-Services Discrimination

This chapter treats four important techniques: (1) sampling, (2) the t test for the difference of two means, (3) the chi-square test, and (4) index construction. As usual, I introduce these subjects in a substantive context, in this case discrimination in municipal services, an important area of class-action litigation. The two significance tests have much wider applicability than this one area; indeed, both are among the most widely used of all statistical inference tests, in and out of the courtroom. Sampling, likewise, is required whenever the population is too large to allow every member to be observed or interviewed. Indexes are important whenever a concept is too important to rest on just one research item.

After an introduction to municipal-services discrimination, the chapter provides many tips on sampling—how large a sample to take and why, how to take it, and how to assess its representativeness. Then I describe how data were collected from a sample in one large (population 200,000) Southern city and how the t test was applied to assess its significance. I introduce the chi-square test and suggest some of its uses in the courtroom. Finally I suggest ways to construct indexes for municipal-services examination and, by implication, for other areas as well.

Municipal-Services Discrimination

For decades, U.S. cities and towns have provided unequal services to the so-called wrong side of the tracks. In Southern towns the contrast was especially acute between concrete streets with curbs and underground drainage in the white part of town, compared to gravel or tar roads with ditches on each side in the black community. Indeed, such roads and ditches became part of our image of "niggertown."

The difference in services has had profound implications. A compact frame home in the black community could hardly appear as attractive as its twin in a white area, where no road dust would settle upon it and no mosquito-filled ditch would assault visitors to its front door. Over many years, the disregard openly implied by cities' unequal services probably took a cultural toll on their black communities, contributing to a tendency in some black families to demonstrate status by improving the insides of their houses rather than the outsides.[1] Whites noted the poorer appearance of black neighborhoods, particularly their public portions, and built a myth in white culture that black neighbors cause property values to fall. This portrait of black neighborhoods and this myth about property values contribute enormously to white flight, causing residential areas to resegregate.[2] Indeed, city services do fall off after blacks move in. In a sense, then, whites move out rationally.

In Northern cities, black areas suffer similar deficiencies in services. Here, since blacks inhabit neighborhoods first built for whites, the discrepancies are not so graphically portrayed on the land. Rather, they take the forms of fewer books in school libraries, inferior garbage pickup, and zoning infractions that lower the quality of life for inner-city residents by juxtaposing industry and homes in ways that would not be permitted in more-affluent parts of town.[3]

A body of law has grown up, following *Hawkins* v. *Shaw* [437 F.2d 1268 (5th Cir. 1972)], regarding the discriminatory provision of city services on the basis of race and class. The decisions in this area have been mixed and complex, and I do not treat their complexity here since this cannot be a law treatise. (I list references and helpful organizations in the first part of the additional resources at the end of the chapter.) Usually, if it can be shown that city services are markedly inferior in black or poor sections of town, a prima facie case of discrimination against the city (or county) has been made. After all, if the disparities are obvious, city officials can hardly claim they are inadvertent because provision of city services is a matter of conscious policy and detailed record. Hence, though it would be hard to find written proof of intent to discriminate, intent can reasonably be inferred from the fact of the discrimination itself.

Studies of municipal services have additional uses besides lawsuits directly on that topic. I was asked to present data on zoning, street width, and paving in the lawsuit attacking Jackson's form of government [*Kirksey et al.* v. *City of Jackson* (461 F. Suppl. 1282)] to show unresponsiveness to the black community by white elected officials. Similar data might also be relevant to city employment-discrimination cases to show a pattern of discrimination that extends beyond hiring and to indicate that present city employees, regardless of their alleged qualifications, are not doing a good job throughout the city. These studies can also have implications beyond the courtroom. In at least one town, once city officials learned of *Hawkins* v. *Shaw* and found out that data were being gathered in their community for a similar lawsuit, they drew up a bond issue to improve sewage and paving in black neighborhoods. No suit was ever filed. Thus, once discriminatory results have been shown by a social scientist, they can be the basis for community awareness and political organizing that may bring enough pressure to bear on city hall so that a political solution can be found and streets can be improved "voluntarily."

Much of the case against a city can be made from its own records. For example, land-use records in the city-planning department or zoning-board office usually show which parcels of properly are residential, commercial, and industrial. These records or maps are matters of public record. So are zoning records and maps, showing how each part of the city is zoned. Comparison of these two data sets yields the proportion of land in each section of the city that is mis-zoned or misused.

Zoning is an important city service, not to be overlooked in favor of more-physical matters like paving. It is established that industry and residences make poor neighbors. The noise, smell, trucks, railroads, and auto traffic generated by industry can only lower property values and the quality of life in residential areas. Industrial zones should be buffered from residences by natural barriers, highways, or commercial districts. When homes and factories do coexist, the residents thus afflicted are usually not affluent whites.

Whether a parcel is miszoned or misused is partly a matter of history. A section of the city may have been industrial for decades and zoned for industry for decades. To realize income from vacant land reserved for future expansion and to house some of their workers, the captains of industry may have put in some rental housing, also decades ago. This is a misuse of their land because it subjects the occupants to the poor living conditions that good zoning is intended to prevent; but what the remedy should be is not obvious. It is unreasonable to suggest the factories be closed, since they antedate the housing and since the site probably is not prime residential land anyway; but tearing down the houses may only worsen a tight low-income housing market. Perhaps the misuse should be ignored.

A more objectionable abuse occurs when industries and commercial establishments illegally enter areas already zoned residentially. At least in one city, this practice has been common, and again it usually afflicts poorer parts of town. Rather than attack each illegal use individually, a lawsuit against the zoning officials would be appropriate, supported by maps showing a clear correlation between percentage minority and percentage misused land.

Miszoning is harder to prove than illegal misuse of correctly zoned land. Again, history is important. Industry and commerce may have been allowed to encroach gradually upon poor and minority residential areas legally through zoning changes and variances. In past decades, some residents of these neighborhoods may not have felt efficacious, may not have believed that city officials would respond to them if they did object to a zoning change. In much of the pre-1965 South, blacks were not voters so they would have particular reason to assume they were impotent to influence officials, or residents may have complained, to no avail.

Miszoning can be demonstrated by mapping the proportion of residential land in each census tract or neighborhood that is located within, say, 100 meters of an industry or commercial establishment. If that map also resembles maps showing percentage minority and percentage of land illegally misused, again a prima facie case of racially biased zoning practices has been established, at least in part. Detailed historic analysis of a few individual zoning cases, showing that the minority residential area antedated the requested changes, would complete the picture.

Other forms of municipal services can also be examined through city records to see if discrimination occurs. Typically, fire and police protection is more intensive in the inner city, owing partly to the commercial and industrial buildup in that area, so there is no need to examine fire station location or police patrol routes. Water department records usually identify size, age, and location of mains and hydrants, but again, these are not usually a problem for poor or minority neighborhoods. Number of books in branch libraries and school libraries can be checked, however, as can their overall budgets on a per capita basis, based on the population of the school or the served neighborhood.

At some point, however, you will probably want to gather some data on-site. When you do, unless you are suing a tiny town, you will probably not want to squander resources by examining every street light, the drainage of every block, and the width of each street. You will want to take a sample.

Sampling

Most people who are not social scientists put too much credence in large samples. Research based on large samples, such as *Equality of Educational Opportunity* (the so-called Coleman Report), is accorded undue praise and importance. When laypeople (and some social scientists) do their own research, they tend to choose too large a sample. Students of sampling know that the famous survey fiascos of the past were based on samples that were too large, not too small. For example, when the *Literary Digest* predicted in 1936 that FDR would lose, the prediction was based on a sample of more than 50,000 persons; Gallup's prediction of Dewey over Truman, leading to the famous photograph of a grinning Truman holding up the Chicago *Tribune* headline heralding Dewey's victory, was based on many more respondents than his more carefully selected samples of recent years.

How can a sample be too large? If it is not random (or if its nonrandomness is not understood and intended or compensated for by the social scientist), then its size is no guarantee of quality and may even mitigate against quality.

How large should a sample be? That depends upon three factors: (1) cost (including such nonmonetary considerations as time, personnel available, and bother to respondents if a survey is involved); (2) plans for data analysis; and (3) the need for representativeness and defensibility.

Cost, broadly construed, is a greater problem than sometimes appears. Many research projects have lacked effectiveness because a disproportionate amount of time and energy was spent on data gathering, owing to an overly large sample. The research process includes most of the following steps and sometimes others:

Consulting with the attorney(s) and client(s);

Deciding upon a research design;

Developing a questionnaire, observation form, or other instrument;

Pretesting it;

Selecting a sample, interviewing its members, and revisiting those absent;

Entering the data into the computer;

Completing a run, locating errors in the data, correcting them, and completing a second run;

Analyzing the results;

Interpreting them;

Creating effective ways to present the data;

Consulting again with the attorney(s) and client(s), not only at the end but also throughout the process.

There are far too many other steps to allow the interviewing, revisiting, and data-entry steps to dominate the undertaking, which they will do if the sample is too large.

Suppose that a company claims to have no data on the race of persons it has rejected for employment but has name/address/phone numbers for them. Suppose further that the company is located in a county with a 35 percent black work force, while its employees are only 8 percent black. It would be tedious to learn the racial identities of all 1,818 disappointed job seekers of the past 24 months at the factory, but if in a sample of 30, chosen at random, 10 are black, it indicates that the proportion, 33 percent black, is not much different from the work force in the county but does differ markedly from the work force at the plant. Even so small a sample thus shows that lack of applications is probably not the problem; some form of rejection after they apply is affecting black applicants differentially.

As a rule of thumb, a sample size numbering 30 (N = 30) provides stable statistics and allows for percentaging. Ns as low as 15 can be percentaged, but 30 is better. When Ns below 15 is involved, I refuse to percentage, instead merely reporting "8 of 11 . . . ."

This need for an N of 30 or 15 applies also to subsets of the sample if these are to be analyzed separately. For instance, to continue our preceding example, if we sought to compare qualifications or test scores of white versus black applicants, then we need 30 in each group, or 60, and if blacks made up only 33 percent of the population of applicants, then to obtain 30 blacks in a random sample of applicants requires an N of 90.

More-complex internal comparisons may be required, necessitating still larger samples. For instance, it may be claimed that a city is not providing its newer black subdivisions with street paving equal to that provided white subdivisions. Some older residential areas of the city may have been built for whites but are now inhabited by blacks; it is not claimed that those areas are afflicted by narrow or poorly paved streets. Accordingly, we use a four-cell research design (see table 9-1). If the city is 70 percent white, and if one-fourth of its streets are categorizable as newer, then to have 30 city blocks in the black post–World War II cell requires a total sample of 400 blocks because (0.3) (0.25) $(400) = 30$. Of course, there are also acceptable ways to oversample a particular category deliberately so that fewer than 400 blocks will nonetheless yield 30 black post–World War II blocks.

Gallup and other national pollsters predict the behavior of the U.S. electorate from samples of 1,700 people, or 0.0008 percent of the nation's population. These small samples are more accurate than earlier larger ones because elements of nonrandomness in the earlier samples have been carefully eliminated or reduced. Nonetheless, the public tends to believe that more is more, and since judges are members of that public, a study of street paving based upon 30 white and 30 black blocks in a city of 200,000 would probably not be convincing, even if statistically sound. It might be charged that the sample neglects the X neighborhood. To be convincing, a sample needs to be representative—large enough, in this instance, to include blocks from each major part of the city. In short, a sample must be defensible, and its defense will be both statistical and commonsense. Hence sample size is a matter for the lawyer and expert to work out together.

One way to approach the matter statistically is to imagine the magnitude of the differences you anticipate finding between groups. If you believe black streets will be about eight feet narrower than white streets, on the average, then the social scientist can quickly do a t test for this difference, using various sample sizes, to learn how large a sample will be required to produce statistical significance.[4] A sample comfortably larger than this minimum should then be selected.

An instance of sampling in a municipal-services investigation I conducted provides some pointers on sample size and on how to take a sample. The task was to study the municipal services of a metropolitan area much larger than the Shaw, Mississippi, site of the landmark *Hawkins* v. *Shaw* decision. The entire

Table 9-1
City Blocks, by Race of Residents and Age of Area

	Mostly White Residents	*Mostly Black Residents*
Pre–World War II (to be ignored regarding street paving)		
Post–World War II		

town of Shaw (population 2,500) could be surveyed, and it was, so no sampling was required. In a city of 200,000, however, a total survey of city streets would be prohibitively expensive.

In order to decide what N would be strategic, Dr. Mickey K. Clampit and I determined how many blocks of streets there were in the city. This was no small task, requiring verification of the city map by driving perhaps one-fourth of the total street mileage, glimpsing all side streets. "One block" was given a uniform operational definition different from a census block, which is appropriate for population but not for analyzing street characteristics. We defined a block as the distance along a street from one intersection to the next, providing at least one house faced onto the street in that distance. (If none did, then such a block was not residential, so we dropped it for it could have no racial identity, having no residents. We did not need to check all such blocks and drop them from our population of all blocks; we simply dropped it if it showed up on our sample and was then found to be uninhabited.) Figure 9-1 gives several examples of blocks.

On our corrected map we now gave every block a unique number. The city was found to contain 6,600 blocks. A sample must always relate to a population, which it is then supposed to mirror accurately; our population N was 6,600. We decided to take a sample of 660, one in ten, because we felt it could be handled by the student assistants available to us and would be logical to ten-fingered judges. For purposes of statistical analysis, an N of less than 200 would have sufficed. If I were repeating the project, I would suggest an N of 330, sure to yield 200 residential blocks, for we did find the data gathering exhausting.

The simplest way to take a sample is randomly. *Random* is a word often bandied about as in, "I took a random sample of undergraduates at the student union." Such a sample is not random. Random has a specific meaning: a random sample is drawn from the underlying population in such a way that every member of the population has an equal chance of being included. (Not every student has an equal chance of being at the student union; thus commuters, for one, may

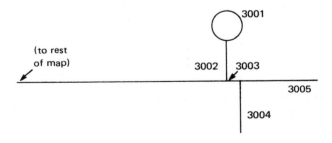

Figure 9-1. Examples of Blocks in a Map Fragment

be undersampled.) A simple random sample is correctly taken by assigning each member of the population a unique number and then using a random-digits table available in the back of most statistics texts. A random sample is crucial because it can be assumed to resemble the total population in all respects. Therefore, if in our sample whites had significantly wider streets, no one could claim that we only examined rich white streets, because our random sample would include rich and poor white blocks in proportion to the population.

Sometimes obtaining a list of the population is too great a burden. This would be the case in a city of one million or more, or when sampling employees in a company with many plants. Target sampling reduces this burden, also cutting down on travel. Sometimes one group needs to be oversampled, to make sure it is represented in the sample by enough members for defensible statistics. Disproportional random sampling can be used to assure the desired representation. Then, by a weighting procedure, the sample can still be used to generalize to the population as a whole. These and other specialized sampling techniques are described in the sampling texts listed in "Additional Resources." All of the techniques relate back to simple random sampling for their justification.

Data Analysis: The *t* Test for the Difference of Two Means

After we took our sample, we surveyed every included block with two instruments: (1) a form reporting physical characteristics such as street width, type of drainage, and number of street lights and (2) an interview schedule inquiring about fire protection, garbage pickup, and other services. We had set up these forms for ease of entry into our computer and had pretested them for clarity and brevity. The forms are included at the end of the chapter. As mentioned, we dropped blocks with no residences, such as downtown streets, highways, and industrial drives. We used an additional randomizing technique to select one household for interview on each sampled block.[5]

The resulting data showed discrimination. For instance, the mean street width in the black community was about 29 feet; in white areas it was 41.

Is a twelve-foot difference important? Parking, for example, could hardly be permitted on both sides of the average black street; the protection to sidewalks and children and the residential quietude that parking lanes provide were lacking in black neighborhoods. Combined with paving and curbing differences, the broad concrete streets compared to narrow tar streets provided a substantial increment in property values for white homeowners.

Is the difference significant? The appropriate statistical test is the *t* test for the difference of two means:

$$t = \frac{\bar{X}_w - \bar{X}_b}{s(\bar{X}_w - \bar{X}_b)}$$

where

$$\bar{X}_w = \text{the mean white street width,}$$
$$\bar{X}_b = \text{the mean black street width,}$$
$$s(\bar{X}_w - \bar{X}_b) = \text{the standard deviation of the difference between the means.}$$

Like other t formulas, we see a difference divided by a standard deviation. (If the reader has not already encountered t tests, she or he should refer at this point to chapter 8.) The standard deviation of the difference of two means must be greater than the standard deviation of a single mean. Each mean could vary, if different samples were taken repeatedly, so their difference could vary more. The formula for this standard deviation reflects this:

$$s(\bar{X}_w - \bar{X}_b) = \sqrt{s\bar{X}_w^2 + s\bar{X}_b^2}$$

The standard deviation of the white mean street width, in turn, will be small when the sample N is large and will be small when the standard deviation of the variable itself (street width) is small, and its formula reflects this:

$$s\bar{X}_w = \frac{s_{X_w}}{\sqrt{N_w - 1}} \qquad s_{X_w} = \sqrt{\frac{\Sigma (X_{w_i} - \bar{X}_w)^2}{N_w}}$$

Based on a sample of 200, our twelve-foot difference would happen by chance far less than one time in 1,000. This fragment of our analysis is ready to go to court, once attractive bar graphs and other exhibits have been constructed to present the findings effectively.

Like the t test for difference of two proportions, this test has many applications. It is usally appropriate wherever the variable (in this case, street width) can be measured parametrically—that is, on a meaningful numerical scale. This holds true for physical characteristics like weight or width, anything measurable in dollars, time units (such as years of education or days of sick leave), and many other items of social importance.

Nonparametric data must be analyzed differently. Chapters 6 and 7 offer examples of nonparametric significance tests. What of the rest of our observation

The easiest way to come to terms with the formulas is by working through a small example; in turn, doing the calculations in the form of a table makes them easier. In reality, all calculations would be done by a computer, but there is no substitute for going through them once to understand how they are done.

Black and White Street Widths in Small Sample, Michigan

	Widths of White Streets			Widths of Black Streets	
X_{w_i}	$(X_{w_i} - \bar{X}_w)$	$(X_{w_i} - \bar{X}_w)^2$	X_{b_i}	$(X_{b_i} - \bar{X}_b)$	$(X_{b_i} - \bar{X}_b)^2$
40	1	1	55	26	676
42	1	1	16	13	169
45	4	16	20	9	81
35	6	36	25	4	16
44	3	9	116	52	942
41	0	0			
247	15	63			

$$\bar{X}_w = \frac{247}{6} = 41.1 \text{ feet} = \text{white mean} \qquad \bar{X}_b = \frac{116}{4} = 29 \text{ feet} = \text{black mean}$$

We calculate the mean white width. We subtract each width from that mean, recording only the absolute (unsigned) difference. Then we square those differences and add them up. Substituting in our formulas:

$$s_{X_w} = \sqrt{\frac{\Sigma(X_{w_i} - \bar{X}_w)^2}{N_w}} = \sqrt{\frac{63}{6}} = 3.24$$

$$s_{\bar{X}_w} = \frac{s_{X_w}}{\sqrt{N_w - 1}} = \frac{3.24}{\sqrt{5}} = 1.45$$

Then we do the same calculations for the black standard deviation, s_{X_b}, and for the standard deviation for the black mean, $s_{\bar{X}_b}$. Then we combine them according to the formula to get the standard deviation for the difference of two means, $s_{(\bar{X}_w - \bar{X}_b)}$:

$$s_{(\bar{X}_w - \bar{X}_b)} = \sqrt{(s_{\bar{X}_w})^2 + (s_{\bar{X}_b})^2} = \sqrt{2.1 + 78} = 8.95$$

$$t = \frac{\bar{X}_w - \bar{X}_b}{s_{(\bar{X}_w - \bar{X}_b)}} = \frac{41.1 - 29}{8.95} = 1.35$$

Checking a t table or normal-curve table,[1] we learn that $t = 1.35$ is not significant. In everyday language, the black mean is less than the white mean by 1.35 standard deviations, and that could happen by chance fairly often—about 10% of the time.[2] Although the black/white difference was substantial, our sample was too small for the difference to achieve statistical significance. A larger sample would surely yield highly significant results.

[1] H. Loether and D. McTavish, *Inferential Statistics for Sociologists* (Boston: Allyn and Bacon, 1974), pp. 293–295, for instance.

[2] This sentence is slightly inaccurate for the purpose of propaedeutic clarity.

Figure 9-2. Working through an Example of the t Test for Two Means

form? (See "Additional Resources" for a copy of the form.) Some variables on it are nonparametric but cannot easily be examined with the sign test or signed-ranks test. One more example of a significance test, the chi-square test, is presented now.

The Chi-Square Test for the Significance of a Table

The significance tests in chapters 6-9 have all been for making one comparison at a time: Hispanic tax assessments with Anglo, for instance, or white mean street width with black. Sometimes comparisons get more complex than that, and when they do, we need a way to show the data compactly and to calculate its significance in a single statistic. In municipal-services cases, street guttering and drainage provides an example of this complexity.

There are four main ways that U.S. communities handle storm-water runoff. The best is underground, through grates at the curb at low points in the streets, connected to large buried concrete storm sewers, eventuating in a lake or river. Next best, but often quite attractive, is a system of graded ditches tied into street grates, often lined with concrete, landscaped, and again leading to creeks or rivers. A distant third are the ungraded ditches at the side of the road, requiring culverts or small bridges at every driveway. Often they collect trash and breed insects, and they too eventually lead to larger ditches and nearby streams. Worst of all, at least in regions with much rainfall, is the complete absence of drainage, so that swampy low spots and flash flooding are recurring hazards.

Table 9-2 shows these four alternatives as dependent variables, for although the race of a neighborhood might influence what system is put in, their drainage system could hardly cause the inhabitants of an area to change race. Composition of neighborhood is divided into three types, by race.

Note first that the table is percentaged vertically, with each column totalling 100 percent, as suggested in chapter 5. This allows us to ask what proportion of black blocks have roadside ditches compared to the proportion among white blocks. Finally, note that the difference, 70 percent versus 4 percent, is shocking, clearly important, and the highlight of the table.

The numbers in the bottom row and right-hand column, marked "Total" are the marginals. In the absence of any racial effect, the right-hand marginal percentages would predict the percentages in each column—that is, since 60 of all 200 blocks, 30 percent, have underground drainage, if race had no effect, then 30 percent of our 100 white blocks would have underground drainage, or 30 blocks. Race is indeed having an impact for we observed 50 white blocks with underground drainage, far more than what we expected.

This difference between observed and expected, combined for all of the cells in the table, forms the chi-square statistic. Its formula is

$$\chi^2 = \sqrt{\frac{\Sigma\,(\text{observed - expected})^2}{\text{expected}}}.$$

Table 9–2
Race and Drainage Types in a Southern City

Drainage Type	Racial Composition of Block							
	White		Interracial		Black		Total (All Blocks)	
	Number of Blocks	Percentage	Number of Blocks	Percentage	Number of Blocks	Percentage		
Underground system	50	50%	5	25%	5	6%	60	30%
Graded ditches	36	36	5	25	9	11	50	25
Roadside ditches	4	4	10	50	56	70	70	35
No system	10	10	0	0	10	13	20	10
Total (all blocks)	100	100%	20	100%	80	100%	200	100%

Obviously, the greater the disparities in the table, the greater the impact of our independent variable (race, in this example), and the greater the chi-square statistic. Tables have been developed to tell if a given size chi-square statistic (or larger) is significant, or if it could occur due to chance.[6] For our example,

$$\chi^2 = \frac{20^2}{30} + \frac{10^2}{25} + \frac{31^2}{35} + \frac{1^2}{6} + \frac{3^2}{7} - \frac{2^2}{2} + \frac{19^2}{24} + \frac{11^2}{20} + \frac{28^2}{28} + \frac{2^2}{8}$$

$$= 93.8.$$

A chi-square table shows this result to have a significance level better than .01, indicating that a table this distorted from what would be expected could hardly happen owing to chance. The independent variable, race, made quite a difference.

Chi-square statistics are two-tailed significance tests. A difference from the expected value contributes to the chi-square statistic regardless of its direction. Thus, if we had observed only 10 white blocks with underground drainage, that result would be as different from 30, our expected outcome, as the 50 we did find and would contribute equally to the chi-square statistic. Of course, with those results an expert witness would testify that race makes a difference in that whites are disadvantaged, and minority plaintiffs would never take their case to court.[7]

Chi-square is sometimes misinterpreted as a statistic of association or importance. It is neither. It does not directly tell how much association exists between the independent variable (race of residents, in our example) and the dependent variable (type of drainage), nor whether that is an important association. It does tell how likely the association is, owing to chance, which is useful to know because if the table possesses statistical significance, then the expert can say its independent variable, race (or something itself related to race), made a difference in drainage. How much of a difference? The expert reads that directly from the table: half of all white blocks have underground drainage, compared to just 8 percent of black blocks, and so forth.[8]

Index Construction

Before leaving the area of municipal services, let me use the observation form (in "Additional Resources" at the end of the chapter) to show one more important technique: index construction. Early in the book, I pointed out that major issues in litigation should not rest on one item in a single study. For defensibility and to achieve compact data presentation, items from a survey or even from various sources should be combined into a single index.

This could easily be done for several items describing the physical character of streets, all taken from the observation form for city services at the end of the chapter. Drainage, item 18, is already divided into four categories. Street width could be divided into four ranges, in feet, each range set so that it includes about one-fourth of all the blocks. The same could be done for item 25, street lights. Curbs might then be divided into three types since item 24 only provides three categories. Each set of categories must then be assigned numbers operating in the same direction. If 1 represents underground drainage while 4 means no drainage at all, then 1 should denote broad streets and 4, narrow ones. The result would be an index of street quality. On it the best blocks in the city would have a score of 5; the worst possible score would be 19; and the median street-quality index scores for white, interracial, and black blocks should provide an effective summary of the physical quality of streets by race in the city.

A refinement would be to weight items in the index. For instance, street lighting is much less important than paving to the image and value of a neighborhood. It has no effect during daylight hours, after all. So it might be weighted 1, meaning that its scores—1, 2, 3, or 4—are included as listed, while all other elements of the index could be weighted 2, doubling their values before adding them into the index. The new index would range from 9 (best blocks) to 34 (worst), and lighting would make less difference, although still included.[9] Additional elements could be added, such as presence and obtrusiveness of utility poles and lines. The median value of the street-quality index could be calculated for each census tract. That value could then be combined with still other measures, such as the proportion of miszoned and misused land, or census data on the proportion of homes lacking some plumbing, to form an overall quality-of-life index.

Other indexes can be used in content analysis, survey research, employment-discrimination cases, and many other areas where more than one item is available to measure a concept. An index is a superior operational definition, usually better than letting a concept be measured by only one operation.

Notes

1. L.M. Stalvey, *The Education of a WASP* (New York: Morrow, 1970), pp. 39–40 et passim.

2. Several studies have shown the property-value myth to be false usually. Because blacks are somewhat restricted to certain segments of the metropolitan housing market, it often follows that prices rise when blockbusting occurs. Often the first wave of panicked white sellers fails to realize any profit, contributing to the perpetuation of the myth, which realtors also encourage because it promotes turnover. Later sellers make profits.

Infrequently, when several areas are undergoing racial transition at once, black buying pressure can be less than the white buying pressure that the first black residents supposedly cause to dry up. Usually, however, changing neighborhoods have not been prime areas for whites for some years before transition, so white pressure has been weak for some time.

School desegregation contributes to the development of stable interracial neighborhoods. Transition should not be assumed and is not automatic, particularly in cities with metropolitan school desegregation. Equalization of municipal services would surely have a similar impact in favor of integration. See two articles and their bibliographies: 38 Social Scientists, "School Desegregation and Residential Segregation," *Transaction/Society* 16 (July 1979):70–76; and J. Loewen, "Desegregating Schools Can Help Desegregate Neighborhoods," *Clearinghouse for Civil Rights Research* 7 (Spring 1979):14–18.

3. Class as well as race contributes to this problem. Less-affluent inner-city renters are almost defenseless against wealthy businessmen who can dominate zoning boards through their status and connections.

4. This is not stacking the deck in one's favor. (The way to do that is by taking a very large sample.) The method requires estimating the standard deviations as well as the means of each sample. A tiny pilot study can help one make these estimates. The social scientist will want a sample larger than the bare minimum to ensure significance even if the standard deviations are unexpectedly large.

5. Each observer had to enter a block at an end. We put a householder number, randomly selected from one to twenty, on each householder interview form, and we told the observer to count households to his left, clockwise, around the block until he came to the designated house or apartment. If there were only three houses on the block and the desired household was number seven, our observer would count around twice and select the first house on the left, with which he began, as the seventh. If it were crucial to our study to interview a random sample of householders, then the interviewer would have made repeated visits to the selected house until he found someone home. Indeed, we might have imposed a further randomization procedure within each household to ensure we interviewed a random sample of sexes and ages within families. However, for our purposes we merely needed one householder on each block to supplement the observation form regarding physical characteristics. Hence we allowed our interviewers to go to the adjacent dwelling if no one was home in the selected household.

6. S. Siegel, *Nonparametric Statistics* (New York: McGraw-Hill, 1956), p. 249. To read chi-square tables requires an understanding of degrees of freedom, or df. This subject is covered in Siegel, pages 44 and 110. A one-sentence summary will allow for the reader to master the tables: df equals the number of columns in the table, not including the marginal or total column, minus one, times the number of rows, not including the marginal, minus one. For our table, df = (3-1) (4-1) = 6.

7. There are few standard rules in the literature as to what procedure to follow when some of the results in a table indicate one relationship, some its opposite. Such mixed results happen only rarely in most researches for courtroom use. Faced with such a table, I would first ascertain why the cell or cells behaved oppositely. Perhaps a variable has been misconceptualized so that a given value of it is out of proper order. For example, concrete streets may have

been ranked first by the researcher, ahead of tar, brick, gravel, and dirt, yet in this city concrete may be reserved for commercial, industrial, state-aided, and major arterial roads, all with four lanes of traffic or more—hardly prime residential streets, even though residences may front on some of them. In such a city, if black residents enjoy concrete streets disproportionately, this shows bad zoning rather than good paving.

A second possibility is that the misbehaving cells are very small in N and should be combined with other categories. This is the situation with one cell of table 9-2, "Interracial-No system," with an expected outcome of 2 and an observed outcome of 0. In no case should a misbehaving difference between observed and expected blandly be added into the chi-square statistic, thus artificially increasing its significance. My suggestion would be to subtract the squared difference, rather than adding it, and that is why one element in the series on this page is subtracted, rather than added. See also W.G. Cochran, "Some Methods for Strengthening the Common X^2 Tests," *Biometrics* 10 (1954):417-451.

8. Chapter 4 mentions statistics for summarizing the amount of association in a contingency table.

9. Weighting should be established before data collection to head off any charge that an item was deweighted because it showed little discrimination.

Additional Resources

Further Reading on Sampling

M. Slonim, *Sampling in a Nutshell* (New York: Simon and Schuster, 1966), is a good first book on sampling for attorneys or social scientists.

S. Sudman, *Applied Sampling* (New York: Academic Press, 1976), is a good followup to Slonim, providing social scientists with a full discussion of size, cost, and different ways of taking samples.

D. Raj, *The Design of Sample Surveys* (New York: McGraw-Hill, 1972), is useful in addition to Sudman because it gives specific surveys in its later pages, with particularly helpful chapters on demographic and employment surveys.

Further Reading on Municipal Services

J. Hodson, *Measuring Urban Services* (Bloomington: Indiana University Workshop in Political Theory and Political Analysis, 1975). This packet includes plans for a roughometer, helpful in measuring paving, and suggests ways to measure police services.

International City Management Association (1140 Connecticut Avenue NW, Washington, DC 20036) publishes several texts and information services on administering cities. They are useful sources as to the nature of good or standard practice; they also tell some of the kinds of data cities customarily collect about themselves, available through discovery or simply as matters of public record.

T. Kemper, "Why Are the Streets So Dirty: Social Psychological and Stratification Factors in the Decline of Municipal Services," *Social Forces* 58 (1979): 422–442, is a scholarly article that provides a framework for using poor municipal services as an argument for affirmative action in employment in order to provide afflicted neighborhoods with workers who care.

Lawyers' Committee for Civil Rights under Law, *A Community Guide to the Equalization of Municipal Services* (Washington, D.C., no date), tells how to conduct a community survey to determine if street paving, parks, garbage collection, and other services are provided on a nondiscriminatory basis.

R. Lineberry, *Equality and Public Policy* (Beverly Hills: Sage, 1977), opposes the notion of equality as the test for the distribution of municipal services and also tells ways of measuring services.

E. Lowe, "The Wrong Side of the Tracks: Measuring Inequalities in Municipal Services," *Clearinghouse for Civil Rights Research* 4, no. 1 (1975), analyzes the difficulties encountered by several unsuccessful municipal-services lawsuits including those in Anacostia, DC, and Fairfax, VA.

National Leage of Cities/U.S. Conference of Mayors, *Urban Affairs Abstracts* (1620 Eye St. NW, Washington D.C. 20006), is a weekly information service covering lawsuits and other developments regarding municipal services.

Trinity Parish, *The Next Step: Toward Equality of Public Service* (New York: Trinity Grants Program [74 Trinity Place, 10006], 1974), is a useful introduction to municipal-services litigation that suggests legal strategies, social science research methods, and even remedies. Although dated, the booklet also contains an extensive bibliography.

Urban Institute, *Measuring the Effectiveness of Basic Municipal Services* (Washington, D.C., 1974), presents ways to make observations systematic, hence defensible, and also surveys cities' complaint-handling services. See also other studies by the Urban Institute, including *Residential Zoning and Equal Hosing Opportunities: A Case Study in Black Jack, Mo.,* and *Inequality in Local Government Services: A Case Study of Neighborhood Roads.*

Example of a Municipal-Services Observation Form

Observation Form on City Services

Purpose: to record actual observations on the quality of city services.

Form # _2_ .   Census tract #_____ .   Block #_____ .   House #_____ .
     col.1   cols.2-3   cols. 4-7   cols.8-9

blank col.#   item

_____10   What kind of houses are in the majority on this block or street?
                1.Good. Medium to large houses, in new or excellent condition.
                2.Average. Small but in good shape, or medium to large but in fair
                    shape. Definitely adequate for the necessities of comfort.
                3.Below average. Small in fair shape, or medium in poor condition.
                    Repairs needed. Probably crowded.

_____11-12   How many dwelling units (apartments, houses, etc.) are on block?
                (If 2 code "02." If 100 or more, code "99.")

_____13   How far to the nearest fire hydrant? 1.within 200ft.   2. 200ft-500ft.
                3. more than 500ft or none visible from house.

_____14   How is street paved? 1.concrete;   2.blacktop(tar);   3.gravel;
                4. none(dirt);   0.other (_____)

_____15-16   How wide is street? (Measure in feet from curb to curb, or from edge
                of pavement to edge of pavement, or if not paved, from ditch to ditch.)

_____17   If street is paved, what is condition of pavement? 1.excellent; 2.good,
                some rough spots; 3.has potholes, needs repair;   4.poor, must drive
                slow; 5.gravel road or dirt road.

_____18   What kind of storm-water drainage is provided?
                1.underground lines.
                2.system of graded ditches
                3.ungraded ditches at the side of the road
                4.none (do not confuse with #1!).

_____19   Are there any large ditches or creeks in the area? 1.yes; 2.no. If
                yes, describe: _____.

_____20   If so (yes on item #19), what condition is it in?
                1. excellent: dry or small puddles (unless it has rained recently);
                    concrete or well-graded grass sides.
                2. plain open ditch or creek, no particular grading. Dry or clear water
                3. same as #2 but with unclear or polluted water and/or trash in stream.

_____21   Is the creek enclosed in any way, to help keep kids away from it? 1.yes;
                2.no.

_____22   Are there   piles of garbage, leaves, trash, etc., in the neigh-
                borhood?   Vacant lots that are littered, have high weeds,
                or abandoned buildings? Other potential hazards? 1.yes; 2.no. If
                yes, describe the problem: _____

_____23   How far is it to the nearest factory, industry, commercial area, or rail-
                road? 1.within one block (300ft); 2.within four blocks; 3.visible
                or audible, but further than four blocks; 4.none visible. Describe
                it (if any): _____.

_____24   Is there any pollution, including smoke, odors, noise, water pollution,
                etc.? 1.yes; 2.no. If yes, what?_____.

_____25   State the number of street lights on the block, including both inter-
                sections (if they exist). If more than 9, enter "9".

_____24   The curb is: 1. ⌐___   2. ___∨   3.none.

_____25   The racial composition of this block's residents is mostly: 1.black;
                2.interracial; 3.white.

Your name: _____ . Today's date: _____ .

10 Social Surveys to Support a Change of Venue

In criminal trials, particularly those with racial, political, or ideological overtones, defense lawyers sometimes ask for a change of venue. They claim that adverse publicity, the place of the victims(s) or criminals(s) in the community, the nature of the alleged crime and its impact, or other factors make it impossible for the defendant to get a fair trial locally. They seek a new location, perhaps in a distant county.

Such a move can have distinct advantages. For one, even if denied, a change-of-venue request can delay trial. In some circumstances, delay can help the defendant. Second, in a remote setting the prosecutor may feel less under eye of his constituents, more able to use plea bargaining or to reduce charges as he might with more-ordinary offenders. Most importantly, some jury members in a publicized local trial may find it hard to avoid being swayed by the many discussions of the case occurring around them, with friends, in the newspaper, and so on. Jurors may be thought of, or may come to think of themselves, as representatives of the (white) community, which may make it hard for them to convict a white or acquit a black. Jurors in a distant community will hear the case discussed less often and will feel less identification with its outcome.

Since juries are supposed to be representative of their communities (chapter 8), if the defense can show that the community in general is aware of the crime and has formed an opinion that the defendant is guilty, then venue may be changed. Also, if the defense can show that the adults in the dominant group are prejudiced against the class of people of which the defendant is a member, that also supports a change-of-venue motion. The best way to find out community awareness or community bias is to survey the whole community or a random sample thereof.

Negative and Positive Aspects of Survey Research

A major problem that afflicts survey research is that surveys do not measure what people do or feel but what they say they do or feel. This problem must be dealt with when interviewing prospective jurors. An intelligent racist, for example, will deny prejudicial attitudes when interviewed, because Americans know it is good form to be egalitarian. A common way of dealing with this problem involves developing subtler and subtler questionnaire items so as to tap the vein of prejudice that may flow beneath the egalitarian verbal exterior of the

143

respondent. This is an inadequate solution however; problems with it have been mentioned in chapter 9 and chapter 4. There is no completely satisfactory answer, so attorneys and social scientists should not seize too quickly upon the attitude survey as the best way to establish some part of the factual situation. Other methods can be used instead of attitude surveys, and this book is full of examples. When survey research is deemed necessary, other methods can be used to complement it.

Surveys also can study things other than attitudes, which are sometimes as ephemeral as a soufflé in the icebox. Items whose measurement is less problematic than attitudes include:

Past experiences ("Have you ever dated a member of another race?" "Have you ever had a member of another race to your home for dinner?");

Social structure (shopping patterns, church membership, other organizational memberships, later analyzed by race);

Future plans ("Have you ever considered moving to another home in Jackson?" "In what area of town would you like to live?");

Behavior ("Do you read the Jackson *Daily News*?" "Is that where you learned of the such-and-such case?").

Each of the items in parentheses might have some relevance to the racial polarization that, if shown, could support a change-of-venue request.

Past practices might be the point of a survey. At the end of the chapter, I include a mailed questionnaire that was introduced in court. It sought information from all Mississippi school-district heads as to their practices in purchasing textbooks. Because of the factual nature of these practices and the questions, the court had no reason to doubt the accuracy of the superintendents' answers.

In some cases, it might be important to survey the distribution of knowledge in society or in an institution. For example, if a police force claims to have in place an aggressive affirmative-action recruitment campaign directed toward minorities and women, a survey of college students and other young adults in the area, asking them where to apply for jobs with the police department, what such jobs pay, what qualifications are required, what diverse kinds of positions are available, and if they have heard of the affirmative-action program, might be useful. In a public high school with a charge of discrimination regarding discipline, rather than asking how folks feel about the discipline procedure—is it fair and so on—instead ask them to describe it through multiple questions. Administrators will know the procedure better than faculty members, probably, and aggrieved students may know even less about the proper procedures than students in general. The inadequate filtering down of knowledge about channels may vitiate the institution's invocation of the procedures as a defense against charges of racism or insensitivity.

Many other kinds of data have been generated by surveys and used in litigation; some are described in the articles cited at the end of the chapter. Survey research will continue to be an important tool of the attorney who is trying to establish a factual base or pattern. There will be times when a traditional attitude survey like a Gallup Poll is appropriate. One example is in change-of-venue requests. If the defendant is black and the incident has been publicized, the attorney may want to show that many people have formed opinions about the matter and the defendant's guilt or innocence, opinions that preclude a fair trial in that community. There is no way to find out what people have heard about the incident, no way to ascertain their attitudes toward the defendant, except by asking them. Even here, however, the attitude survey results should be complemented by other data and methods. For example, racial polarization in the community can be shown by census data, indicating radical socioeconomic differences between white and black residents, as shown in chapter 5. Recent elections can be analyzed to see if racial bloc voting occurred, another indicator of racial polarization (chapter 14). Residential segregation can be measured (chapter 11). The alert attorney and social scientist can suggest other ways to provide a mix of methods, rather than letting a questionnaire stand alone.

Attorneys should not devise their own questionnaires, however. Neither should clients. Too many pitfalls exist, both as to form and content. Some kinds of errors will work against one by cutting the response rate or making responses hard to interpret. Other errors can make easy targets for criticism by an informed social scientist or layperson on the other side. A qualified social scientist is needed, also, to explain why questions were asked in the order and manner they were, to defend the response rate, and to assess the strengths and weaknesses of the methodology against standard practices. Many social scientists have had little or no experience in conducting questionnaires, particularly in doing survey research that will be subjected to searching critique by others. Therefore the attorney may need to help direct the study, at least by pointing to possible weaknesses and by making suggestions as the work gets underway. Accordingly, this chapter, covering survey research in a compact form and offering some hints that may be new to the social scientist as well as to the attorney, is an introduction to the subject. Many large books have been written on survey research, so this chapter can hardly claim to provide readers with proficiency in the area; I do describe some sources, at the end of the chapter, from which this proficiency can be gleaned.

Before plunging in, an ethical caution must be emphasized. Survey research bothers people, uses their time, and can worry them. When done for legal use, surveys can cause still greater worry. To the usual possibility for abuse of privacy in the research instrument is added the potential harm from failure to keep respondents' identities secret. Lawyer and researcher should reread chapter 3 on ethics before going farther. They must agree on procedures that will safeguard respondents from harassment during the data collection or afterwards. A third opinion, such as the judgment of a research-review committee, should be sought because they may be more objective, being less involved.

The attorney should also consider submitting the proposed survey instrument to the other side and asking for its comments and agreement before finalizing it. The court's opinion may also be sought. Even if agreement is not forthcoming, a good-faith attempt to modify in order to deal with the other side's comments and suggestions can enhance the credibility of the survey. Of course, if the survey is not of the general public but within an institution or other smaller milieu, then the other side might be able to sabotage the process by notifying would-be recipients before they had a chance to participate.

Varieties of Survey Research

Survey research is a method of generating or collecting data. The various methods grouped under the heading survey research can be placed along a formal/informal continuum:

Formal ←————————————————————————————————→ Informal

Mailed questionnaire	Handed-out questionnaire	Questionnaire in interview form (interview schedule)	Focused interview (structured interview)	Unstructured interview

As we move from left to right, we see more and more input from the observer, and that input grows harder to standardize, analyze, or defend in court. If an item on a mailed questionnaire is said to be highly biased, the judge can read the question and decide for himself. However, if the observer uses an unstructured interview, her respondent may say what he thinks she wishes to hear, or she may interpret his words as she wishes, or at least such distortion may be charged by the other side in court. That kind of bias is hard to pin down, hence hard to defend against. Thus, most survey research presented in court is of the three types on the left side of the continuum.

The techniques toward the right offer several benefits to compensate for their several drawbacks. One is response rate. It is hard to say no to a request to talk from a person on the scene; it is much easier to put aside a mailed questionnaire, eventually forgetting to return it. Moreover, the respondent in the forms of data gathering on the right is in interaction with the researcher so he can make greater input, tell things the researcher never knew to ask. Thus the right-hand methods are better for pilot investigations.

If the researchers have enough funds, usually they will settle on a scheduled interview or questionnaire in interview form. This maximizes returns while standardizing the interview, and both increase courtroom defensibility.

Specific Hints for Scheduled Interviews

Like pencil-and-paper questionnaires, scheduled interviews are best kept brief. Short interviews are less of a burden on respondents so they pose less of an ethical issue. Also, if the interviewer can state that the interview will take only about five minutes, she will get fewer refusals than if the interview will last half an hour.

The interview must begin with some introduction or statement of purpose. This introduction should be direct and short. It should introduce the interviewer by name and usually by institutional affiliation, say that a short interview is involved, introduce its subject and purpose, quickly reassure as to anonymity, and ask for cooperation.

The introduction is especially crucial when the interviewer is not in eye contact with the respondent (the telephone poll). Introductions customarily tell the truth, but not the whole truth, regarding their purpose. Thus, a survey designed to record community attitudes toward a specific defendant with a well-known racial membership or political flamboyance might be introduced as a "survey regarding recent events in Jackson, including the RNA eleven," to cite a case I once was involved with, rather than a "survey to see if Imari Obadele can get a fair trial." Neither statement is false; the second introduction has greater potential for biasing the responses (in either direction) and cutting the response rate.

Here is a possible introduction for a structured telephone interview to assess community attitudes toward a black defendant accused of a crime with potential ideological implications:

> Hello, My name is Jane Doe. I'm a sociology student at the University of Vermont, and we're doing a survey on people's attitudes toward recent events in Burlington, including the Ernie Smith murder. I want to ask you just eight questions, and your name will never be released to anyone in conjunction with the survey. It'll take less than five minutes. May I continue?

As this introduction implies, the interviewer must have some believable role. The role should be true, too, and if a university's name is mentioned, the survey must be done by students under a professor's direction, who will have obtained departmental approval for the mention.[1]

After answering any questions from the respondent, the interviewer plunges into the body of the interview. The first question should be interesting but not controversial. What social scientists call hard data or socioeconomic background information should never be placed first, always last. Attitude questions are like straws in the wind—the slightest breeze can bend them, including the influence stemming from having just identified and thought of oneself as a member of a certain occupational group, race, or age category. How one has just replied to an attitude item only rarely influences one's reported race, job, or age, however. Hence attitude items should precede hard-data items.

There is one major exception to the considerations in the previous paragraph. Often the first item(s) should help legitimate the entire questionnaire. For example, "How long have you lived in Burlington?" flows logically from the sample introduction, and "Are you a registered voter?" follows logically from that. Both questions may have to be asked sooner or later to establish that the respondent is part of the potential jury pool whose attitudes have possible legal implications. Asking them early may cause the respondent to take the questionnaire seriously and allows the interviewer to talk some someone else if the first interviewee is a transient nonvoting fourteen-year old.

The questionnaire should usually be organized logically, sometimes even with subheadings, so that it does not seem jumpy and disruptive to the respondent. The exception is when you do not want respondents to surmise what the focus or purpose of the poll is. In that case, the questions might be titled "Attitudes toward Current Issues" so respondents will not expect continuity.

More than one item should be used to inquire about attitudes or issues important to the expert's testimony. These items should be phrased so that agreement with them indicates one position on some of them, the opposite position on others.[2] The items should approach the topic in various ways so that a person who indicates the same general sentiment on each has shown what might be called a syndrome. Several sophisticated statistical measures can then be applied to this subset of questions, including item-to-scale correlations and factor analysis. Several items can be combined mathematically into the index—of racism, say, or of high future aspirations. These multi-item indexes then constitute operational definitions of the important concepts in the research.

When several questions are asked regarding one item, it is useful to include one open-ended question. Most items on a survey for courtroom presentation should probably be closed—that is, with alternatives provided to the respondent for his selection. For example:

Regarding black employees, this company on the whole

___ treats blacks better than whites in some ways,

___ treats both groups equally,

___ treats whites better than blacks in some ways.

is a better question than "Regarding black employees, this company
                                        ." Some respondents will fill in the blank with "is biased," and the investigator will never know if the implication is bias toward or against the minority. Others will reply cryptically. Even in face-to-face interviews, comments will not be clear, especially to the principal investigator who will be reading them later. Also, comments in the blanks must often then be coded—divided into meaningful categories by the researcher. Whenever this is

planned, consider sharing the code categories with the respondent—that is, closing the question.[3] In a context of good closed questions, one open-ended item gives the respondent an opportunity for putting things his own way. In the process, he may disclose a fact not otherwise inquired about, suggesting a line for further questions. Or he may utter a phrase that can be excerpted in court to make the data sing, a phrase that helps clarify the position of others answering the closed questions in a like manner. Meanwhile, the closed questions provide grouped results so that the open-ended question need not be coded and one's procedures need not be defended in court.

Steps in the Process

To develop a questionnaire or interview schedule, gather data, analyze them, and present conclusions in court is a multistage procedure that requires, at the very least, two weeks of full-time work and is much more likely to stretch out part time over four months. Six months would be a safe span of time to allot for the project.

The first step would be an exploratory conference between attorney and social scientist. Indeed, all the steps in this developing relationship described in chapter 2 should be followed. After the social scientist has an understanding of the points to be explored in the survey, she should explore with the attorney its form and approach. The following questions must be answered:

If a survey is needed, should it be a questionnaire or interview? Structured or unstructured? Why?

How large a sample will be required and how should it be taken? (Chapter 9 discusses sampling.)

How will the data be analyzed? What kinds of percentages and graphs will be used in court? What must be learned about the respondents—for example, will women's responses be compared to men's? (If so, then sex must be asked on the questionnaire.)

A second step would be for the social scientist to develop a pilot or trial questionnaire or interview schedule. She may go ahead and administer it to half a dozen would-be respondents who were picked representatively from the population to be surveyed. She must do this herself. She should also have one assistant do five or six interviews if assistants will be doing some or all of the data gathering once the project is underway. Then she should assess the results by asking what questions were difficult for respondents to answer or understand. What questions led to results that were hard to interpret, especially when filled in by the assistant? She should also show the questionnaire and results to the attorney (and perhaps the client) for evaluation and comment. (See figure 10-1.)

Small changes in item wording can cause enormous differences in responses. One way to become sensitive to wording effects is by critiquing items. Before looking at my criticisms, write down what you feel is the matter with each of the following questionnaire items, which are taken from or parallel to items used in actual surveys.

1. You are preparing for a state budget hearing. You represent a small but effective program on alcohol abuse that tours public high schools. Within a questionnaire given to students before the program, designed to show their ignorance or knowledge about alcohol, is this item:

    "Every year Americans spend more money on alcohol than on religion, but less than on education."

    _____ Agree
    _____ Disagree

2. As part of a change-of-venue motion, you want to show that the opinion leaders of the community, those with more income and status, are particularly aware of and opposed to your defendant and his alleged crime. You ask,

    "My family income is $ _____."

3. You are Senator Orrin Hatch and say you want to survey public opinion regarding right-to-work legislation. You ask,

    "Are you in favor of allowing construction union czars the power to shut down an entire construction site because of a dispute with a single contractor, . . . thus forcing even more workers to knuckle under to union agents? Yes _____ No _____"
    (his ellipses)

4. You want to see if black students at a state black university are more conservative than at a nearby private black college, part of a climate of orthodoxy you hope to show. One question you ask of a random sample is,

    "Black people should have all the rights white people have."

    _____ Strongly agree
    _____ Agree in general
    _____ Disagree in general
    _____ Strongly disagree

5. You plan to challenge an affirmative-action program at the university on behalf of a nonpromoted female faculty member. You ask a sample of the faculty:

    "Do you believe the University of Vermont is doing all it can to enhance the position of minorities and women on campus?"
    _____ Yes _____ No

Figure 10–1. Words Make a Difference

Item 1 is double ended. A yes answer is correct and meaningful, but disagreement could come from a respondent who feels we spend even more on alcohol than on education or from one who believes we spend less on it than on religion. Hence, a disagree answer is ambiguous and cannot be interpreted. (There are other problems, among them the fact that most Americans have no idea how much Americans as a whole spend on any of these three items.)

Item 2 is an invasion of privacy. Moreover, the answers will surely be coded eventually, so that $10,000-14,999 rather than $13,446.72 will be entered. Why request specificity only to discard it? Supply the code categories and ask for the appropriate X. Another problem is the fact that this wording will cause underreporting because some sources of income will be overlooked—for example, investment appreciation, children's earnings, and so on.

Senator Hatch uses catchwords including *czars, forcing,* and *knuckle under* as well as the gentler distortion in phrases such as *power to shut down* and *union agents.* Only a fool could agree with the question as worded, so Hatch is obviously not trying to see what people know or think about this complex topic. His alternatives are also poorly spaced.

Almost no young black adult believes that blacks should be denied equal rights. Hence everyone at both schools on item 4 will check strongly agree. There will be no dissent, so there will be no way to see if that dissent is rarer on the public campus.

Item 5 is almost as biased by a catch phrase as item 3—that phrase is *all it can.* No person or institution can really do all it can, so a no answer has very little meaning.

Figure 10-1. *(continued)*

The pilot data gathering should lead to a pilot analysis to ensure that the interview form is easy to read and punch from and to provide actual preliminary computer output. The scientist and attorney should go over this output together. The expert describes the results she anticipates on the basis of this tiny pilot study. She even tells the statistical tests she plans to use. The lawyer responds, perhaps suggesting that the analysis looks too complex to be readily understandable by the court. In sum, the discussion after the pilot should be full because it will likely be the last extensive communication between expert and attorney until data are in and analysis is complete.

After problems have been resolved, the data gathering can begin in earnest. The social scientist must stay in close touch with this process. I must warn lawyers that many social scientists seem to be shy, so they avoid fieldwork. Nevertheless, our social scientist must make at least half a dozen of the contacts with respondents so she will have a sense of the process and can claim in court that she did some of the work, from start to finish, herself. She will learn first-hand what people say. She can also assess the quality of subordinates' work much more effectively after learning what some of the pitfalls of the procedure are.

While data gathering continues, two steps preliminary to data analysis can be taken: coding and punching. We have already argued that most items should be closed, with alternatives supplied, which keeps coding to a minimum. The interview forms should have been laid out with computer punching (data entry) in mind. Now only a little work may be needed to get them ready for punching, including checking for completeness and legibility, spot checking for accuracy, and adding information where necessary, such as where census block data are added to the form after it has been filled out. Then the data are punched into the computer for storage.

It is often tempting to begin to analyze the data before they are all in. That is a mistake. The energy should go into checking the work of the gatherers, tying up loose ends, and completing the data-entry process because if the survey is not quite complete, the analysis will simply have to be repeated. Otherwise, analysis of survey results parallels analysis of any other data set and need not be discussed here.

Let me close with the by-now familiar admonition to think creatively about what other data, from the census or elsewhere, and what other methods might provide a context to enhance the survey results and make the factual presentation much more effective. Supported by other evidence, surveys are very useful in court. In a change-of-venue request I would supplement the survey with content analyses of media coverage of the crime for which the defendant is on trial. If using survey research to ascertain female employees' aspirations in a manufacturing firm and their knowledge of promotion avenues, I would also content analyze the company's promotional material and in-house publications for possible sexism. With that kind of complementary evidence, survey data can be highly effective.

Notes

1. If you do not, respondents may phone the department later, seeking more information, only to be told no survey exists. Because of this mention and because of the possibilities of harm to individuals that could result from unethical practices, the enterprise will need to be reviewed by the departmental or institutional research ethics committee (see chapter 3).

2. Otherwise it may be charged (and may be true) that respondents are merely agreeable. See Arthur Couch and K. Kenniston, "Yeasayers and Naysayers," *Journal of Abnormal and Social Psychology* 60 (1960):151–174.

3. Stanley Payne, *The Art of Asking Questions* (Princeton, N.J.: Princeton University Press, 1951), chapter 3.

Additional Resources

Further Reading

Irvin Deutscher, *What We Say/What We Do* (Glenview, Ill.: Scott, Foresman, 1973). To the social scientist, this book offers a sophisticated discussion of the pitfalls of relying on survey data. To the lawyer, the book suggests tough questions to put to survey researchers regarding the adequacy of their research dedesigns.

J. Fiedler, *Field Research* (San Francisco: Jossey-Bass, 1978). This book suggests ways of managing social surveys, particularly if the survey must be large scale.

Leonard H. Goodman, ed., *Sources and Uses of Social and Economic Data: A Manual for Lawyers* (Washington, D.C.: Bureau of Social Science Research, 1973), contains a chapter, "How to Conduct a Survey," providing well-written introductions to issues such as question bias, format, supervision or interviewers, and coding. Chapter 1 also offers a useful, though overly restrictive, view of surveys and the hearsay rule.

Des Raj, *The Design of Sample Surveys* (New York: McGraw-Hill, 1972), is useful because it gives specific surveys in its later pages, with particularly helpful chapters on demographic and employment surveys.

Stanley Payne, *The Art of Asking Questions* (Princeton, N.J.: Princeton University Press, 1951), stays in print because it helps anyone making up a survey ensure that the questions are clear, the answers meaningful.

Example of a Small Survey Used in Court

The following one-page questionnaire was mailed to all Mississippi public-school superintendents in 1979. About 60 percent replied after a follow-up. Data were used in *Loewen et al.* v. *Turnipseed et al.* (488 F. Supp. 1138) to show that most districts had little or no money available to purchase textbooks that were not on the state list. Exclusion of a text from the state list was therefore tantamount to excluding it from use in the public schools.

'(letterhead)

(date)

to: all Superintendents of Schools,
     State of Mississippi

Dear Superintendent:

We are doing a survey to determine whether and to what extent local school districts in Mississippi use local funds to purchase, for classroom use, textbooks
that are not on the state-approved list and for which state money is not available.

Results will be compiled for the state as a whole. No information about individual
district practices will be released, so confidentiality is assured. The questionnaire will take only five minutes -- and your cooperation is most appreciated.

1. As a practical matter, how much money in local funds did your school district
spend last year for the purchase of textbooks not on the state-approved list?
         __less than $1000.
         __between $1000 and $5000.
         __more than $5000.
Can you indicate in the following blank an approximate dollar amount? $_____.

2. In the past two or three years, has your district used local funds to purchase
textbooks for classroom use which are not on the state-approved list? __yes; __no.

3. If so, which of these alternatives describes your use of local funds? (Check
as many as apply):
         __We purchased textbooks for regular classroom use as the required text.
         __We purchased auxilliary books for required classroom use.
         __We purchased auxilliary books for optional classroom use.
         __Other (please explain:

4. Finances aside, as a matter of school district and educational policy, would
your district give consideration to the state-approved list in selecting textbooks?
         __Yes, we would probably choose from the state-approved list in any event.
         __Perhaps; the fact that the state had considered and approved the book
           would influence us in its favor.
         __Perhaps not; the fact that the state had considered and approved the
           book would influence us to consider alternative texts.
         __No; we would probably avoid any book on the state-approved list.

This survey form was completed by:

        Name _____

        Position _____

        Address _____

        _____

Please use the enclosed stamped envelop to return your completed survey form to:
(name, institution, address). Thank you for your cooperation!

11

Using the Index of Dissimilarity to Determine the Extent of Segregation

Segregation can take many forms. Not all of them relate to race, or even to persons or families. Therefore, the index of dissimilarity about to be discussed has uses far beyond school or residential segregation.

Basically, it can be used to assess whether or not one item is clustered or distributed unequally within a population. For example:

Are home-improvement loans concentrated in certain neighborhoods?

Are women restricted to certain departments and offices in a large industrial firm?

Do defects originate disproportionately in certain production lines and shifts?

Are Native Americans treated only in the first two chapters of a history text, then forgotten?

The index of dissimilarity can help answer these questions.

Four Sources of Segregation

Racial segregation was institutionalized consciously by whites in the United States as a way of implying white supremacy and keeping blacks "in their place." It did not always exist. Although elements of segregation were present during slavery, the Civil War, Reconstruction, and the fusion period following Reconstruction, most analysts date the development of segregation as a system to approximately 1890. Thus in the South, many streetcars, cemeteries, restaurants, and so forth were not segregated until the 1890s; in the North, it is instructive to remember that Jackie Robinson was not the first black major-league ball player, but the first in the modern era, blacks' having first been shut out of organized baseball in 1889. Political posts reserved for blacks in the nineteenth century were turned over to whites in the twentieth. The final blow was the segregation of federal facilities in Washington, D.C., by Woodrow Wilson.[1]

Segregation can be defined as a system of social relations that keeps two groups separate whenever they are doing the same thing, such as swimming or learning math or thinking, but allows close contact when they are doing different tasks that imply hierarchy, such as being one's janitor or secretary or nursing one's baby. Segregation implies inferiority, because it is imposed by one group upon the other—that is, if there were nothing wrong with the subservient group, then it would be perfectly allowable for the two to mix while doing equal tasks. The courts have long noted the stigmatizing aspects of segregation.[2]

Segregation can arise from four distinct sources: law, policy, practice, and choice. De jure segregation has been most common in the South, is now illegal in most forms, and when shown, poses no particular courtroom problem and requires no particular social-science expertise. Even in then segregationist Mississippi, however, officials recognized as far back as 1962 that they must not claim to be operating segregated institutions. So it was that state officials claimed that the University of Mississippi was not segregated and had not excluded James Meredith because of his race but merely happened to have no blacks enrolled. Therefore de jure segregation in the present usually cannot be shown. De jure in the past, even the distant past, is legally relevant, for courts have usually held that officials have an affirmative duty to desegregate, to dismantle a once-segregated institution, and few officials have ever done that.[3] Hence a high level of segregation in the present combined with the de jure segregation of the past can be used to make a strong argument for desegregation steps in the future.

Many communities and institutions where there was no de jure segregation nonetheless have contained minorities by policies. For example, some employers have stated, formally or informally, that certain types of jobs were for men, others for women. As recently as 1981, I knew of universities that openly reserved the posts of president and full dean for men "because some faculty members are not ready for a female dean." School districts have drawn attendance zones to conform to racial boundaries, when use of more-obvious natural barriers would create interracial zones, "because homogeneous school populations are easier to teach and promote good learning." Slavish adherence to the policy of neighborhood schools, particularly when neighborhoods are defined racially, can promote residential segregation; thus the relationship between school segregation and residential segregation is reciprocal, with segregated schools helping maintain segregated neighborhoods as well as the reverse.[4]

Practices of the majority can also lead to segregation of the minority. Steering is a practice of realtors that I have personally encountered in Mississippi and Maryland vis-à-vis blacks and in Vermont vis-à-vis French Americans. Realtors fail to show houses in interracial neighborhoods to white would-be purchasers or do so in such a way as to stigmatize the home and neighborhood. The result is to encourage blockbusting to maintain white and black parts of town.[5] City officials sometimes reduce services in interracial areas, thus condemning them to a wrong-side-of-the-tracks appearance and causing white flight.[6] The practice of requiring certain physical size or test scores, if those attributes are not job related, can segregate jobs by sex or race.

Expert testimony on the resulting segregation, using the index of dissimilarity, can help end such practices. The defendant may claim that the segregation results from individual choice: "Blacks are more comfortable where there are other black families"; "women feel it would be unladylike to be a lineman." Undoubtedly choice is a factor. With regard to race, however, choice has been discounted as a major cause of the high residential-segregation indexes of blacks. The much more-moderate indexes found for various white ethnic groups might represent the levels of segregation we would expect among blacks if choice alone (black and white choices) prevailed.[7] Choice as an explanation also cannot explain the existence of plaintiffs—black, female, or other.

Segregation has basically the same unfortunate consequences whether it originated in law, policy, practice, or choice. Separating one group from another makes it unlikely that the lower group will know of paths of mobility to upper positions. Multitudes of new skills, attitudes, and even bits of etiquette may be required in the transition from telephone operator to lineman or from secretary to associate editor, and if one job is reserved for women, another for men, it is hard for women to acquire the new knowledge or to be motivated to do so. Residentially, if blacks are contained in one part of the city and one set of schools, it can be difficult for them to believe they can acquire or to actually acquire the kinds of verbal facilities needed for good performance on standardized tests and so on. This statement of the ills of segregation hardly scratches the surface (see "Additional Resources" for a bibliography).

Courts have sometimes made much of the de facto/de jure distinction. My aforementioned causes of segregation blur this line deliberately because no clear two-part distinction can be drawn. Courts have usually held that segregation caused by policy is as actionable as that caused by law, particularly where intent can be shown, and intent can often be inferred from results. Segregation by choice has been held to be constitutional, and I would agree, provided that free choices of blacks and whites are involved. (Whites must not constrain black choice by choosing to sell only to white home buyers; men must not choose to work only under a male dean.) Segregation by practices, particularly when those practices originate in persons or institutions other than those sued, has proven to be a complex and troublesome area. For example, school officials may know that realtors are maintaining racial segregation through a host of practices. School administrators may even be abetting the practice by refusing to zone and bus in ways that could cause school desegregation and promote residential desegregation. It is not clear that such practices are currently unconstitutional.

Whatever the legal terrain, the attorney needs, as a first step, to determine the extent of the segregation. To do this, he needs a measure that is not directly affected by the proportion of each race or group in the system.

The Index of Dissimilarity

At one time DHEW (now the Department of Education) considered a minority child to be segregated if she or he attended a school in which that minority was in the majority. Proportion of minority students in majority-minority schools then became a rule of thumb to compare districts for degree of school segregation. How simplistic! Any school system that was more than 50 percent black and was totally desegregated, so that each of its schools was identical to racial ratio, would by that rule appear to be completely segregated.[8]

Social scientists have developed at least half a dozen more-sophisticated indexes to measure the extent to which a community's schools or neighborhoods are racially segregated. Each has validity for some purpose, but perhaps the most popular and one of the easiest to compute is the Taeuber index, the index of dissimilarity, D.[9] It has the advantage of being unaffected by the overall proportion of minorities in the area. If a city is 10 percent black but clusters all its black pupils in two 45 percent black schools, the Taeuber index will pick this up; some measures would not. Hence, D allows comparison of different districts and of a single district across different time periods.[10]

Its uses in civil-rights cases are manifold. For example, suppose you are suing a school district that is alleging employment discrimination. It would be useful to show that the district also operates its elementary schools in a segregative manner to show that a pattern of racism or insensitivity exists and to indicate that prior employment discrimination has had unfortunate effects upon current institutional practices. The Taeuber index offers a quick way to assess the amount of segregation among elementary pupils.

The analyst needs the number of black pupils and white pupils at each school. (A decision must be made regarding others: Asian Americans, Hispanics, Native Americans. One way is to leave them out, doing only blacks and whites, and then do the third group against whites, leaving out blacks.) D is then found by:

$$D = \Sigma(B_i/B - W_i/W)$$

For all schools where the term in the parentheses in positive. This formula is not at all forbidding. B_i means the number of black children at the first school. Dividing it by B, the total number of black children in the district, yields the proportion of the district's black children at the first school. If this fraction is larger than the proportion of the district's white children at that school, shown by the second fraction, W_i/W, then the result for the first school will be positive and becomes a component of D. Usually D is then multiplied by 100, so it varies from 0 to 100. Figure 11–1 offers an example of the entire analysis for a district with five elementary schools. These schools are rather segregated, by visual inspection of their enrollments, and the Taeuber index does not disappoint, coming out at a high 82.7.

This index, D, is not only easy to compute but also has a quickly graspable meaning; it represents the proportion of minority students who would have to be transferred to majority schools in order to obtain perfect desegregation, an

After obtaining the data in the first two columns of the table, compute column three, B_i/B, by dividing the number of black pupils in each school by 220, the number of black pupils in the system. Do the same for the whites. The final column is the subtraction of column four from column three; negative outcomes are omitted. Its sum, .827, is D, the index of dissimilarity, or 82.7 on a scale from 0 to 100.

School Enrollments by Race, Mythical School System, 1982

School	Number of Black Pupils	Number of White Pupils	$\dfrac{B_i}{B}$	$\dfrac{W_i}{W}$	$\left(\dfrac{B_i}{B} - \dfrac{W_i}{W}\right)$
Adam	0	100	.0	.36	negative
Baker	10	90	.045	.32	negative
Charles	20	80	.09	.29	negative
Dexter	90	10	.409	.036	.373
Efron	100	0	.454	.0	.454
Total	220	280			$\Sigma = .827$

Figure 11-1. Computing the Index of Dissimilarity to Measure Racial Segregation

index of 0. (This is not an efficient means to desegregate and is not proposed. Any efficient means would involve two-way transfers so that majority students were also being moved to previously minority schools. In that event, the proportion of all students who would have to be moved would be much less.) An index of 0 means the proportion of blacks in all schools is the same, while $D=100$ represents total apartheid, with not one black in a white school and not one white in a school with blacks. So we have here clear evidence of school segregation, whatever its cause. Most school systems in the southeastern states, which operate under some form of desegregation plan, have indexes of dissimilarity between 7 and 25.[11]

A school district can desegregate its schools but still segregate its children by placing them in segregated classrooms within ostensibly desegregated schools. Intact busing, the sending of entire classes from one school to use vacant rooms in another school, is one way to do this. Another method is through tracking so that college-preparatory students rarely encounter vocational types. The index of dissimilarity can be calculated for classrooms within a school or schools, just as was done for schools within a district. D can also be calculated for districts within a metropolitan area. Careful work can distinguish the amount of segregation owing to within-school classroom differences, school-to-school differences within districts, and districtwide differences within a metropolitan area.

Turning to housing, we find it even more segregated than schooling in most U.S. cities. The unit of analysis is usually the block, smaller than the school-attendance zone. Since some desegregated schools draw students from all-white or all-black blocks, such schools will obviously have lower indexes, indicating less segregation than their constituent neighborhoods. Few citywide housing plans or court orders have seriously attacked residential segregation either, unlike school desegregation.

Residential-segregation indexes have been published for more than 200 cities, based on 1960 and 1970 census data.[12] Cities range from about 60 to 98, with a median of about 88, and are so highly segregated that no city can be much higher than the median. These data can be used irresponsibly to claim that, for instance, city policies could hardly have been responsible for a segregation index of 89 in a city's public-housing units, since after all, the entire United States is about equally segregated. This argument would resemble a claim by the University of Mississippi that it was no more segregated than other Southern universities and school districts, hence could not be at fault! The four sources of segregation have been at work for decades across the United States so it cannot be a surprise that they have had an effect. Therefore it would be hard to single out a particular set of housing projects as particularly segregated compared to the nation, but it would be easy to demonstrate that those projects were segregated in the abstract or compared to desegregated parts of the city.

A complete showing of actionable segregation in an institution requires several witnesses and proofs in complementary areas. At least one of the witnesses should be experienced in these kinds of lawsuits if the lawyer is new to the area. A huge literature exists in the social sciences regarding desegregation, some listed in "Additional Resources" at the end of this chapter; also listed there are some sources of legal advice.

The index of dissimilarity can also be used for many other tasks. Like the Lorenz curve and its Gini index,[13] it can be used to measure income inequality. Instead of B_i representing the number of black pupils in the first school, I_i would represent the number of dollars of income received by the first group, the lowest income category, and would be divided by all income received by the entire population under study, or I. The next column would be P_i/P, or proportion of the total population in that group. D would again vary from 0 to 100 and would represent the percentage of all income that would have to change hands for income equality to prevail. D for income is about 40 for the United States, smaller for some political subdivisions within it. A higher D indicates that the differences in a county are unusual, showing marked income inequality, indicative of a continuing legacy of discrimination.

Notes

1. On the increasing segregation of the late nineteenth century, see Howard N. Meyer, *The Amendment that Refused to Die* (Radnor, Pa.: Chilton,

1973), pp. 117–137; Rayford W. Logan, *The Betrayal of the Negro* (New York: Macmillan-Collier, 1965), also published as *The Negro in American Life and Thought; The Nadir, 1877–1901* (New York: 1954); and C. Vann Woodward, *The Strange Career of Jim Crow* (New York: Oxford University Press, various editions).

2. See *Brown* v. *Board of Education,* 347 U.S. 483 (1954); see also plaintiff's argument in *Gong Lum* v. *Rice* [treated in James W. Loewen, *The Mississippi Chinese* (Cambridge, Mass.: Harvard University Press, 1971, pp. 66–68)].

3. *Columbus* v. *Penick,* 99 Sup. Ct. 2941.

4. 38 Social Scientists, "School Desegregation and Residential Segregation," *Transaction/Society* 16 (July 1979):70–76.

5. Rose Helper, *Racial Politics and Practices of Real Estate Brokers* (Minneapolis: University of Minnesota, Ph.D. dissertation, 1969); and Diana Pearce, *Breaking Down Barriers: New Evidence on the Impact of Metropolitan School Desegregation on Housing Patterns* (Washington, D.C.: Center for National Policy Review, 1980).

6. See chapter 9.

7. 38 Social Scientists, "School Desegregation," p. 74.

8. Readers will recognize that a heavily black but itself desegregated system surrounded by white systems is still segregated in the larger metropolitan context.

9. See Karl Taeuber and Alma Taeuber, *Negroes in Cities* (Chicago: Aldine, 1965), pp. 195–245, for a full discussion of this index.

10. There are some problems with the Taeuber index, summarized by H. Becker, "The Measurement of Segregation," ERIC Document No. ED171-825 (1978).

11. Indexes for many school districts are given by Karl Taeuber and F. Wilson, *Project Report No. 1: Analysis of Trends in School Segregation* (Madison: University of Wisconsin Institute for Research on Poverty, 1979).

12. Taeuber and Taeuber, *Negroes in Cities,* pp. 39–41; Annette Sorensen et al., "Indexes of Racial Residential Segregation for 109 Cities in the United States," *Sociological Focus* (1975):125–142.

13. For an introduction to the Lorenz curve and Gini index, see Howard Alker, *Mathematics and Politics* (New York: Macmillan, 1965), chapter 3. For an example of their use in comparing two counties regarding race relations, see James W. Loewen, *The Mississippi Chinese* (Cambridge, Mass.: Harvard University Press, 1971), pp. 15–17.

Additional Resources

Further Reading on School Desegregation

The school desegregation literature is vast. The sources listed here provide the barest of beginnings.

A small article by Ronald D. Henderson and Mary von Euler, "What Research and Experience Teach Us about Desegregating Large Northern Cities" (*Clearinghouse for Civil Rights Research* 7 No. 1 (1979):2-14), really amounts to an annotated bibliography of many of the most recent sources on how to desegregate effectively. It mentions and cites some eighty-five different studies on the subject, thus offering a quick way into the literature.

The relationship between school segregation and residential segregation is explored in a social-science statement signed by thirty-eight social scientists and appended to the defendant's brief in *Columbus Board of Education* v. *Penick*. It is most easily locatable as reprinted under the title "School Desegregation and Residential Segregation," *Transaction/Society* 16 (July 1979):70-76.

Three bibliographic works summarize much of the literature on school desegregation prior to 1980, particularly as it affects individual students. They are Nancy St. John, *School Desegregation* (New York: Wiley, 1975); Meyer Weinberg, *Minority Students: A Research Appraisal* (Washington, D.C.: National Institute of Education, 1977); and Robert Crain and R. Mahard, *Desegration and Black Achievement* (Durham: Duke University Institute of Policy Sciences and Public Affairs, 1978).

Four continuing sources should be surveyed by the social scientist who wants to be current in this area, which is marked by continuing publications and ongoing controversies among scientists. They are: ERIC (Educational Resources Information Center), a computerized microfiche information storage and retrieval system located at most major university libraries; the U.S. Commission on Civil Rights, Washington, DC 20425; the Desegregation Studies Group at the National Institute of Education, 1200 19th Street NW, Washington, DC 20208; and the National Review Panel on School Desegregation Research at the Duke University Institute of Policy Sciences and Public Affairs, Durham, NC.

Sources of Legal Expertise in the Area of School Desegregation

Attorneys for local plaintiffs in school cases will want to be in touch with some of the national legal groups with emphasis in this area: the Office for Civil Rights, Department of Education, Washington, DC 20201; the Center for National Policy Review, Catholic University Law School, Washington, DC 20064; the Lawyers' Committee for Civil Rights under Law, 733 15th St. NW, Suite 520, Washington, DC 20005; or the NAACP Legal Defense and Educational Fund, Inc., 10 Columbus Circle, New York, NY 10019.

Further Reading on Indexes of Segregation

H.R. Alker, Jr., supplies a general introduction to Lorenz curves in his *Mathematics and Politics* (New York: Macmillan, 1965), chapter 3.

H. Becker, "The Measurement of Segregation," ERIC Document No. ED171-825 (1978), critiques the Taeuber index of dissimilarity.

Annette Sorensen et al., "Indexes of Racial Residential Segregation for 109 Cities in the United States," *Sociological Focus* 8 (1975):125-142, provides Taeuber indexes of residential segregation based on the 1970 census.

Karl Taeuber and Alma Taeuber, *Negroes in Cities* (Chicago: Aldine, 1965), proposes the index of dissimilarity, explains at length the problems with some other indexes, and analyzes residential segregation using 1960 census data.

Karl Taeuber and F. Wilson, *Project Report No. 1: Analysis of Trends in School Segregation* (Madison: University of Wisconsin Institute for Research on Poverty, 1980), provides recent indexes of school segregation for many locales.

12

The Runs Test to See whether Minorities Are Being Clustered

Even if an institution is wise or progressive enough to avoid outright segregation so that it does not keep blacks in certain schools or restrict women to certain parts of the work force, nonetheless it may practice segregation on a smaller scale—we call this clustering. A college that is leery of "inflicting" minority students upon its majority undergraduates may know better than to keep minorities out of its dormitories altogether or segregate them into one dorm but may nonetheless group or cluster them within certain rooms or sections inside its dorms. To the degree that majority and minority students are aware of this practice, it is stigmatizing toward the minority student, and to the degree that minority students are restricted in their choice of rooms, it is discriminatory toward them.

Similarly, a housing project may confine minority families largely to certain buildings or areas, preserving the facade of an integrated policy while maintaining de facto segregation. An employer may hire female managers, but only in its marketing division, so that all decisions as to personnel, production, and policies are still made by men.

Of course, clustering can occur by chance. There is no reason to assume that every dormitory floor would contain the same number of minority students or that minorities would in every case be assigned majority roommates. Voluntary choice is also a factor in roommate choice, particularly in postfreshman years. Although often there is not a great range of selections available when one rises to the top of the public housing list, chance and choice play roles there too.

A statistical test exists to tell whether a given sequence of residences shows unusual clustering or could have occurred by chance. (To rule out voluntary choice would require some on-site investigation.) It is the one-sample runs test.

The Runs Test

Suppose a coin was tossed ten times and the following sequence of heads and tails occurred: H H H H H T T T T T. This is akin to a housing project with minorities in one wing, whites in the other. A run is a series of identical occurrences; here only two runs occurred. This would seem to be too few for a fair coin or a fair tossing procedure. Even though both groups are included, something segregative is going on. Nonchance clustering seems to be involved. Like other statistical inference tests, results from the runs-test table[1] parallel common sense: the chance of getting only two or fewer runs when intermixing five items of each type is less than 5 in 100 (5 percent significance level).

Siegel provides clear instructions as to how this simple test is performed.[2] Attorneys can learn how to do it in just a few minutes. He also includes the necessary runs-test table.

Applying the Runs Test to Clustering

I used the runs test to determine if Chinese-American students were clustering at Mississippi State University and the University of Mississippi. (They were, but choice was at least partly involved.) The runs test can be used wherever small-scale segregation is suspected, such as when it is claimed that:

A teacher assigns most minority students to seats in the back of the room;

A history text treats women, but only in special women's boxes not integrated with the sweep of U.S. history;

A newspaper prints stories and photos of black weddings, but only once a week, clustered together on a page by themselves.

All of these examples are based on fact, incidentally. I recall being sent a page of a New Orleans newspaper when I complained that the paper apparently covered only white weddings. Not so, claimed the editor, and sure enough, running consecutively at the bottom of the page he enclosed were several small stories on black weddings. Perhaps he honestly failed to perceive the stigma connoted by such treatment, but I suspect some black newlyweds preferred no coverage of their nuptials rather than to subject their happy days to such humiliation.

Three of my students once infiltrated a high-school classroom in Madison County, Mississippi, whose (white) teacher assigned all her black students to the rear of the room. She took attendance by calling out each white name and then asking, "Are all the niggers here?" Hence it took three days for my three black interlopers to be noticed and apprehended! The usual existence of black high-school students in a class such as this is pretty dreary. What black child could ever be anything other than alienated from such a teacher? Minority students in such a setting would probably hate school, study little, and fail achievement tests. Yet the school looks statistically desegregated, classroom by classroom. Black failures might even be blamed on desegregation by some parent or educator!

These examples point to the importance of doing microlevel analyses of clustering within allegedly desegregated units, whether these are classrooms, newspaper pages, chapters, or divisions of a company. Each example also indicates a potential application for this easy-to-use technique.

Notes

1. S. Siegel, *Nonparametric Statistics,* (New York: Mc-Graw-Hill, 1956), p. 252.

2. Ibid., pp. 52–58.

13 Evaluating Standardized Tests in Equal-Opportunity Cases

A footnote in Justice Powell's swing opinion in *Bakke* [98 Sup. Ct. 2733 (1978)] indicated a judicial need for more information about test bias in medical-school admission. So did Justice Douglas's earlier minority opinion in *DeFunis* [94 Sup. Ct. 1704 (1974)] regarding law-school admission. It seems only a question of time before a number of legal challenges are mounted concerning the role of so-called standardized testing for admission to higher education.

The use of tests for hiring or promotion in working-class jobs has already come under a great deal of scrutiny, particularly since *Griggs* v. *Duke Power Company* [401 U.S. 424 (1971)]. The results of litigation as well as the "Uniform Guidelines on Employee Selection Procedures" [43 Fed. Reg. 38, 290 (1978)] agree on the four-fifths rule for adverse impact. This rule holds that whenever a test (or other selection procedure) results in a pass rate or selection rate for a minority that is less than 80 percent of the rate for the majority, adverse impact probably obtains, and the employer must demonstrate that the test is job related in order to continue using it.[1] If 100 Hispanics and 1,000 Anglos have taken the test in recent years, and if 50 of the Hispanics have passed and been hired compared to 800 of the Anglos, the pass rates are different: 50 percent versus 80 percent. 50 percent is less than 4/5 of 80 percent (which would be 64 percent), so the test is having an adverse impact and must be justified.

The reason why similar legal and other challenges can be predicted in higher education is factual—the "standardized" tests used by colleges and universities do discriminate against minorities. This chapter first surveys some of the discriminatory problems with "standardized" tests. Then it discusses whether the tests are job related, for if they are, following the line of reasoning of *Griggs* and *Webber* [563 F2d 216 (1979)] their use can be defended even if they do hurt minorities. Finally, some of the common defenses likely to be encountered in litigation or research on this subject are examined, and I suggest ways to overcome these obstacles. This approach parallels the examination of testing in employment so the attorney or expert in that area may also find useful suggestions in this chapter.

"Standardized" Tests Discriminate

Simply in terms of results, which is how impact is measured, "standardized" tests have an adverse impact on blacks, Hispanics, Native Americans, and nonaffluent persons, and sometimes on women, older persons, and rural Americans. Afro-Americans average about 125 points below whites on the Scholastic Aptitude Test (SAT), for instance, where 100 points equals one standard deviation. Thus the average black student (mean score) is outscored by almost 90 percent of all whites taking the test. To the extent that test cutoffs are employed, or even to the degree that test scores are weighted in as part of the admissions process by schools that do not use absolute cutoffs, blacks are certain to be disadvantaged.

Several reasons exist as to why more legal challenges have not yet been mounted against bias in higher-education admissions due to the use of "standardized" tests. For one, admissions procedures are neither precise nor explicit. Few programs admit that they use a test-score cutoff. Admissions officers point to a host of other factors that influence the admissions process: grades in previous schooling (grade-point average), recommendations, essays and other responses on the application forms, extracurricular activities, the intangibles conveyed in interviews, and other particular characteristics of each applicant. Test makers suggest that tests should be used only in conjunction with other factors and that no cutoffs be utilized. Hence it is hard to pinpoint the role that bad test scores played in the rejection of one applicant or even a class of applicants.

The difficulty is increased by the fact that admissions procedures are usually kept private. Colleges also infrequently give individual applicants any reason as to why they were accepted or rejected. The disappointed applicant is in the same position as the black would-be voter in parts of the Deep South before 1965 who was told he or she failed to meet the requirements but not how.

Further complicating the picture has been the wall of secrecy thrown up by the test makers, particularly the Educational Testing Service (ETS). For many years, ETS even refused to give out mean scores by race, and it still fails to release much data that might bear on the question of test bias. Adverse impact exists by the mere fact of the test-score gap. To justify using the tests, universities and test makers need to be able to show two things: (1) that the gap in test scores is caused by a similar gap in the abilities of minorities or women, rather than by bias in the construction or use of the tests, and (2) that this ability gap is job related in that it predicts future performance. Test bias does exist, however. The rest of this section demonstrates its existence.

The bias inheres, first of all, in the test format. The format is excessively white, middle class, and biased in favor of persons with verbal quickness and a high reading rate. Now, it might be argued that verbal quickness and a high reading rate are qualities valued by colleges, qualities that therefore are perfectly reasonable to test for and to use for admissions. However, the kind of verbal facility called for by "standardized" tests is peculiar and narrow. Nowhere in the occupational world are we called on to read a paragraph quickly and then to select the best of five alternatives to some question about it. Even within colleges, most of one's education does not consist of that kind of exercise but of studying at home, listening and interacting in class, and writing papers and

Within college populations, precisely those students who lack quick verbal facility often request multiple-choice tests, thinking that they can mark X's as well as anyone else, while believing they will be disadvantaged on an in-class essay exam by their inferior writing skills. It is true that between two students who both know A- worth of sociology, the inferior writer is likely to receive a B on an in-class essay, owing to his anti-eloquence, while the glib A- student may balloon his answer into an A+. However, my experience, testing white and black college students simultaneously, shows that verbal skills will make a much greater difference to their relative performances on a multiple-choice test. Black students who did equally well on difficult essay questions fell behind while students on multiple-choice items. My conclusion is that the "standardized"-test format unfairly advantages students with quick reading skills.[2]

The content of most "standardized" tests is similarly biased. Tests of "reasoning" or of "verbal aptitude" build their analogies from words like *Herodotus, Thucydides, baroness, argentum, minotaur, cuneiform, Runnymede, Michelangelo*—not words like *spline, mitre, kerf, hawk,* or *fox* (the last two from black argot). Hence their items test exposure, not reasoning or verbal aptitude, and residential and school segregation in the United States limits the exposure of minorities to this kind of information. Black students are not going to do as well on such items as whites; urban students will outperform rural Americans; rich kids will outscore poor kids.[3]

A third source of bias is the setting. The tests are created by white institutions, typically administered at white institutions, and are for admission to still other white institutions. The minority student is playing on the other fellow's turf and knows it. Test anxiety has been shown to depress scores and to be greater for minority children.[4] One way to overcome test anxiety is with repeated practice, perhaps through test-preparation courses, and these courses have been shown to increase test scores. However, affluent majority children have much greater access to such courses and to schooling that incorporates them. Finally, minority children build up a history of failure on standardized tests. Since these tests are labeled intelligence tests and aptitude tests, the students may conclude they do not have intelligence or aptitude, or at least the kinds of aptitudes valued in education. Hence, when confronted by the next in a long series of examinations, they are likely to be affected by their own low self-expectations, causing them to avoid taking the test seriously. To the degree that they do not take it seriously—leaving early, answering without concentration, and so forth—they do not have to take their own (anticipated) failure seriously. To that same degree, however, they miss questions they really could answer correctly and depress their score further below their real performance level.

Although test bias is pervasive, it does not account for all of the test-score gap between blacks and whites, say, or poor and rich. Spokespersons for ETS are forever warning that we must not "slay the messenger" for bringing bad tidings. Social structure is unequal, they point out—that is, minorities get worse schooling and live in homes with less income so inferior test scores merely indicate this deeper inequality.

Proponents of this line of reasoning have a point. Societal inequities do matter. But the messenger is much more than a mere bearer of bad news to minorities. The messenger—the test— is part of the news, part of the inequity, due to the biases I have described. This is why I have placed quotation marks around "standardized" whenever it has been used. Tests are not standardized. Some people claim they cannot be. I think they can—but they are not at present, not in form, content, or setting.

The Tests Are Not Job Related

Even though the examinations are biased, perhaps their use could be defended if it could be shown that they nonetheless are job related—that is, if test scores do accurately predict college or graduate-school performance, then perhaps they should be used. Of course, if bias is involved, then it might follow that some bias exists within college grading as well, and that bias would be as unacceptable as any other. But we shall ignore that mare's nest of issues and address the relationship between test scores and college performance.

This relationship is not strong. We have seen, for instance, that blacks do 1.25 standard deviations worse than whites on the SAT. I know of no study in higher education that suggests a deficiency of 1.25 standard deviations in black performance in college, once admitted, compared to whites. Several studies show, on the contrary, that blacks do almost as well as whites, even if their test scores are far below white means.[5]

On another age level, Jane Mercer studied the effect of IQ tests on Mexican-American children. She found that, on the one hand, although a huge proportion of them tested retarded, many were rated normal by a social-skills test of their behavior. Not one retarded white child, on the other hand, rated normal on the behavioral test. So the Mexican-American children were doing far worse on the IQ test than they should have.[6]

Whenever the huge test gaps that separate minority children from white middle-class children are not accompanied by equally huge performance gaps, the minority test scores are almost surely artificially depressed by some bias in the test content, format, and/or situation.

Moreover, whether comparing minority to majority children or within either group, test scores do not relate strongly to later performance. For example, the correlation between scores on the Miller Analogies Test (MAT), used by many graduate schools and some professional programs for admission, and students' performance in those schools and programs averages a dismal .2. The next chapter describes correlation at some length. Here let me just note that r, the correlation coefficient, can vary in magnitude from 0 to 1, with 0 being no relationship between the two variables, 1 being a perfect relationship. Thus, correlation of .2 shows a very weak relationship. If we square r, the result, r^2, .04 in this case, tells the percentage of the variation in graduate performance explained by the MAT score: it is just 4 percent.

Scores on ETS exams—the SAT, Graduate Record Examination (GRE), and Law School Aptitude Test (LSAT)—show slightly higher correlations, averaging $r = .3$ to .4 in most studies. Again, those correlations are rather dismal, and the test explains only about 9 to 16 percent of the variation in college or graduate performance. The Medical College Admissions Test (MCAT) and American College Test (ACT), which are not ETS exams, are just a little better, showing rs closer to .4.

Test makers will assert that psychology is a field beset by unpredictable individual variation, the kind of thing I have called noise in the system (chapter 2), so that $r = .4$ is not so bad. They may also claim that, since decisions about admission have to be made, any source of information that decreases the uncertainty faced by admissions officers should be utilized, including tests.

However, data exist to suggest that even the modest relationships between observed test scores and performance are largely artificial. First, the correlations of .3 and .4, mediocre as they are, are between test scores and first-year grades in the program. Those correlations then decrease as later years are examined. For example, at the University of Vermont there is a 100-point gap between in-state scores and out-of-state scores on the SAT. Vermont is much more selective in admitting out-of-state students and uses test scores as an important criterion for them; moreover, its out-of-state applicants come mostly from the affluent suburbs of Boston, New York, and other East Coast metropolises where test taking is taught and scores are high. In line with findings regarding minorities, there is a small first-year gap between the grade-point averages of rural Vermonters compared to suburban out of staters, although the gap is nowhere near the standard-deviation gap in test scores. By their senior year, in staters have closed the gap or even edged on top.

Similarly, correlations between the MCAT and medical-school grades are modest for the first year, then deteriorate so that the test does not predict performance in the important clinical year(s). Moreover, since the purpose of medical education is to train good doctors, true validation of the MCAT would be to some measure of performance in the field, and no such measure has been developed, let alone correlated with MCAT scores.

Two reasons stand out to explain the modest correlations between scores and first-year performance. First, although the tests are a very imperfect indicator of aptitude or ability, they do indicate familiarity and ease with upper-middle-class culture. Colleges and professional schools are the ultimate expression of upper-middle-class culture—even black colleges or community junior colleges. In *The Feminized Male,* Patricia Cayo Sexton has argued that one reason boys do worse than girls in elementary school is because of the feminine nature of school culture.[7] This is a subtle argument, probably transferable to college on a class and racial basis. In other words, culture shock can particularly afflict nonwhite or nonaffluent students, depressing their first-year performance. The same students probably received lower test scores. Second, first-year studies are most like "standardized" tests, particularly in their testing procedures. Freshman classes often are large, and most grading is on the basis of multiple-choice exams. Later, smaller classes rely more on research projects, papers, and essay tests. We would thus expect correlations to be highest in the first year.

The most pervasive problem with "standardized" tests is with their labels. They are said to be aptitude or intelligence tests. Thus their justification is said to be that they tell which students have more law-school aptitude (in the case of the LSAT), more intelligence (in the case of the Stanford-Binet), or more high-level reasoning ability (in the case of the MAT). These labels are not justified. The tests do not predict who will do well as lawyers or even who will do well in law school. Logically, I should now examine two related topics: the stigmatizing effect of these labels, once students receive bad scores, whether or not they are then admitted to college (perhaps through some special admissions door), and the alternatives to testing that would be fairer. However, these topics are of tangential relevance to litigation in this area. Let me instead summarize this section by noting that so-called aptitude, ability, and intelligence tests are all types of achievement tests. They test what one has learned, just as a Spanish test or welding test does. Aptitude tests are merely much vaguer as to subject matter than Spanish tests; intelligence tests are vaguer still. What one has learned may possibly predict what one is capable of learning, to be sure, but only among people who have had the same chances to learn in the first place. Without equality of prior opportunity, then, aptitude tests measure exposure to upper-middle-class urbane material more than any kind of ability, verbal or otherwise. To use them as a bar to further learning means completing a vicious circle, using past discrimination to legitimate discrimination in the next step of the educational process.

Dealing with the Other Side's Defenses

Let me first caution the would-be plaintiff and his attorney and expert that litigation in this area will be difficult. The legal terrain is rocky, and if a major standardized test is attacked, the plaintiff can expect that immense resources will be thrown into the fray on the other side. So no frivolous suit should be contemplated.

The first problem will be to obtain good data. To attack the use of "standardized" tests at a given institution, it will not do to cite the low correlation between the test and performance in higher education generally. Data from that school will be needed. Hence it would help to have a friendly opponent—that is, to launch the suit with the cooperation of the university. There are some reasons why this is not farfetched. For example, if an institution wanted to start or maintain an affirmative-action program, it would be helped by a finding of prior discrimination. This is a ticklish subject because no school wants to be found guilty of discriminating in favor of whites, say, in 1970, lest it face possible lawsuits from minorities barred in the past; but it can be dealt with. Also, some institutions are using the tests against their will. For example, every law school in the United States is virtually forced to use the LSAT, even though some of them offer alternatives to traditional legal education and might want to use alternatives to traditional admissions techniques. Even if the institution as a whole is not friendly to the suit, individuals or departments within it might be, and they might share data or make it easier to obtain that data through discovery.

The second problem is to show adverse impact. At many schools, the tests' adverse impact against blacks is compensated for by a special admissions door that allows blacks to attend even with inferior scores. The plaintiff and attorney will have to decide if that procedure lets discriminatory testing off the hook. Stigma still attaches to the special admits, both in the eyes of the faculty and in their own eyes. In the worst case, a university may admit minority students but, because of their test scores, think badly of them. Professors may expect less from them, and expectations are all important in the educational process; they may then flunk out or be given undeserved grades. In neither case do they receive equal educational opportunity, and tests are partly to blame.

It would be easier to attack tests on behalf of plaintiffs who were not admitted. Subtle analysis indicates, for instance, that women are discriminated against on the LSAT, even though their scores are equal to the norms of men, because a select group of women apply to law school, better qualified than men, so the test-score equality really shows discrimination. Tests also discriminate against groups for whom no special admissions programs have been devised, such as older returnees to higher education, poor whites, and rural Americans.

At some point, test makers will introduce the issue of validity. A method is valid in social science when it measures what it purports to measure. Thus an aptitude test is valid if it really measures aptitude. Aptitude is usually defined as capability to perform, in this case in higher education. Tests are often claimed to be valid in three ways: face validity, construct validity, and criterion validity. Face validity, also called content validity, is sometimes put down by psychologists as unscientific, but I believe it is basic to all other forms of validity and perhaps to the accumulation of knowledge in general.[9] Face validity refers to a measure that, on the face of it, by its very nature, seems to measure what it claims to measure. An example, not from aptitude testing, would be a prejudice test that asked respondents to agree/disagree with a series of statements, each of which indicated prejudice or tolerance toward blacks, Jews, and so on. A person with replies in the prejudiced direction on these items could be presumed to be more prejudiced than another respondent.

Criterion validity means a strong relationship between a measure and an output variable. An aptitude test that correlated strongly with performance in later schooling would have criterion validity. Some tests will have both forms of validity at once, such as a typing test for a prospective secretary. Typing is part of her job, so the test possesses obvious face validity; it also relates to how well she will do in her job. Hence, typing-test scores would undoubtedly correlate at least moderately with some measure of secretarial performance.

Construct validity is harder to define. I will let the American Psychological Association (APA) do it:

> The process begins with an identification of job behaviors which lead to successful performance. The next step is to identify, based on psychological theory, the essential skills for those job behaviors. The next step in the process is to identify related positions that have similar required skills and abilities and for which there exist selection procedures with known construct validity that have been empirically validated and for which validity studies are available for quotation. It is then noted that these tests measure these constructs and are valid in these previously defined positions. The final step in the construct validation process is to demonstrate, through similarity of the positions, that the constructs defined from the previous contexts ought to be considered on an a priori basis to be valid in the new context. This assumption of validity is justified only when practicalities preclude the possibility of empirical validation in the new context.[10]

Taken seriously, this is a Herculean task.

It is difficult for test makers to assert face validity for their products for two reasons. First, even in diploma mills, not much of a student's education consists of reacting quickly to paragraphs through multiple-choice tests. Second, obvious content bias and content irrelevancy pervade the tests. What difference can it make to my graduate education in sociology if I do or do not know *Runnymede, minotaur,* and *Herodotus*? Clearly none. That claim is not even directly made, but it sometimes is, indirectly, such as when tests are described as ability or aptitude tests, which might imply to the unwary that something is being tested that itself relates to graduate-school work.

The claim that tests test aptitude actually amounts to a claim of construct validity—that is, the use of *aptitude* implies that although it is not relevant to my progress through sociology graduate school to know Herodotus, the kinds of abilities, lumped together as verbal aptitude, that the Herodotus analogies test are relevant to my graduate progress. However, no test maker has even attempted the job of proving, rather than merely claiming, construct validity along the lines suggested by the APA.

Whether or not tests possess criterion validity is shown by their correlation with some criterion, some output variable such as graduate-school grades or completion of medical school. We have already indicated that such correlations are extremely weak. Moreover, they are not usually even sought with true output variables such as performance as a lawyer or publications as a scholar. Thus this defense will probably fail, too.

Test makers may make it hard to study their tests by claiming confidentiality. There is some kind of property-right claim here so that ETS, for instance, has claimed that their expenses would go up and the tests might even be vitiated if they were forced to share scores and questions with students or plaintiffs. For most tests, this is nonsense. ETS is constantly changing questions, putting some into inactive files, developing new questions, and even altering test formats. If it did not, then a test-preparation center could simply hire someone with spy techniques or a retentive mind to take the test and supply a copy; students would then know specifically what to study in order to get a perfect score on the test's next administration. The number of items in a test bank for a national exam is in the thousands, perhaps even tens of thousands. It does not compromise the test to release old copies of the 50 or 100 items used in any one administration of it.

Because of the resources the defendants may marshall, the plaintiff's attorney should plan to use more than one expert. One should be expertly conversant with psychological tests and measurement theory, either as a psychologist or researcher in education. Another might be a sociologist, linguist, social psychologist, or perhaps anthropologist who could speak to the ways a given test disadvantages the group under question—blacks, Native Americans, women, rural Americans, poor whites, or whomever. Because the literature in the field is vast, the social scientists need to be already familiar with it. They also need to be conversant with its deficiencies. For example, almost no published studies discuss test bias with actual data showing the answering patterns of majority versus disadvantaged students. Almost no studies relate test items to later performance but only test scores as a whole, and the range of test items has been circumscribed by the procedures by which new items are added. New items must correlate with old ones and with the test as a whole. The result is that the establishment bias of the test, built in long ago, maintains itself automatically.[11]

Notes

1. Ronald B. Rubin discusses this rule in "Testing and Employment: The New Uniform Guidelines on Employee Selection Procedures," *Clearinghouse for Civil Rights Research* 6 (1978):35-37.

2. James W. Loewen, "Breaking the Vicious Circle," *Clearinghouse for Civil Rights Research* 6 (1978):24-29.

3. James Fallows, "The Tests and the 'Brightest'," *Atlantic Monthly* 245 (February 1980):37-48.

4. M.B. Goldfarb et al., "Recent Developments in IQ Research: What Policymakers Need to Know," *Clearinghouse for Civil Rights Research* 6, no. 1-2(1978):7-8.

5. William M. Boyd, II, "SATs and Minorities: The Dangers of Underprediction," *Change*, November 1977, pp. 48-50; Rodney Hartnett and Benjamin

F. Payton, *Minority Admissions and Performance in Graduate Study* (New York: Ford Foundation, 1977); Michael Genz, "Back to *Bakke*: Testing and Medical School Admissions," *Clearinghouse for Civil Rights Research* 6 (1978): 19–23.

6. Mercer, "Institutionalized Anglocentrism," in *Race, Change, and Urban Policy,* edited by P. Orleans and W. Russell (New York: Sage, 1971).

7. P. Sexton, *The Feminized Male* (New York: Random House, 1969).

8. Note Betsy Levin's discussion of *Washington* v. *Davis* in *The Courts as Educational Policymakers and their Impact on Federal Programs* (Santa Monica: Rand, 1977), p. 31.

9. B. Lerner, "Employment Discrimination: Adverse Impact, Validity, and Equality," in *Supreme Court Review, 1979* (Chicago: University of Chicago Press, 1980), pp. 18–19. Lerner is contradicted by C. Lindblom and D. Cohen, *Usable Knowledge* (New Haven: Yale University Press, 1979).

10. American Psychological Association, Committee on Psychological Tests and Assessment, "Statement on the Uniform Guidelines on Employee Selection Procedures," 17 February 1978:6–7. Reprinted with permission.

Additional Resources

The testing literature is too large even to suggest here, but I do list several organizations active in this area. They might supply bibliographies or suggest experts in the area.

American Psychological
Association
Test Fairness Network
1200 17th Street NW
Washington, DC 20036
(202) 833-7600

Huron Institute
123 Mt. Auburn Street
Cambridge, MA 02136
(617) 491-5450

The Measuring Cup
Savannah, GA
(912) 233-6311

National Center for the Study of
the Professions
Washington, DC
(202) 232-2204

14 Correlation and Regression in Voting-Rights Litigation

The most common single measure of association, in or out of the courtroom, is r, the coefficient of correlation. Association is what most class-action lawsuits are trying to demonstrate. For example, to return to the sign test with which we began our exposition of inferential statistics (chapter 6), if our blind expert found there that 9 of 10 women were more qualified than their male counterparts, then an association between femaleness and greater qualification has been shown. The tables and associated tests we have presented thus far in this book have compared one group against another, such as men versus women, or black blocks, integrated blocks, and white blocks. However, we are often confronted by parametric or continuous variables that do not easily lend themselves to grouping. To see if two such variables are associated with each other, the correlation coefficient is usually the method of choice.

For example, in voting-rights cases it is important to prove that whites are usually bloc voting—voting en masse for white candidates only. If precincts were all white or all black, the way a college professor is male or female, then we could look at the voting behavior of the all-white precincts and stop, for we would thereby have shown the voting behavior of the white population.[1] Precints vary, however. Some are all white, some black, but most are mixed. In one small county, for instance, they have the racial composition shown in table 14–1.

Table 14–1
Race and Voting Behavior, Shell County, Arkansas

Precinct	Percentage of Registered Voters Who are White	Percentage of Votes for the White Candidate
Able	39.0%	45.9%
Baker	44.1	51.3
Charlie	100.0	99.1
Dorado	98.4	97.4
Emerald	1.0	2.6
Flag	44.2	53.6
Given	96.2	95.9
Hay	75.4	75.1
Impulse	47.2	49.1
James	1.0	4.0

Inspection of the table indicates an association. On the one hand, precincts low in white voters show little support for the white candidate; Charlie Precinct, on the other hand, voted overwhelmingly for the white office seeker. Other precincts such as Able and Flag are in the middle in both variables, proportion of whites and voting pattern. We need a statistical measure to summarize these data so we can make a compact definite statement about the relationship and compare it to other relationships in other counties or in social science generally. Grouping the precincts into white, mixed, and black would be artificial and would throw out some information such as the difference between precincts that are 100 percent white and 92.7 percent white. The measure we need is the correlation coefficient.

The Coefficient of Correlation and the Scattergram

As a rule, when confronting two sets of parametric data that may be associated, the first analysis that the social scientist should do is a correlation to see if the two variables are associated. It summarizes the strength of the relationship between variables with a single number, r, and indicates the direction of the relationship with a plus or a minus sign (a negative, indicates an inverse relationship, such as the whiter the precinct, the more votes for the black candidates). If only a dozen precincts are being analyzed, it is possible to use a hand calculator; otherwise a computer is necessary.[2]

Figure 14-1, a scattergram, is an illustration of this analysis. Each point represents a precinct with the percentage of voters who are white and the percentage of votes for the white candidate serving as the coordinates of the point. This particular scattergram shows a strong positive correlation between the percentage of white voters and percentage of votes for the white candidate. The line is the best-fit line, or least-squares line, and is a way to summarize the detail and approximate the pattern of the points. The closer the points fall to the line, the stronger the correlation.

The coefficient of correlation, r, tells how close the points are to the line; it can vary in size from 0 to 1. When $r=0$, there is no relationship between the two variables: points on the scattergram form a vague cloud. When $r=1$, the relationship is perfect: all the points fall on a perfect straight line. In sociology and political science a strong r is in the neighborhood of .5 to .7. Because psychology deals with individuals, not groups of individuals such as precincts, psychologists are often happy to obtain rs of .4. Obviously r has an intuitive meaning.

It has in addition a statistical meaning. Typically, one variable can be conceptualized as the prior, or independent, variable that may cause or lead to some change in the dependent variable. Race of voter may influence who that voter votes for, while the reverse is not true—no one has ever changed race as

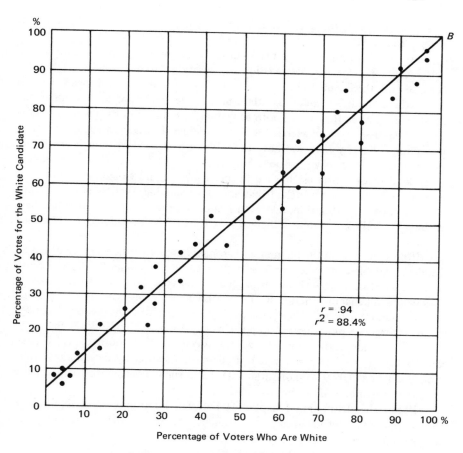

Figure 14-1. Ecological-Regression Line

they emerged from the polling place. Accordingly, race of voter, by precinct, is our independent variable; outcome of the election is the dependent variable. We are trying to learn if the first causes the second. The correlation coefficient can help tell us.

There is a variation in outcome. In one precinct the white candidate garnered 99 percent of the votes; in another he received only 2.6 percent. This variation can be described statistically by the range, as in the previous sentence, or the variance (or its square root, the standard deviation).[3] We want to know how much of this variance is due to the independent variable, race. The answer is provided mathematically by r^2, the square of the correlation coefficient.[4] For figure 14-1, $r^2 = .884$, meaning that 88.4 percent of all the variance in votes received by the white candidate can be "explained" by race of voter. For the data in table 14-1, the correlation is still greater: $r = .995$, and r^2 is an astonishing 99 percent.

Explained is in quotations marks in the previous paragraph because the expert must not move from association to causation without some thought. Just because two things are found to be highly correlated does not mean the first causes the second. We could have the whole matter backward so that the second causes the first, or they could both be caused by a third prior variable. The next chapter discusses how to search for third variables. For now, it suffices to make two points. First, we do not have the relation backward. Although we cannot prove statistically that voting does not cause race, such an assertion contradicts every kind of causation established in social science and violates common sense as well. Second, it is farfetched that any third variable, such as poverty, could account for the relationship, and even if it could, that variable itself would have to be so closely correlated with race that it could be considered a racial characteristic.

If $r=.5$, we are still explaining a reasonable chunk of the variance in the dependent variable, but when $r=.3$, $r^2=.09$, meaning that only 9 percent of that variance is associated with our independent variable. Sometimes there may be lots of unexplainable variation in the dependent variable—noise in the system— or our measurement of either variable may be imperfect, causing more slippage. In voting-rights cases, this can happen when, instead of registration figures by race for the independent variable, we are forced to rely on outdated census data on the voting-age population. Such problems can artificially deflate the correlation coefficient (they cannot inflate it), so in such cases an expert may nonetheless consider an r of .3 to be important.

Recall the distinction (chapter 4) between importance and significance. The correlation coefficient and r^2 are direct measures of the importance of an association or relationship. This is why they are so useful. It is easy to go another step and assess whether the relationship thus unearthed is likely to have occurred owing to chance. This entails computing the significance of the correlation coefficient. Loether and McTavish explain how this is done, but almost all computer routines that compute r also compute its significance. Frankly, the significance level of a correlation coefficient can usually be ignored because most rs that have importance also possess stastistical significance as a matter of course. For example, based on a sample of 30 cases, even an r of .3 approaches significance (at the .05 level). All higher rs based on that many cases, and many lower rs based on larger samples, will likewise be significant.[5]

The Uses of Correlation

Many are the cases to which correlation analysis might be applied. When two variables are both parametric, r is usually the appropriate first step in the analysis to see if they are related. Here are some examples:

Employees in a bureaucracy share the same basic rank, with substantial salary variations. These pay differences are supposed to be based in large part on job-performance ratings as reported on an elaborate multi-item form that results in a performance index. Correlation analysis between index scores and salaries will tell if the relationship is a strong one, or if other factors (age, race, sex, nepotism, and so on) may have greater influence.

In Chicago public schools, an important r persisted for many years between proportion of whites in student bodies and number of books per student in the school library.

Banks claim they do not redline but loan without regard to race. Among their criteria are income of borrower, age of house, and size of loan. Correlation and its allied analysis, regression, can determine the relative importance of each of these factors and can help assess if racial discrimination is additionally involved.

The miszoning maps suggested in chapter 9 can be summarized by r to describe the relationship between percentage black and percentage of land miszoned, by census tracts.

An employer may try to rebut a charge of sex discrimination in promotion by claiming that seniority ties his hands and has resulted in the observed pay differentials by sex. Besides being a problematic defense that relies on past discrimination to explain ongoing differences, this claim is open to analysis by correlation coefficient. To the degree that the relationship between seniority and pay is not strong or robust, factors other than seniority are entering in.

Created data can be tied to existing data through correlation analysis. For example, a diverse small sample of employees might be shown a list of the many positions or job titles in a company and asked to rank their status from 0 to 10. The composite rankings can then be correlated with percent female among the employees holding that job, to see if women hold lower-status jobs in the organization.

Another strength of correlation analysis is its ability to handle more than two variables at once. It is an easy matter to plug both seniority and performance rating into the analysis at once, for instance, and then to see how much of the variance in pay has been explained. The next chapter, "Controlling for Third Variables," tells how this is done.

Correlation can also be used when one of the two (or more) variables under analysis is not parametric. To do this, artificial quantitative values are assigned to the nonparametric variable. For example, sex can be treated numerically with 0 = female, 1 = male, and those values correlated with pay, or with seniority and pay. This is a violation of the principle "thou shalt not apply parametric techniques to nonparametric data," but the distortion is not severe: usually r is lower than it would be with parametric data. The advantage of doing this is that r is a useful measure of the strength of an association, one that you may already be presenting to the court regarding parametric variables. Hence it is also an effective way to show the impact of a nonparametric independent variable like sex.

Correlation can be overused, however. Recall that we used the t test for the difference of two means to compare the widths of black and white residential streets (chapter 9). Street width is parametric—it has a meaningful zero point and is measured in numerical units (feet or meters). Indeed, that is why we could compute means. Proportion of blacks is also parametric: 0 percent is meaningful, and a 4 percent black block is twice as black as a 2 percent black block. Instead of treating race as a discrete variable, then, using the t test, we could have considered it to be parametric, varying from 0 to 100. Then we could have computed r to see whether percentage white on the block was related to width of the street.

Doing so would have meant much more work, however. Our old method required dividing the blocks into three types by race of residents: white, integrated, and black. A block's location, its apparent inhabitants based on quick visual inspection, or old census data sufficed for this rough trichotomy. Now we would have to obtain a percentage figure. Moreover, since most blocks are overwhelmingly black or white, using exact percentage figures would not add a great deal of precision to the analysis. Finally, although a correlation coefficient can be made perfectly intelligible to the court, the difference between two means, as used in chapter 9, already is obvious and clear.

The Ecological Fallacy

The biggest weakness with correlation is that even if r is high, so that r^2 indicates we have explained a considerable part of the variance, we cannot be quite certain sometimes that we have proved a relationship between the independent and dependent variables owing to the ecological fallacy. This fallacy does not refer to the problem of prior causes or other third variables—that problem is discussed in the next chapter. I shall return to our voting-rights example to show the ecological fallacy.

A high r does not tell which group—white, black, or both—is doing the bloc voting. The only assertion that can be made without chance of error, based on correlation analysis, is that a whiter precinct will produce a greater proportion of votes for the white candidate. This is an assertion about groups, precincts. To go beyond this, to state that whites are voting white, is to commit the ecological fallacy of imputing to individuals a relationship found to exist among groups.

It is possible, for instance, that in whiter precincts the black voters vote for white candidates, perhaps fearing or seeking the approval of their white neighbors. Meanwhile, perhaps white voters are splitting their votes, as they supposedly do in blacker precincts, hence are not guilty of racial bloc voting at all. Possible but farfetched. In fact, if we inspect Dorado Precinct in table 14-1, we see that it is not even possible—black voters could never have accounted for the overwhelming margin rolled up by the white candidate; and there are no black voters at all in Charlie Precinct. So the entire line of reasoning in this paragraph is weak, and the ecological fallacy is almost a nit-pick.

There is a stronger possibility of an ecological fallacy, however. If all the whites in Shell County split down the middle in this election, half voting black, while all the blacks bloc voted for the black candidate, the resulting scattergram would be a straight line, and the correlation would be well nigh a perfect 1.0. Again, a high r does not in itself tell which group bloc voted. The group-level statement ("A whiter precinct will produce more votes for the white candidate") is still accurate, but the individual-level claim ("Whites are bloc voting for the white candidate") would be wrong.

Again, mere inspection of Dorado Precinct throws this hypothetical fallacy into doubt, for the white candidate did so well there that the white voters could hardly have divided 50/50. This conclusion from Dorado Precinct leads to the method by which we can evade the ecological fallacy in general: the method of bounds, or overlapping-percentages analysis.

Overlapping-Percentages Analysis

Correlation has shown us if groups high in one characteristic (for example, percent white) are high in another (for example, votes for white candidates). Overlapping-percentages analysis allows us to determine whether the individual cases within those groups that have the given characteristic (for example, whiteness) manifest the expected characteristic in their dependent variable (for example, voting white). Overlapping percentages allow us to determine, using simple arithmetic, how whites and blacks actually voted in overwhelmingly white or black precincts.

In a heavily white district we start with the assumption that all blacks who voted did so for white candidates (maximum racial crossover). We can then compute the minimum amount of white bloc voting that must have occurred (see table 14-2). For example, in Dorado Precinct, 98.4 percent of the voters were white. The white candidate received 97.4 percent of the votes, the black candidate, 2.6 percent. Assume that all of the whites who could have voted black did so—assume, in other words, that 2.6 percent of all voters were white and voted black. Subtract that from the percentage of whites. That leaves 95.8 percent of the voters who were white and voted white, which means that

Table 14-2
Overlapping-Percentages Analysis, Shell County, Arkansas

Precinct	Percentage of Whites among Voters	Percentage of Votes for White Candidates	Minimum Percentage of Whites Who Had to Vote White
Charlie	100.0%	99.1%	99.1%
Dorado	98.4	97.4	97.4
Given	96.2	95.9	95.7

97.4 percent of the whites (95.8/98.4 percent) had to have voted white. This is a minimum; the actual proportion will be still higher. Even assuming maximum possible racial crossover, the proportion of whites voting white is still very high.

The great strength of overlapping-percentages analysis is its simplicity.[6] Only arithmetic is involved. Judges and other nonstatisticians grasp it at once. Moreover, the resulting minimum is indisputable. Anyone would have calculated it. No elaborate test, subject to varying interpretations, is involved. It is a good first step for the attorney or plaintiff to take since it can be done in a few minutes by hand.

Its utility goes beyond voting issues. For instance, if you know the proportion of employees receiving merit increases or year-end bonuses in each division or part of a company, you can use overlapping percentages to see if women or men (or racial or ethnic groups) were particularly advantaged. All that is required are some overwhelmingly unisexual (or uniracial and so forth) departments or divisions. Another application would be to obtain the proportion of white and black students sent to the principal's office for discipline. In both cases, individual data are not needed—data by department or classroom suffice for overlapping-percentages analysis. Because it is so simple, it is effective in the courtroom.

The problems with overlapping-percentages analysis are three: it gives us only the minimum amount of racial bloc voting (or whatever is at issue), it is computed for only one precinct or other unit at a time, and it can be calculated only for overwhelmingly (more than 90 percent) uniracial precincts. (It requires units that are lopsided in one or another of the values of the independent variable.) Another technique, ecological regression, avoids these problems.

Ecological Regression

Ecological regression provides a better estimate of racial bloc voting or other potential associations between two variables. It is based on the entire data set and can be computed without an overwhelmingly uniracial precinct. It works with the best-fit line of figure 14–1 that shows the relationship between the race of the voter and the outcome of the election. This line is projected to the point where there are 0 percent white voters, which is where the line crosses the Y axis. Point A is the point at which there are 0 percent white voters. The percentage of votes for the white candidate at this point, 5 percent, must have come from black voters, since there are no white voters to produce them. So we conclude that black votes across the county went 95 percent to the black candidate, 5 percent to the white, and our conclusion is based on information from all the precincts since the best-fit line is based on all the dots. By locating the point at which there are 100 percent white voters, B, we can find the percentage of white votes that were cast for the white candidate. This figure, almost 100 percent, shows that whites are bloc voting white.[7]

It is possible to put confidence intervals around these percentages that we obtain from ecological regression. This means that we can draw a band on either side of the regression line and assert that we are 99 percent sure that the actual line falls within that band. Depending on the number of precincts or other cases in our sample, those limits will be 2 percent to perhaps 20 percent in width.

In conjunction with correlation and overlapping percentages, ecological regression provides a powerful statement of the effect of one variable upon another. We shall now see the application of all three techniques to a voting-rights case. The application shows how each technique complements the other and suggests an order of testimony.

Applying Correlation and Regression to a Voting-Rights Case

Because election rules and districts are typically drawn up by persons in power, and because those persons are usually white, those rules and districts are often biased against minorities. Blacks in Shell County, Arkansas (not the true county or state), cannot elect any member of the county board of supervisors. The county is 63 percent black (1980 census), but that does not translate into anything like a voting majority. The voting-age population is less black than the total population, the proportion of blacks registered to vote is usually smaller than the proportion of whites, and the proportion of black registered voters who turn out at the polls is still lower, owing to a host of socioeconomic factors. Because black residents are concentrated in the southern half of the county, if there were elections by fairly drawn districts, blacks would likely elect at least two of the five supervisors, allowing them some representation in county decision making. In 1970, redistricting was ordered, but the supervisors instead switched to at-large elections. The white electorate, which constitutes an effective voting majority, elects all five.

If whites frequently voted for black candidates, then the lack of a black countywide voting majority would not deter black political candidates. If whites bloc vote for white candidates, however, then in conjunction with data showing the voting-age population in the black and white populations, a social scientist can prove that blacks are effectively shut out from the political process in the absence of redistricting.

To discover whether two variables are associated, it is necessary to have a measure of the independent variable (the variable that may cause or influence the other variable) and dependent variable (the variable that is caused). In the analysis for racial bloc voting, the dependent variable (votes for black and white candidates by precinct) is easy to obtain from newspaper reports or formally filed election returns. The best measure of the independent variable is actual turnout at the polls, by race, by precinct. There are several ways to get it:

Observer-report data from the Justice Department, if observers were ever assigned to the county;

Sign-ins at the polls matched with racial designation on registration lists;

Sign-ins at the polls with racial designation from local experts and addresses.

Next best is the registration roll by race by precinct, as of the time of the election, recently purged. If race is not shown, it can be added by local experts and from addresses. If neither of these is available, then voting-age population data by race from the census can be used. Tedious work is needed to divide census enumeration districts to match precinct lines.

When using a poor data source for the independent variable, such as unpurged registration lists, it is almost impossible that the problems with the data would be patterned in such a way as to create a spuriously great correlation between race of voter and outcome. Therefore the expert who finds strong evidence of bloc voting, even using inferior data, should be able to tell the court that the results would doubtless be yet stronger if better data were available. This is a general principle.

The expert then enters the data into a computer (unless very few precincts—fewer than fifteen—and very few elections—fewer than five—are involved, in which case a calculator could be used). She first forms a table like table 14-1 and requests a correlation analysis. This output provides a scattergram (figure 14-1), r, r^2, and the information needed to determine the best-fit, or regression, line. It also states whether the correlation is statistically significant. The expert uses the regression line to determine the proportions of whites voting white, voting black, and not voting for this office.

The election practices that were at issue in the lawsuit—in our case, at-large elections rather than election by districts—are the subtle contemporary counterparts to the old poll tax and interpret-the-constitution requirements. More than a demonstration of white bloc voting is required to challenge these practices successfully. Census data, information on public services, and employment data could also prove useful. In conjunction with the age structure of the populations, socioeconomic deterrents to black registration and voting, and near-total white bloc voting, these election practices seriously hinder black political participation. This conclusion is the overall point of the expert testimony.

Included in the "Additional Resources" at the end of the chapter is a question-and-answer-type abbreviated run-through of part of the testimony in a voting-rights case. It should help lawyers frame questions and teach witnesses what to expect.

Whenever correlation and regression are used, the expert should present census data, other statistics when available, and a framework of social-science theory and findings so as to provide a context for the association demonstrated through correlation/regression. Then the court will understand not only that the association is significant, but also what its importance is in the day-to-day functioning of the social structure.

Additional refinements in correlation and regression analyses include multiple correlation/regression (looking at the effect of two or more variables at once on a dependent variable) and partial correlation/regression (looking at a variable's effect on another while holding a third variable constant). They are not usually needed in voting analyses, although sometimes the defendants will throw them in to create confusion. These techniques are introduced in the next chapter, along with other methods of treating third variables.

Notes

1. This is the method of overlapping percentages presented later in the chapter.

2. N. Nie et al., *Statistical Package for the Social Sciences* (New York: McGraw-Hill, 1975), pp. 292–300, supplies a computer program for correlation/regression that generates a scattergram and r.

3. The range, standard deviation, and variance are presented in chapter 4.

4. A good expert witness should be able to explain why r^2 has this property in a manner that is understandable and convincing to a judge or attorney. This is a useful test in selecting an expert witness and a useful part of the expert's preparation for the courtroom.

5. H. Loether and D. McTavish, *Inferential Statistics for Sociologists* (Boston: Allyn and Bacon, 1974), pp. 229–235.

6. A complexity might be added. Using percentages instead of actual numbers of voters and votes makes the assumption that rolloff is equal by race; it usually is not. Once rolloff has been calculated from ecological regression (see next section), the corrected figures can be inserted here. The correction will be trivial, however.

7. A more accurate result can be obtained by using a slightly different scattergram and regression line for this analysis. If it is available, the expert should use percentage white in turnout at the polls for the independent variable.

For the dependent variable in the regression analysis, use number of votes for white candidate(s) divided by number of voters at the precinct. This is proportion of voters for the white candidate and will always be lower than the proportion of votes cast for that office that went to the white candidate, which figure 14-1 used.

The latter proportion, familiar in common parlance ("Smith got 52 percent of the vote"), is the appropriate dependent variable for the correlation analysis. If it is used for ecological regression, however, slight distortions can lead to estimates of more than 100 percent in some cases for the proportion of intrarace bloc voting—clearly impossibly high.

When proportion of voters voting for the white candidate has been used for the dependent variable, the estimate of percentage of white voters voting for the white candidate will always be lower because some voters failed to vote at all for the office. The expert should then do the analysis a second time, plotting proportion of votes for the black candidate against percentage white among voters. This line slants oppositely, in the declining or negative direction, and when read at 100 percent white, provides the estimate for the proportion of white voters who voted black.

For our data these calculations were: 91.5 percent of whites at the polls voted white, and 0.5 percent voted black. Accordingly, 8.0 percent of those at the polls failed to vote for this office (rolloff). Dividing 91.5 percent by (91.5 percent plus 0.5 percent) tells us the proportion of white voters (for this office) who voted white—the key fact we wanted to learn. (It was 99+ percent.) The analyst can similarly calculate racial bloc voting, crossover voting, and rolloff among blacks at the polls.

If we began with registration data instead of turnout data, this same analysis would lead to conclusions regarding turnout (combined with rolloff) by race. If we started with voting-age population figures, we would obtain proportion of the entire population by race that voted for each candidate. And if we did all of these analyses, we would be able to calculate the racial proportions as we go down the line from total population to voting-age population to registration to turnout to rolloff to outcome.

Additional Resources

Further Reading

J. Cohen and P. Cohen, *Applied Multiple Regression/Correlation Analysis for the Behavioral Sciences* (New York: Wiley, 1975), is for the researcher needing more information than supplied in general statistics texts. This book offers a thorough presentation and argues that regression/correlation can be applied much more widely than it has been. Substantially more difficult than Loether/McTavish.

O. Duncan and B. Davis, "An Alternative to Ecological Correlation," *American Sociological Review* 18 (1953):665–666, describes overlapping-percentages analysis.

L. Goodman, "Some Alternatives to Ecological Correlation," *American Journal of Sociology* 64 (1959):610–625, is the first description of ecological regression.

E.T. Jones, "Ecological Inference and Electoral Analysis," *Journal of Interdisciplinary History* 2 (1972):249–269, applies ecological regression to voting behavior, as does J. Kousser, *The Shaping of Southern Politics* (New Haven: Yale University Press, 1974).

L. Langbein and A. Lichtman, *Ecological Inference* (Beverly Hills: Sage, 1978), is the standard compact reference on ecological regression, also treating overlapping percentages.

H. Loether and D. McTavish, *Descriptive Statistics for Sociologists* (Boston: Allyn and Bacon, 1974), chapter 7, is a readable introduction to correlation and regression. Chapters 8 and 9 cover multiple regression and partial correlation.

F. Parker and B. Phillips, *Voting in Mississippi: A Right Still Denied* (Washington, D.C.: Lawyers' Committee for Civil Rights Under Law, 1981), shows the role of voting analyses in winning lawsuits that challenge discriminatory electoral practices.

W. Robinson, "Ecological Correlations and the Behavior of Individuals," *American Sociological Review* 15 (1950):351–357, is the classic statement of the ecological fallacy.

S. Verba and N. Nie, *Participation in America* (New York: Harper, 1972), is a useful introduction to political-science generalizations regarding voting behavior.

Q and A on Correlation/Regression

Because it is often crucial to show that two variables are associated, and because correlation/regression is by far the most common measure of association, at least for parametric data, it is likely that an attorney and expert will need to make correlation analysis clear to the point at some point. The following questions and answers suggest a way of doing so. Data are taken from table 14–1.

Q: Dr. Smith, what do the data in exhibit 6 [table 14–1] show?

A: Well, first, your Honor, just by looking at the table you can see there is a relationship. Dorado Precinct, for instance, is overwhelmingly white, and it votes overwhelmingly for Mr. Whyte, the white candidate. Able Precinct is mixed, and its votes are mixed. Emerald Precinct, overwhelmingly black, voted predominantly for the black candidate, Mr. Jones. So just by looking, it seems that race, the independent variable, is having an important effect on the election results.

Q: Did you apply any statistical analyses to these data?

A: Yes. The most common statistical analysis for data of this type is called correlation. It is used to see if the first variable, race, has an impact on the second variable, election results. The correlation coefficient is called r—that's little r, underlined—and it ranges in size from 0 to 1. An r of 0 means that there is no relationship between the two variables. When r is 1.0, you have a perfect relationship, so that if you know race of voters, in this case, you can predict votes for the precinct perfectly, with no error whatsoever.

In sociology we're usually quite satisfied to get an r of .5 to .7, indicating a strong relationship between the two variables. Indeed, .3 is usually meaningful. We can compute a second figure, r^2, simply by multiplying r by itself. r^2 is useful because it tells the proportion of the variance in the dependent variable that is explained by the independent variable.

Q: Can you explain that for us more simply?

A: Yes. If you look at the right-hand column of exhibit 6, you see that there's a lot of variation among the precincts in percentage of the vote going to Mr. Whyte. Some precincts are high, some low, some in between. That happens in most elections. Now, the question is, what causes that variance? We answer that question by seeing what independent variable might predict or be associated with those differences in outcome. If we find something that has a high correlation, say .5 or .6, then we know that more than 25 percent of the total variance in election results is accounted for, because $.5^2$ is 25 percent.

Q: Did race have an impact on this election?

A: The correlation coefficient, r, between race of voter and outcome of the election, by precinct, for this election was .995. The whiter the precinct, the more votes for Mr. Whyte, and the relationship was almost perfect.

Q: Is this a strong relationship?

A: Extremely strong. I mentioned earlier that an r of .5 or .7 would be considered strong. Correlations above .9 are extremely unusual.

Q: What does this mean?

A: It means that if I knew the racial composition of a precinct I could predict its vote almost without error. r^2 was 99 percent, meaning that 99 percent of all the variance in electoral outcome can be predicted just knowing this one fact, race of voters.

Q: Can you break it down for us, doctor? What does this high r imply regarding racial bloc voting?

A: It certainly indicates that most of the whites voted white. However, there is a possible fallacy in our analysis to this point, called the ecological fallacy. This fallacy is defined as imputing to individuals a relationship we know to hold for groups, without being sure it holds for the individuals within the groups. In this case, it may be possible, however implausible, that the blacks in heavily white precincts are responsible for lots of the white votes, not the whites in those areas. Actually, that's farfetched, for there aren't enough blacks in those areas to account for the votes received by Mr. Whyte, but nevertheless, there is an easy way to see if I have committed the ecological fallacy.

Q: And what is that?

A: That is overlapping-percentages analysis. I have an exhibit, exhibit 7, I believe, that explains it. [Delay while attorney, expert, and judge turn to exhibit 7, previously supplied, identical to table 14–2.]

Q: Tell us about overlapping-percentages analysis.

A: It's very easy. Let's look at Dorado Precinct. Now, this precinct is 98.4 percent white, overwhelmingly white. To do overlapping-percentages analysis requires precincts that are overwhelmingly white or overwhelmingly black— 90 percent or more is a good cutoff. We assume that the maximum amount of crossover voting—whites voting for blacks, in this case—that could have occurred did occur. In other words, we assume that there was the least possible amount of racial bloc voting within the white population, and we calculate what that least amount is. In Dorado Precinct, the black candidate received only 2.6 percent of the votes. If all those votes came from whites, then that still leaves 95.8 percent of the total population that was white and had to have voted white, because 98.4 percent minus 2.6 percent leaves 95.8 percent. Now we do a simple division: we divide this percentage by the proportion of whites in the population, 97.4 percent, because we seek the proportion of whites, not of the total population, that was white and had to have voted white. The result, which happens also to be 97.4 percent, goes in the right-hand column as the minimum percentage of whites in Dorado Precinct who voted white.

Incidentally, this is even easier to calculate for Charlie Precinct, because since that precinct is all white, we know immediately that 99.1 percent of the whites at its polls voted white.

Q: So according to exhibit 7, the actual proportion of whites voting white in this election is somewhere between 95.7 percent and 100 percent?

A: Yes. The problem with overlapping-percentages analysis is that you cannot use it on the county as a whole, only on those parts of the county that are overwhelmingly white or black. Also, it doesn't yield a single best figure as the proportion of whites voting white, or blacks voting black. But there is a method that avoids all these problems.

Q: And what is that?

A: Ecological regression. Basically, ecological regression is similar to overlapping percentages, except it makes use of all the information from all of the precincts just the way that r, the correlation coefficient, did, and it comes up with one figure for the percentage of whites voting white and another for the percentage of blacks voting black.

Q: And what were those figures?

A: 99 percent of whites voted white. 93 percent of blacks voted black.

Questions would follow in order to see if the expert considers these levels to be examples of racial bloc voting, to see if she is certain of the figures or would place confidence limits around them, and to see if she believes that ecological regression is the most accepted measure for this kind of analysis in social science.

15 Controlling for Third Variables

To convince others of the soundness of one's conclusions, reasonable alternative explanations must be explored and discounted. It is not enough to show that two variables are related, inferring from theory that one causes the other. We must also look for the effects of potential third variables. Before going to court with a finding or relationship, then, the social scientist and attorney should anticipate the major competing findings or explanations that exist in the literature or that are alikely to be put forward by the other side, and control variables should be investigated so as to be able to comment on these explanations. How to do this is the subject of this chapter.

I begin by illustrating the process with a single example. Then I present all the ways that a third variable can make hash of what would otherwise be a straightforward cause-and-effect relationship. From this discussion, it follows that the search for third variables must be assiduous and intensive. The final section of the chapter demonstrates that such a search can also be conducted in a wrong-headed manner so that third variables are invoked unnecessarily. The result, sometimes thrown up by defendants in class-action cases, is the spurious use of third variables to mask a real cause-effect relationship in order that an expert witness can incorrectly claim to have found a null result—no discrimination.

Example of Three-Variable Analysis

Women at Hyperbolic Litigation, Ltd., a multistate law firm, claim discrimination in hiring. While it is true that the firm employs many women, it does not seem to do so for long. Most women who work for the firm, including all receptionists, most secretaries and paralegals, and even many junior attorneys, appear both young and beautiful. Older women seem not to be hired; younger women seem not to be retained long enough to grow old. Table 15-1 shows a modest but important relationship between sex and age: men are more likely to be old, while women with the firm are somewhat younger. The finding has statistical significance.[1] Perhaps some prejudice does exist against hiring older women or some process mitigates against retention of women. But there are alternative explanations.

The firm may claim that it implemented an affirmative-action program during the last five years and hired many women in that time, while its male

Table 15-1
Age and Gender at Hyperbolic Litigation

Age	Men		Women	
	N	Percentage	N	Percentage
40 and over	494	52%	108	40%
Under 40	456	48	163	60
Total	950	100%	271	100%

work force has slowly aged, augmented by fewer new hires. This is quite a different explanation than the claim that the firm employs only attractive younger women, showing them the door when they show signs of age. However, both explanations are identical in outcome: both assert that the firm will not have few older women. The discriminatory hypothesis and the benign hypothesis each account for the observed present relationship between sex and age. At this point we cannot choose between them. In litigation, this means a court would have no reason to believe the plaintiff's argument over the defendant's. The plaintiff has not proved discrimination.

To choose between the two explanations requires some investigation of the third variables, recency and beauty, that each side claims are responsible for the observed relationship between sex and age. We check out third variables by controlling for them, or partialling. We might control for recency of hiring by looking among part of the data set: the recently hired. Table 15-2 allows us to do that. Among the recently hired (those in the entire left-hand side of the table), we can see that sex is not associated with much difference in age. 42 percent of the men are over 40, compared to 38 percent of the women. The 4 percent difference is not enough to build a case around. Among longer-term employees, who are even more central to our hypothesis of discrimination, the difference caused by sex or gender is a mere 2 percent.

Table 15-2 shows that the sex difference washes out, in short. Among the recently hired, sex makes little difference to age; neither does it among the previously hired. The apparent effect of sex on age in table 15-1 was really due to recency of hiring; a third table, with hiring across the top and age on the side, men and women combined, would show this hiring effect. With additional theory and investigation and additional controls, it might be possible to resurrect the hypothesis that sexism is rampant at Hyperbolic, but without more analysis, it looks as if their affirmative-action explanation does hold.

Types of Third Variables

We have just found the existence of a prior variable. We had imagined that sexism was responsible for the paucity of older women at Hyperbolic. Schematically, we thought that

Table 15-2
Age and Gender at Hyperbolic Litigation, by Recency of Hiring

| | Recently Hired (within 5 Years) | | | | Previously Hired (5 or More Years) | | | |
| | Men | | Women | | Men | | Women | |
Age	N	Percentage	N	Percentage	N	Percentage	N	Percentage
40 and over	82	42%	80	38%	412	55%	28	53%
Under 40	118	58	131	62	338	45	32	47
Total	200	100%	211	100%	750	100%	60	100%

$$X \longrightarrow Y,$$

where X was sex (femaleness), Y was being young, and the arrow was a causal chain including elements such as male chauvinism among the men who determine company personnel policy, a sense of beauty that is culturally tied to youthfulness, and decisions to let older women go or not hire them. Instead, we now accept the existence of a third variable, A, which causes both X and Y:

$$A \underset{\longrightarrow Y.}{\overset{\longrightarrow X}{}}$$

A is recency of hiring, X is still femaleness, and Y is still being young. X and Y are still associated or related, but this is because a prior variable, recency of hiring, causes both sex (more women) and age (younger employees).

Prior variables are common. Analysts and attorneys must become proficient at thinking of them and then searching for them. Here is another example, one that should be more familiar because it comes from civic life. Throughout the Vietnam War, polls showed that the higher the educational level of U.S. adults, the greater their support for the war; X = education, Y = hawkishness. Table 15-3 is an example of the relationship at one point during the war.

Since 40 percent hawk is much higher than 20 percent hawk, table 15-3 implies that college education caused hawkish sentiment. However, it is possible that a prior variable, higher parental social class, caused many of these persons to have gone to college long ago and also socialized them toward greater allegiance toward the status quo, including government policies such as this silly war. Other explanations also come to mind, but if this hypothesis is correct, then A, parental social class, causes both X, education, and Y, hawkishness.

Almost as important as prior variables are intervening variables. Again, X and Y are associated, just as they are when both are caused by a prior variable. However, now they are related because X in fact causes some third variable, A, and A in turn causes Y. Without A, X does not cause Y:

$$X \longrightarrow A \longrightarrow Y.$$

Table 15-3
Relationship of Education to War Sentiment in the Adult Population, January 1971

	Educational Level		
War Sentiment	0-8 Years	9-12 Years	Some or All College
Percentage Hawk	20%	25%	40%
Percentage Dove	80	75	60
	100%	100%	100%

Source: Data from Gallup Poll, January 1971. Some rounding for ease of exposition.

An example might be support for U.S. intervention in a Central American country embroiled in civil war. Conceivably, men might favor our intervention more than women, but sex (gender) might really be irrelevant. Men (and women) who had been in the armed forces might be much more interventionist. Without that involvement, men would be no different from women. Thus, sex does not make the difference but merely correlates with the important causal variable, veteran status. The key importance of intervening variables in class-action litigation is that they will often be invoked by the defense. An employer might defend against the charge of sexist promotion policies by claiming that sex (female) does not itself mitigate against promotion; rather, sex is tied with a lack of desire for higher-paid positions, perhaps because women feel more family responsibilities, are loathe to travel or to be transferred, or feel uneasy about being in positions over men. The plaintiff's lawyer and expert must be sure, then, that the defendants have proved those claims—that is, that they have demonstrated the existence of the intervening variables. Moreover, many intervening variables that are tied to race or sex, such as child-care responsibilities, can be mitigated. For example, a firm may set up child-care centers at the factory or may arrange flexible work hours for its workers or managers. These allow for more participation and advancement by women in its work force. If certain skills are required for promotion, and if those skills are not widely found in the minority work force, the firm may set up training programs to teach them. In short, before intervening variables are allowed to excuse an apparently discriminatory relationship between X and Y, they should be examined carefully.

Qualifying variables are third variables that do not eliminate the effect of our first or independent variable but that may drastically limit its impact. Schematically,

$$X \longrightarrow Y.$$
$$\uparrow$$
$$A$$

X still causes Y, but only for one group, only in a certain situation, or only in the presence of some other condition or value of a variable, A. There are many examples of qualifying variables; several are important in courtroom situations. For example, formal education may relate positively to income in a firm's work force, but only among men. Among women, higher education may not be tied to more pay, because women with college degrees may be mostly secretaries. Such statistics might indicate discrimination, particularly if the firm has promoted men from dead-end jobs when they obtained more training or education, while making no such gestures toward female office workers.

The Coleman Report, *Equality of Educational Opportunity*, provided a well-known example of the operation of a qualifying variable. It reported that differences in school quality made little difference to the educational achievement levels of majority students but did cause greater effects among minority children.[2] One reason why qualifying variables need to be located, if they exist, is that a relationship between X and Y may otherwise seem very weak or nonexistent. Suppose Hispanic-American parents are pressing for the retention of a special bilingual education program for their children, for instance, a program to increase literacy in English. If school officials argue that the program has been ineffective by releasing comparative reading-level scores for schools that do and do not have the special teachers, they have certainly overlooked a qualifying variable: ethnic-group membership. There is no reason to expect that a bilingual program will improve reading skills of students who speak English at home. Adding the multitudes of such speakers to the school mean scores would mask even a strong relationship that held only for Hispanics.

Although these examples might seem obvious, many qualifying variables go unexamined. Their key roles in litigation are two, to summarize: (1) they may be introduced to show that a given relationship between X and Y really is important and significant, at least among part of the population, or (2) they may be used to show that for some reason, probably actionable, a relationship that should occur between X and Y is not occurring among part of the population.

The most important types of third variables are prior, intervening, and qualifying variables. Other third variables that can interfere with our understanding of whether X causes Y are third variables that themselves cause Y or decrease the occurrence of Y. These third variables can be correlated or uncorrelated with X; names assigned them in the literature include nullifying variables, masking variables, and enhancing variables. Good social-science methodologists will know how to search for and eliminate their effects.

Using Third Variables to Hide a Relationship

Unfortunately, competent social-science methodologists can also use third variables to hide a relationship between X and Y that does exist and should not be hidden. It follows from the form of most class-action litigation that defendants in particular may resort to this misuse of social science. After a prima facie case of discrimination has been made by a plaintiff, the burden shifts to the defendant to show why his policies and actions do not amount to discrimination but are justified on other grounds. Witnesses hired by the defendant may therefore do their best to invoke other variables to explain away what seems to be a real relationship between X (perhaps racial- or sex-group membership) and Y (perhaps lack of promotion).

An example of this practice seems to be Hauser and Elkhanialy, *The Hauser Report on Lending Practices of Savings and Loan Associations in Chicago–1977,* so I use this report to supply the factual arena for a discussion of the mistaken use of third variables. Their first table apparently portrays the worst sort of redlining, for in 53.4 percent of Chicago's predominantly black census tracts, savings-and-loan associations granted not a single residential loan, while only 7.9 percent of the white tracts went without a loan during the year. Hauser and Elkhanialy then insert six other factors to try to explain this apparent racism. Each of these is by census tract; they use no data on individual loan applicants. Their variables are median family income (for the tract), median value of home, percentage of homes in the census tract that are occupied by their owner, percentage of single-family dwellings, percentage of homes in the tract built before 1949, and population stability. By the time they are done, Hauser and Elkhanialy come to the following conclusion:

Table 15–4
Percentage of Census Tracts with Varying Numbers of Loans Made, by Race of Tract

	Race of Census Tract		
Number of Loans	Predominantly White	Racially Mixed	Predominantly Black
None	7.9%	28.4%	53.4%
1–5	23.2	37	31.2
6–10	15.4	12.3	6.9
11–30	32.6	17.3	7.7
31–50	14.4	4.9	0.8
Over 50	6.6	0	0

Note: Predominantly white = 90–100 percent white; racially mixed = 26–90 percent white; predominantly black = 75–100 percent black, according to the authors.

Source: Philip M. Hauser and Hekmat Elkhanialy, *The Hauser Report on Lending Practices of Savings and Loan Associations in Chicago, 1977* (Chicago: Shapiro, 1978), p. 4. Data are for Chicago, 1977, from twenty-two federal savings-and-loan associations.

It is easy to understand why the differential incidence in numbers of loans and the differences in the amount of the loans and total investment give rise to charges of "redlining." But, as the data show, the differentials are attributable to a number of factors of which the racial composition of neighborhoods is but one and one that derives its importance largely from its relationship to other variables. Lending practices, in some part, reflect the disadvantaged position of blacks in American society and the American economy which cannot be remedied by individual sectors of the economy or society, including the savings and loan associations.[3]

Several of their six other factors are partly redundant to race, however. For example, if blacks live in older inner-city neighborhoods, lenders could claim that their refusal to lend is not based on race but because homes in those areas are too old and make bad investments. As an intervening variable, age of house would make apparent sense, particularly if lenders could also demonstrate a higher risk of losing their money through default, uninsured fire loss, or the like in older neighborhoods.[4] Note also that this is a matter of theory, of interpretation. If we lay all of the joint difference made by race and house age at the doorstep of house age, then we are making an assumption about what is in the mind of the lending officials—that is, we are assuming that race makes no difference to them. We have not proved it, just assumed it. Such an assumption intrinsically gives the institutions carte blanche to continue to redline in any black neighborhood that is also old.

Actually, Hauser and Elkhanialy found that age of housing made no difference to lending because, as a whole, black areas and white areas did not differ systematically in the age of their housing. Population stability also made little difference. These investigators did claim that median income made a much larger difference than anything else, largely accounting for racial differences. Now, we know that black Chicagoans make less money, on the average, than white Chicagoans. So again, if we allow the claim to stand that income, not race, is responsible for the redlining of black neighborhoods, then we justify redlining in any black neighborhood where the median income is low. It is merely a question of which variable is put first.

In this analysis, Hauser and Elkhanialy are also committing the ecological fallacy described in chapter 14. The argument they or a lender would give as to why income makes more difference than race probably would include topics such as qualifying for the loan and ability to repay. If a family wants to borrow so much that, in the lender's judgment, its payments would be too great a proportion of its income, the loan will be denied. Income does matter; this process is familiar to any homeowner who has ever qualified for a loan. Within a black census tract, however, incomes differ. Probably the homeowners seeking improvement loans or the would-be homeowners seeking mortgages command

higher incomes than the renters who seek no loans. Accordingly, to test the
hypothesis that income, not race, makes the difference, Hauser and Elkhanialy
need data on individual loan seekers. If they had such data, their hypothesis
about income might be invalidated because it is inconceivable that so many
black census tracts hold within them not a single family whose income would
have qualified them for the loan they sought, while it is quite conceivable that
those tracts do not hold within them a single family whose race would have
qualified them for their loan.

Sometimes the question of which variable can be disregarded, which is really
causal, can be settled empirically. If we have lots of rich blacks and poor whites,
then we could compare lenders' performance by race, holding income constant,
and by income, holding race constant. Both factors might have independent
causal effects, and if they did, then to the extent that race made a difference
independent of income, we could charge discrimination in the lending process.
As noted, we really need individual-level data to do this analysis, not data by
census tract. The Chicago study does allow some analysis, even though on the
tract level. Table 15-5 shows the results. It is clear, within each part of the table,
that race still makes a huge difference.[5] Among the poorer tracts, more than five
times as many black neighborhoods received not a single loan. Among the richer

Table 15-5
**Percentage of Census Tracts with Varying Numbers of Loans Made, by Race of
Tract, Controlling for Income of Tract**

Number of Loans	Race of Census Tract		
	Predominantly White	Racially Mixed	Predominantly Black
Poor Tracts (Median Family Income below $10,000)			
None	12.7%	44.9%	63.9%
1–5	45.7	38.8	32.2
6–10	15.6	12.2	2.9
11–30	21.9	2.0	0.0
31–50	3.5	2.0	0.0
Over 50	0.6	0.0	0.0
Rich Tracts (Median Family Income $10,000 or More)			
None	4.5%	3.1%	2.4%
1–5	12.1	34.4	26.2
6–10	15.5	12.5	26.2
11–30	38.3	40.6	40.4
31–50	20.0	9.3	4.8
Over 50	9.6	0.0	0.0

Source: Philip M. Hauser and Hekmat Elkhanialy, *The Hauser Report on Lending Practices
of Savings and Loan Associations in Chicago, 1977* (Chicago: Shapiro, 1978), p. 25. See
note at table 15-4.

tracts, the effect of race is weaker but still definitely present: 28.6 percent of rich black tracts were awarded very few loans (0–5), while only 16.6 percent of white tracts received so few loans. Given the results of table 15–5, the conclusion of the authors, cited earlier, seems obfuscatory. Perhaps the source of their funding (the Federal Savings and Loan Council of Illinois) influenced their wording.

The alert reader will see that there is still room for class-based effects within the poor and rich tracts. If the predominantly black poor tracts are poorer than the predominantly white poor tracts, then economics rather than racism account for some of the huge difference (12.7 percent versus 63.9 percent) across the top of table 15–5. This is unlikely for several reasons. First, there is a floor effect in grouped income data so that by 1977 the median income of the poorest census tract in Chicago was probably above $6,000, not close to $0. The income band $6,000 to $9,999 is narrow enough to render differences within it minor. Second, some of the white poor tracts are undoubtedly as poor or poorer than some of their black counterparts. The lower incomes of black families cause more black tracts to fall into the poor classification, but within that classification we would expect a great deal of economic overlap between white and black tracts. Finally, even if the economic explanation held, for reasons already given we would be simplistic if we assigned the loan differences to economics rather than race.

There is a way to circumvent the problems involved in grouping the data. Since median income, percentage black, and number of loans granted are all parametric variables, partial correlation and multiple regression could be used to analyze these data. Multiple correlation/regression works just like simple correlation/regression, described in the last chapter, combined with the partialling or controlling shown in table 15–5. Table 15–5 asks the question, "What is the effect of race when we remove any effect from income?" However, as we saw, the effect of income was not entirely removed, since small income differences still exist within poor or rich. Multiple correlation/regression eliminates even these small differences for it considers each item individually, removing the effect on the dependent variable (loan approval) that owes to income, and then seeing what further effect exists owing to race alone.

The foregoing paragraph did not explain the difference between partial and multiple correlation. If we are interested in maximizing the correlation coefficient—that is, explaining as much of the variation in the dependent variable, loan-approval, as we can—then we would use multiple correlation to see how great an r we could obtain with both race and income as independent variables. This might be useful for a sociological research paper, but for litigation we are interested in the effect of each variable, race and income separately, upon the dependent variable, loan approval. Multiple regression tells us the amount of change in loan approval that each variable, race and income, makes, but the r that tells how strong is the correlation for each variable separately is called the partial correlation. For this problem, we would compute the partial correlation between race and loan approval after the effects of income have been removed; squaring this r would then tell us what proportion of the variation in loan approval is due to race alone, in the absence of any income effect.

The total effect of race would be greater than this because race as a variable is antecedent to income differences, besides having its own independent effect on loan granting. Schematically, we are dealing with this interplay of factors:

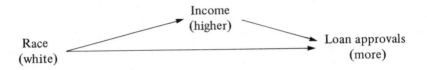

Thus, even though in this case we still find substantial direct effects owing to race, it would be a mistake to assign the income effects to income alone; they also derive in part from race.

In short, partial correlation and multiple regression do not solve the problem of putting the variables into their proper order. Hauser and Elkhanialy fell into this problem in their partial-correlation analysis when they first plugged in all variables except race, then looked to see if race had any remaining effect. Here is a subtler example of the problem: one of their variables was percentage of owner-occupied units, which had a small negative correlation with proportion of blacks in the census tract, so that the blacker the tract, the lower the percentage of owner-occupied homes. When Hauser and Elkhanialy put this variable ahead of race, they assumed that bankers would rather loan in areas of homeowners and that this, not the white race of those owners, caused them to avoid black areas. However, one likely reason for the higher rate of white homeownership would be that past racism in Chicago's lending institutions has made it harder for blacks to obtain mortgages; hence more of them rent. Thus, to place percentage of owner occupancy ahead of race, so that it now decreases the impact apparently made by race, is to use the result of past discrimination as an allegedly nonracial explanation for current redlining.

In all, Hauser and Elkhanialy introduced six variables in addition to race; nevertheless, racial effects did not disappear. Sometimes they will, though. More generally, sometimes the introduction of many third variables, some of which are partly redundant to or correlated with our independent variable, will succeed in eliminating all of its effect. When this happens, the social scientist must examine the order of the variables in the partial correlation, multiple regression, or contingency-table analysis.[6]

As this example shows, it is not always easy to know when to stop an analysis—when enough variables have been investigated, not too few or not too many. Too few and you leave important stones unturned so that your claim that X causes Y is inadequately grounded. Too many and you obfuscate, invoking a host of third variables, each of which itself relates somewhat to your would-be independent variable, X, until finally you have explained away the relationship between X and Y even though it exists. Both the attorney and the expert witness need to be alert to these issues so they can make sure their own presentation controls correctly for appropriate third variables and so they can critique presentations by opposing experts.

Notes

1. The appropriate significance test would be the t test for difference of two proportions (chapter 8).

2. I suspect that schooling makes a big difference for white children too, but Coleman et al., failed to find it for two reasons. First, his variables were not very good. His output variables, achievement-test results, are not good measures of what is demanded or taught in academia (see chapter 13), and his input variables, his measures of school quality, were crude and failed to tap intellectual differences in schools. Second, he assigned joint home-school variation to the home. Children in richer suburbs have homes that are better educationally, to be sure, but they also get better schooling. Even within a multiclass school, affluent children often indicate to teachers that they are affluent and educable through their neatness, clothing, prior knowledge, and other cues. Thus, they receive a different and better education within that school. To assign their resulting better test scores entirely to home background is one sided.

3. Philip M. Hauser and Hekmat Elkhanialy, *The Hauser Report on Lending Practices of Savings and Loan Associations in Chicago—1977* (Chicago: Leo Shapiro, 1978), p. 15.

4. For the record, almost none of the kinds of variables *The Hauser Report* investigates is among those that cause foreclosures. In fact, foreclosures are exceedingly rare among first mortgages where down payments are 10 percent or more. See J. Herzog and J. Earley, *Home Mortgage Delinquency and Foreclosure* (New York: Columbia University Press, 1970).

5. These differences would show up even more graphically in bar graphs. Each half of the table would make a marvelous bar graph modeled after figure 4-4.

6. Sly choice of table categories can also lead to null findings, as can multicollinearity and overfitting in multiple-regression analysis. See D. Baldus and J. Cole, *Statistical Proof of Discrimination* (Colorado Spring: Shepard's/McGraw-Hill, 1980), pp. 174, 247-278. On page 243, however, Baldus and Cole are far too negative regarding multiple regression, claiming it can merely describe statistical relationships. Although technically true regarding statistics, this passage amounts to know-nothingism and does not take into account the interplay of data and theory that is involved in the scientific method and was introduced in chapter 15.

16

Confronting the Other Side's Experts: Assessing Their Data

Dealing with the other side's expert is intrinsically frustrating for both attorney and social scientist, particularly in the courtroom. The social scientist knows what to ask because she knows the literature and has assessed the weaknesses in the other expert's work, but all questions in the courtroom must be asked by the lawyer. The lawyer has a list of questions to ask, but he may be frustrated by the expert's replies because he does not have the background to understand them fully or ask the most penetrating follow-ups. If the expert keeps passing suggestions to the attorney, she may find that her little slips of paper do more harm than good, for they can puzzle the lawyer and interrupt his train of thought and line of questioning. Many is the time I have wanted to stand up and confront the opposing expert myself, instead of going through counsel. This is especially a problem when dealing with complex statistical issues.

There is only one way to reduce this frustration (it cannot be wholly eliminated). That is through coordinated preparation ahead of time, in which the attorney helps lay out the other side's probable legal strategy and the expert helps him anticipate what the other side's factual presentation is likely to be. This chapter presents specific suggestions to make that preparation effective.

Deposing Their Expert

It is a good idea to depose the other side's expert in order to better prepare to deal with him in court. (Throughout this chapter, the other side's expert is referred to as he in order to avoid confusion with our expert, she.) Our expert should attend these sessions, or they will lose most of their value. Our expert can confer with the attorney during breaks and suggest additional lines of questions. More important, she learns firsthand of the nature and work of the opposing expert; otherwise it would only be reported to her via the lay mouth and ears of the lawyer.

The purpose of deposing the other side's expert is to learn as much as possible about his qualifications, previous testimony, methods of research, data, methods of statistical analysis, and findings. This information helps the attorney and his expert prepare questions that will challenge their expert. It also clarifies the points that we need to establish in our presentation. However, a deposition should not give away too much to get this information. In particular, we must take care not to tip our hand, not to signal each area of weakness that we think we have uncovered.

In the heat of the deposition, it is easy to try to win it, to try to destroy the other expert, to show him what is wrong with his own testimony, and essentially to display effective lawyering and social science. It is also a blunder because no one is listening except their attorney; the judge is not there. The greatest courtroom use likely for a deposition is perhaps to quote back a couple of the expert's own sentences if he seems to have changed his mind since saying them.

The deposition will be informal and comfortable. Our expert should make use of the opportunity to meet their's and should learn whatever she can from or about the opposing expert during breaks. Questions about his qualifications should go on until our expert knows enough about their expert to have an opinion and a sense for any weakness. Most important is to get full citations and transcripts, if available, of any previous testimony by this expert. His vita should list his publications, and he should be asked if it is complete. It is also useful at this point to ask him in passing who some of the recognized authorities in this area of study are.

Next, his research methods and his data should be fully explored. It is likely, especially if he is testifying for a government agency, that he has data we do not have. These should be furnished for our own expert's review before trial.

His statistical methods should be elicited only cursorily, if they are entirely familiar to our expert. Our expert can then save any hard-hitting questions for trial. If she is not familiar with the technique or with this application of it, however, she should suggest wide-ranging questions to discover where it is treated in the literature, the exact formula and its use, and what citations apply the technique to this kind of issue.

If their expert has been informed of our expert's work or of other aspects of the nature of our case, he should be asked about our case extensively. For example, what are his major criticisms of our approach? Do they vitiate our work? What citations support his critique? This part of the deposition may yield a statement of bland approval toward our methods that would be useful in court.

While deposing their expert, the atmosphere should be kept informal and friendly. Our expert should be cautioned against becoming overly ego involved with defeating their expert. Sometimes I have become angry, because of the slipshod or distorted research done by the other expert, because I believe his posture to be unethical, or simply because his work opposes mine. These emotions should be reserved for trial. An expert has the chance during deposition of the other expert to ride the elevator with him, talk about the difficulty of the analysis, and perhaps learn more about his work. Attorneys are used to opposing other attorneys while maintaining professional respect and cordiality; social scientists should follow their example.

How to Prepare for Their Expert's Court Appearance

Immediately after deposing the other side's expert, our expert and attorney should confer about him, beginning with his background. Are there weaknesses in his qualifications? (And are there weaknesses in our expert's?) Usually it is counterproductive to try to keep an expert off the stand because it can seem as if he poses a real threat and must be headed off by any means. The judge will probably make a decision later on as to which expert he believes. He will usually want to hear both before deciding, so if asked to bar the expert's testimony he will only rule in favor of the expert. About all that can be accomplished in a qualifications review is to sow a seed of doubt in the court's mind. Particularly if their expert has never testified before and has never published in this specific area, his inexperience can be stressed while making no real objection.

The expert and attorney should then discuss weaknesses in the other side's research methods, data, and statistical techniques. Are these weaknesses serious? Or are they merely the kinds of potshots that can be taken at any research?[1] If additional data should be demanded from the other side, interrogatories should be prepared immediately. Working jointly, our expert and lawyer can frame these interrogatories to obtain what is needed in order to learn just what their expert did. It should be easy to get a copy of their computer output, including the program as well as the results. Our expert will suggest whatever else she needs to replicate their study. The lawyer should also ask his own witness how their study stacks up against ours. Do they disagree? If so, how is the disagreement to be resolved? What are the weaknesses in our presentation?

After this conference, the social scientist has work to do. The attorney should locate copies of the opposing expert's transcripts and exhibits if he has testified before. After reading them, our expert should locate his published articles and books and read them. She may find he has used, hence legitimated, the methods and statistics she is using; this would be useful in case he attacks her methods in court. Our expert may also find citations to sources she is relying on or conclusions about the social world that tie in with her reasoning. She should also skim his footnoted sources to be sure they say what he says they say. She may also wish to raise directly with him some of the ethical implications of his work for the defendant. (Before contacting him, our expert should review her approach with our attorney to be sure she will not jeopardize her own role in the case.)

She should then redo the opposing expert's work. If possible, she should enter his data (if they differ from hers or are on a somewhat different point) and obtain a computer run using his analysis to check his work. If that cannot be done, she can do an approximation by inventing a few cases of imaginary data and using a hand calculator. She also should look most seriously at his criticisms of her own work.

Our expert should draw up a list of major references on the methods and findings at issue. She should make this list no longer than about a dozen items, because the attorney may use it in court to query their expert, may even enter it as an exhibit, and it must be manageable. Perhaps on separate sheets, she should include the most telling quotes from a couple of the sources. For example, S. Verba and N. Nie state that lower socioeconomic strata usually participate less in politics, and they would predict blacks would be less likely than whites to register and turn out to vote in most cases.[2] If their expert claims that a slight black-population majority means blacks have been accorded an equal chance to influence election outcomes, a quotation from Verba and Nie might be useful on cross-examination.

The reference list can put their expert into a difficult double bind, particularly if he is poorly prepared or ill read. If he admits to unfamiliarity with the sources, he impugns his own expertise; if he recognizes them as authorities in the field, then he is confronted with authorities whose conclusions or methods diverge from his. Their expert might finally be asked to cite authorities in the area whose methods and conclusions do agree with his, particularly if our expert believes he cannot come up with anybody. The following questions suggest a line or cross-examination on the literature:

Q: Have you read (authority) or (authority)?
A: No (if yes, see below).
Q: (if no) Have you read the work of (third authority) or (fourth authority)?
A: No (if yes, see below).
Q: (If no) Aren't these the recognized authorities in this area?
Q: (If yes to earlier questions) Which of them agrees with your methodology?
A: None (none will hardly be volunteered, but hopefully will be the correct answer; this will have been explored with our expert previously).
Q: (If yes to earlier questions) Which agrees with your conclusions?
A: None (hopefully).
Q: (Then cite a quotation from one of the named sources that contradicts his methods or conclusions.) Does not this passage from (authority) contradict you?

A related technique is to get their expert to critique his own work. Questions might go like this:

Q: This is a difficult topic to research, isn't it?
A: (Bland assent)
Q: If you had unlimited resources of time and money, obviously your study, like any in social science, could have been improved, couldn't it?
A: (Bland assent)
Q: If you had unlimited resources, how would you have done this research?
A: (May suggest a larger sample, additional studies, and so on.)
Q: What additional work would you have done?

Each response then leads to a potential follow-up because each points to a potential weakness in the work that has been done. The follow-up questions can be difficult to manage, however. The attorney may not discern the right question to ask because he does not know that a statistical weakness has been displayed, while the expert cannot ask because she is not a member of the bar. Attorney and expert should agree to a procedure for communicating follow-up questions from expert to lawyer in the midst of his cross-examination of the opposing witness. Some lawyers can handle submissions on small slips of paper in the midst of trial, and some experts can handle having their questions omitted without explanation if the lawyer so decides. Other lawyers may want to confer with their expert for a few moments just before signaling the end of cross-examination, rather than risk having their concentration shattered by cryptic notes during the interrogation.

The opposing expert should also be asked directly. "What are the major weaknesses of your research design? of your statistical analysis? Who are the major authorities who reach different conclusions? who take a different approach methodologically?" Again, such questions put the expert into a difficult situation. If he says he knows of no major weaknesses, no conflicting authorities, and so on, then he admits ignorance, especially if there are weaknesses and so on. If he does admit to weaknesses or opposing views, then he partly undermines his own testimony.

This line of questioning should be carefully prepared by attorney and expert working together. If their expert can cite no opposition, for example, then the attorney needs to ask about certain authorities by name, having been prepared by our expert as outlined previously. If their expert can cite no weaknesses in his work, then the lawyer should perhaps inquire about some of the following problems, having first prepared with our expert:

Validity,

Reliability,

Ecological fallacy,

Operational definitions,

Statistical assumptions,

Causation,

Research design,

Third variables,

Null hypotheses.[3]

These terms do not comprise a shopping list of problems to throw up to any expert, regardless of his work. Which of them should be invoked depends on what weaknesses vitiate his research.

If no weaknesses severely impair their expert's work, then our expert and lawyer must be able to explain why their findings are not telling but are beside the main point. Otherwise, if the research has been well done and does undercut our posture in the litigation, then according to my understanding of ethics in social research, our expert should recommend to the attorney who employed her that he settle the case.[4] I do not believe in "doing one's damnedest for the lawsuit" by throwing up a mud barrage of elegant-sounding, nontelling, nitpicking criticisms.

Usually, however, it is the other side, the defendant in class-action lawsuits, who throws up the mud barrage. There are several reasons for this, one being that discrimination along various lines is still common in U.S. life. One defense against the charge is to muddy the statistical waters, developing confusing counterresearch that purports to prove that nothing significant in the way of discrimination (or racial bloc voting, or trademark infringement, or whatever is at issue) was going on.

Rebutting the Null Hypothesis

How can we rebut the expert witness who tries to poke holes in our study while presenting his own findings that seem to indicate no significant results? First we will shore up our own research by making sure it commits no major research or statistical blunders. It might also be useful to hire a second witness, one who has had no connection with the case before and who has never met the plaintiff, defendant, attorneys, or either side's experts before. Have him read the depositions or affidavits of both sides and then testify as to their relative merits.

Regarding their null findings, be aware that several kinds of research errors can cause even a strong cause-effect relationship between two variables to be missed or masked. Most obvious is a small N. Chapter 9 on sampling introduces the idea that a sample of certain minimum size is required to show statistical significance, even if a strong and important relationship exists in the data. Our expert can quickly determine, assuming a moderate but important relationship between two variables, whether the sample size used by the other side was capable of showing a significant result. If it was not, then the fact that no significance was shown is meaningless.

The next problem I have called noise in the system. Noise is the buildup of so many countless small errors in the way data are collected, variables measured, indexes constructed, and statistical analyses performed that it would be a miracle for any strong relationship to push its way through and be heard. One famous example of noise is in the Coleman Report, *Equality of Educational Opportunity*, which puts forth the basically null finding that schools make little difference to academic achievement levels. Socioeconomic background is telling, according to Coleman et al.; "when these factors are statistically controlled, however, it appears that differences between schools account for only a small fraction of differences in pupil achievement."[5] There was substantial slippage throughout this study. Response rate was a problem, for only about two-thirds of the sampled schools responded. It is reasonable to assume that those who did not respond might have reasons for their nonresponse—they might be less organized or more discriminatory, for instance—so the full range of schools may not have been sampled. Steps taken to deal with this nonresponse problem were inadequate. Another problem was the reliance on self-reporting by school administrators to measure between-school differences. Indexes relied overly on tangible elements of the school experience, such as presence or absence of a school psychologist or typing classroom; little effort was made to investigate the intellectual quality of teachers or curricula. Null findings from such a large, poorly done study are not more surprising than the *Literary Digest's* 1936 prediction of Alf Landon over Roosevelt for president.

The most elegant way to demolish a null finding that results from noise in the system is to replicate it artificially. Begin with invented data showing the important relationship you believe obtains. Subject the data to the collection procedures, coding techniques, index construction, and statistical analyses used by the other side. At each point, note the possibilities for error and slippage, and develop crude statistical estimates of the resulting variability. Methods textbooks can help in calculating these estimates. The final product is an exhibit that shows a null finding—a showing of no significant relationship—derived from data that did contain the relationship—an exhibit that attacks both the conclusion and the methods of the other side's study.

Research can also be faulty in its basic design. This is a different and more-specific problem than noise in the system, but it can be handled the same way. Let me illustrate. Once in a voting-rights case I had demonstrated that whites bloc voted for white candidates. More than one white sometimes opposed a black candidate; in those cases I added the white candidates' votes together to find the proportion of all votes cast, by precinct, for white candidates. I then correlated these proportions with the proportion of persons at the polls who were white. The correlation was above .95, and ecological regression (see chapter 14) further indicated that more than 98 percent of the white voters had voted white—convincing evidence, I imagined, of racial bloc voting. It held in election after election.

Then the other side's expert presented his analysis. He used the same turn-out and outcome statistics I had used so there was no noise in the system. However, he claimed that the important issue in politics was who won or lost, so he tested whether or not whites had bloc voted for the winning candidate. When one white opposed one black, his results were identical to mine and showed overwhelming bloc voting. When two or more whites and a black ran for office, however, he put the winning white on one side, the loser on the other with the defeated black, and now he found white votes on both sides of the outcome, seeming to disprove the claim of racial bloc voting by the white electorate. The correlation coefficient had dropped to .5 or so between proportion white at the polls and proportion for the white (victorious) candidate.

Of course, I claimed that this was a faulty research design. Probably the most telling method I used to show the flaw was to invent a small county with a few hundred voters in ten precincts. Because these voters were my creation, I could claim to know exactly how each of them voted, and I had every white voter vote for a white candidate. However, because two white candidates were in the race and one black, and because support for each white candidate was uneven, concentrated in that part of the county where he lived, the correlation coefficient by my opponent's method was a mere .3 in an election in which every white had voted white (and most blacks had voted black). This invented situation proved that my opponent's research design could not detect racial bloc voting where it occurred totally, so his null findings were themselves nullified.

Even if you anticipate no courtroom use of your invented data, it is still a good idea to make up numbers to test every index or other statistical manipulation used by their expert. What looks like a perfectly reasonable index of classroom quality, mainstreaming of the handicapped, or whatever can suddenly become unstable and undefined as its denominator approaches zero. Other measures inadvertently are contaminated by N so they indirectly measure population size, not what they claim to measure.

Another form of design error can occur in the grouping of data. There is probably some way to group almost any data that will obscure even a strong relationship the data otherwise show. A graphic way to show this is through the map-shading examples in figures 16-1 and 16-2. These maps show graphically, for the state of Mississippi, the very strong relationship between percentage of blacks in the population and support for Hubert Humphrey, candidate for president in 1968. Figure 16-3 shows the same data as figure 16-2, but equal-N shading has been abandoned. Instead, our analyst might now claim that 50 percent or more is required in politics to win so that 50 percent should be the center of symmetrical shading categories. Now, although the actual data forming figure 16-3 still correlate highly ($r = .92$) with figure 16-1, the maps look much less alike. The relationship, though still visible, has been partly masked by the grouping.

Unconsidered third variables can also mask a relationship. More often, the opposing expert will consider too many third and fourth variables, claiming that they and not our independent variable really account for the effects on the dependent variable. If this is the direction taken by the defense, our attorney and expert should be sure they understand the principles in chapter 14. The basic error of this approach, which is also the reason it is invoked, is that these third variables often contain within themselves aspects of the independent variable itself.

For instance, chapter 13 noted that Afro-Americans score more than 100 points lower than whites on the SAT for a host of reasons. To require blacks to have the same scores as whites using some cutoff or weighted index ensures that far fewer blacks will be admitted than whites, even as a proportion of applicants.

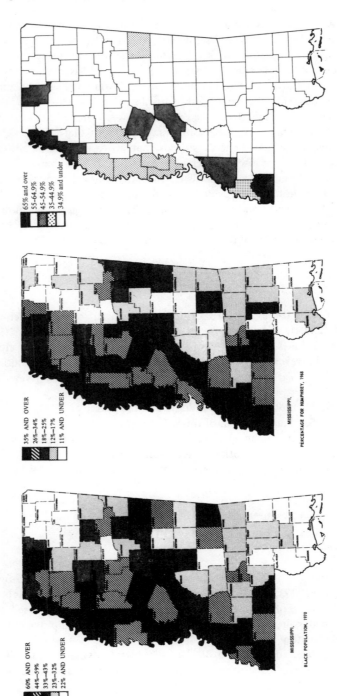

Figure 16–3. Percentage of Votes for Humphrey, 1968: Unequal-N Shading

65% and over
55–64.9%
45–54.9%
35–44.9%
34.9% and under

Figure 16–2. Percentage of Votes for Humphrey, 1968: Equal-N Shading

35% AND OVER
26%–34%
18%–25%
12%–17%
11% AND UNDER

MISSISSIPPI,
PERCENTAGE FOR HUMPHREY, 1968

Figure 16–1. Black Population Mississippi, 1970 Census

60% AND OVER
44%–59%
33%–43%
23%–32%
22% AND UNDER

MISSISSIPPI,
BLACK POPULATION, 1970

We also could imagine a company with almost no women in its managerial work force, "not because we discriminate against women but because we don't hire managers who wear lipstick." Obviously the merit of using these third variables depends upon the case. Statistically, it is easy to insert enough of them so that the main causal relationship under investigation has been explained away. This is the abuse, not the use, of third variables.

Often the defendants in class-action lawsuits hope to confuse the court with irrelevant data, misapplied statistics, or methods that cannot help but produce the results needed—hence, methods that prove nothing at all. Often they get away with it, because, as Michael J. Saks put it, "the agents of the law are such strangers to empirical methods of understanding behavior they cannot tell that they have not been provided with the necessary empirical data."[6] My hope is that the attorney and his expert can develop the suggestions in this chapter into a powerful line of questions and exhibits that will make plain to the court the factual deficiencies in the arguments made by the other side.

Notes

1. For 100 examples of critiques of research designs, see Schuyler Huck and H.M.Sandler, *Rival Hypotheses* (New York: Harper and Row, 1979). Some of these critiques are telling; others are nitpicks. The examples are fun to think about, however, and they sharpen one's ability to spot faulty studies.

2. S. Verba and N. Nie, *Participation in America* (New York: Harper, 1972).

3. Each of these terms is defined in the glossary.

4. See the discussion of this point on pages 30–31.

5. J.S. Coleman et al., *Equality of Educational Opportunity* (Washington, D.C.: Government Printing Office, 1966), pp. 21-22.

6. "Ignorance of Science is No Excuse," *Trial* 10 (November 1974):20.

Additional Resources

Further Reading

D. Copus, "The Numbers Game Is the Only Game in Town," *Howard Law Journal* 20 (1977):374-418, emphasizes the point that variables contaminated by prior forms of institutional discrimination must not be used statistically to excuse ongoing racism or sexism. His article treats employment but is generalizable to other areas.

Irwin Deutscher, *What We Say/What We Do* (Glenview, IL, Scott, Foresman, 1973) offers, to the social scientist, a sophisticated discussion of the pitfalls of relying on survey data. To the lawyer, the book suggests tough questions to put to survey researchers regarding the adequacy of their research designs and would therefore be useful in preparing for cross-examination of one's own or an opposing expert witness.

Richard Light discusses the abuse of third variables with clear examples in a judicial setting in pages 63–67 of Michael J. Saks and C. Baron, eds., *The Use/ Nonuse/Misuse of Applied Social Research in the Courts* (Cambridge, Mass.: Abt, 1980).

Michael J. Saks, "Ignorance of Science Is No Excuse," *Trial* 10 (November 1974):18–20, gives a good account of why some studies show no difference and accept the null hypothesis. He treats small Ns and the inappropriate use of third variables in the context of recent jury size decisions.

Hans Zeisel, "The Deterrent Effect of the Death Penalty: Facts and Faiths," *Supreme Court Review 1976* (Chicago: University of Chicago Press, 1977), pp. 317–343, shows on page 335 an interesting example of how the other expert could not help but find what he was looking for because of his method. Since this publication is aimed at lawyers, the article can help them become more familiar with subtle problems of social-science inquiry.

Glossary

Actionable Legally questionable. A practice, policy, or law that can be altered by lawsuit.

Adverse impact A practice, policy, or law that has a harsher effect on a protected group, usually on women or a racial minority, rather than on the majority. For example, a test for police patrolmen that is passed by half of all white men, but by only one fourth of nonwhites or women exhibits adverse impact. As a rule, the minority must pass at 80 percent of the rate at which the majority passes, or a practice is said to have adverse impact. Such a test or practice must then be justified by the institution using it.

Affidavit A sworn statement by a witness. For the expert witness, an affidavit can be analogous to a small article or paper. She signs it in the presence of a notary, and the attorney then uses it to indicate her findings and conclusions. Because an affidavit cannot be cross-examined, it has less legal significance than a deposition.

Assumption of a test Basic premises that must be met before a given statistical test may correctly be applied. Usually these premises are assumptions about the nature of the data. For example, before a t test for difference of two means may be used, we must be able to calculate means, which in turn requires data that can be added and divided. If we calculate mean student status for students taught by male and female professors, where status is measured by 1=freshman, 2=sophomore, 5=M.A. candidate, and so on, we are technically erring, for these numbers are only ordinal. However, if the overall mean for students taught by men was 3.9 and for students taught by women was 2.2, clearly women are assigned to introductory courses while men are assigned the graduate students. A social scientist or statistician can determine when the rigid requirements of a text can be relaxed and when they must not be.

Bargraph A way to show data visually by means of bars of varying lengths. Bargraphs are effective in court because they are clear, interesting, and even dramatic.

Binomial, *binomial distribution,* or *binomial expansion* The mathematical formula that tells how likely it is to get different outcomes by chance. If there are just two alternatives and each appears to be equally likely, such as drawing jurors in a county equally divided along racial lines, figure 6-1 shows the probability of the number of black jurors selected on a ten-person jury. The formula need not be learned by attorneys. Only the main point needs to be understood: outcomes of six or five black jurors out of ten are likely; one or two or ten blacks are not likely by chance. As the number in the sample gets larger than ten, such as 30 recent masonry apprentices or 500 faculty appointments in a medical school, the binomial distribution looks more and more like a normal curve. The binomial distribution forms the basis of the sign test and several other statistical tests useful in court.

Chi-square test or χ^2 test The upper-case Greek letter chi (pronounced kai) is a significance test used to tell if frequencies in a table deviate markedly from what would be expected by chance.

Cohort All the people who entered a system at the same time. Most common are birth cohorts, such as everyone born in 1942 or in the 1970s, and students in a year in school, such as all Reed entering freshmen in 1982. By tracing the careers of cohort members over time, the social scientist can compare the effects of an institution on men and women, for example.

Construct validity Showing that a concept actually measures what it purports to measure, by means of a complex process. The social scientist begins by identifying subsections of the concept, such as attitudes and responses that form elements of the concept *sexist,* or skills that form job behaviors required for managerial success. She then uses accepted instruments for measuring these subsections, instruments that have been validated by other researchers in other institutional settings, perhaps including attitude scales or standardized tests.

Content analysis Subjecting verbiage (or photographs, and so on) to systematic analysis, often including word counts by computer.

Contingency table A double (or multiple) frequency table, involving two (or more) variables. If one variable is logically prior, the way that gender is to employment, it may influence the second, so that men are promoted before women. Thus promotion may be contingent on sex and the table will show very different promotion rates in its columns (set up by gender).

Continuous A variable that can be measured along an unbroken dimension, such as age (young to old) or income (in dollars). *See also* Parametric; Discrete.

Controlling Assessing the effect of one variable on another while holding constant a third variable. For example, to examine the relationship between family income and home ownership among whites only is to control for race, so that any effect of race has been removed. Multiple regression offers another way to control for a third variable.

Correlation In general, correlation is a way of assessing how strongly two or more variables are related to each other. Specifically, it refers to the analysis of two parametric variables as portrayed in a scattergram and it results in r, the correlation coefficient. This is the Pearson product-moment correlation coefficient. Less common but useful for ordinal data is the Spearman rank-order correlation coefficient. *See also* Correlation coefficient.

Correlation coefficient A single statistic that summarizes the strength of the relationship between two variables. Often called r, it can vary from –1 (perfect negative relationship) through 0 (no relationship) to +1 (perfect positive relationship). A large negative correlation ($r = -.8$, for example) would occur between percentage black, by precinct, and percentage of votes for President Reagan in 1980. Correlating height and weight would result in a large positive correlation (+.7 or +.8, for example).

Criterion validity Demonstrating that a concept actually measures what it purports to measure, by associating the concept's operational definition with an output variable or performance criterion. For example, if people whose favorite color is green can easily learn to weld in ten hours, while people whose favorite color is not green require one-hundred hours to learn welding, then color choice is valid as an admissions test for a welding apprenticeship program. It is valid, although on its fact it has nothing to do with welding, because it correlated with welding ability or aptitude. *Compare* Face validity.

de facto As a matter of practical fact. A job classification system may not specify sex, but if some jobs require qualifications that only men are likely to possess, then it is de facto segregated by sex. School systems in some Northern metropolitan cities require students to attend the school nearest their homes, resulting in de facto school segregation since residential areas are segregated racially.

de jure As a matter of law. The Catholic priesthood bars women as a matter of church law.

Demography The study of population.

Dependent variable The variable or characteristic that may be affected by a prior variable or influence. How one votes on a referendum may depend, among other things, on whether one is white or black, so vote is a dependent variable. Racial membership does not change as one leaves the polling booth, so race is independent of voting.

Deposition Taking a witness's sworn statement before a court stenographer, usually for use in litigation. Attorneys for each side are present and ask questions.

Descriptive statistics Ways of summarizing and presenting data. Examples include frequency distributions, measures of central tendency, and measures of dispersion.

Discovery The pretrial process by which one party to a lawsuit tries to obtain from the other two things: information useful to its case and hints as to the nature of the other side's case.

Discrete A variable that can be measured only in separate categories, such as Baptist, Catholic, and Buddhist. Some discrete variables can be measured in an ordered direction, such as freshman, sophomore, junior, and senior, but these categories are still discrete and do not form a continuum. *Compare* Continuous.

Dispersion Variability; the amount of variation there is among the different examples of a variable, such as the salaries in a university. *See* Range; Standard deviation; Variance.

Ecological fallacy Imputing onto individuals a relationship that you have found to be true on the group level. For example, suppose that counties with more farmers show more votes for Republicans. This does not mean that farmers are voting Republican. There are plenty of other residents who might be providing the Republican majority in rural counties, while farmers split or lean toward the Democrats.

Empirical Based on actual data. Often contrasted to theoretical or philosophical.

Equal-N shading Dividing a map into 3, 4, 5, 6, or 7 categories based on the values of a variable and setting boundaries on those values so that each category has the same number of cases. For example, if shading to show income in a city with 95 census tracts, divided into higher, middle, and low income, about 32 tracts should be shaded "higher." The dollar definition for "higher" should be raised until all but 32 tracts are excluded.

Estimate The best calculation for a statistic, usually based on a sample that is smaller than the total population. In lay language the term implies imprecision, which may be an erroneous implication, so it should be avoided.

Face validity Showing that a concept actually measures what it purports to measure by pointing out that its operational definition is clearly part of the meaning of the concept itself. For example, content analysis of the illustrations in history texts, set up to identify any text less than 2 percent of whose illustrations included nonwhites, could validly form part of an index of racism, since unfair exclusion is part of what racism can entail.

Frequency curve A way of showing how a variable is distributed. Figure 4–2 is such a curve, similar to the bargraph that is figure 4–3. Although the curve possesses technical accuracy, it possesses also the drawback that its vertical scale loses meaning. The number of bars in the bargraph has been increased by making each bar vanishingly narrow, so now we can no longer measure the number of people who fall into the category represented by a given bar. Therefore, for courtroom presentation even of a continuous variable, a frequency curve is usually less clear than a bargraph. Frequency curves underlie many statistical tests.

Frequency distribution The entire range of possible values of a variable and the frequency with which each of them occurs. A frequency distribution can be shown by a bargraph, frequency polygon, frequency curve, or even a table. Bargraphs are usually the most effective.

Gamma A measure of association; a statistic that summarizes whether two variables are related to each other. Used for ordinal data (or for equal-interval or ratio data) and for any two-by-two table.

Gini index A single statistic that summarizes the amount of inequality in the distribution of a variable as shown on a Lorenz curve. For example, a Lorenz curve of income distribution for families will have a Gini index of about .3 if the society is fairly egalitarian, and an index of perhaps .5 if its class structure is rather harsh. A Gini index of 0 means complete equality, with every family (or other unit) possessing identical incomes (or other variable), while 1.0 denotes complete inequality, with one family having all the income (or one part of town having all the nonwhites), and the rest none.

Hard data Socioeconomic information, such as the income, race, sex, and occupation of a person (or group).

Hypotheses, alternative and null The two possibilities established by the social scientist before running a statistical test. The null hypothesis means nothing unusual is going on, the independent variable has no significant effect on the dependent variable and the results could have occurred by chance. The alternative hypothesis rejects the null and prophesies that the independent variable will affect the dependent variable. Sex (female) will affect (decrease) probability of promotion, for example, and as the words in parentheses imply, usually the alternative hypothesis is directional or one-tailed.

Importance The theoretical or practical meaning of a finding or statistic.

Independent variable The variable or characteristic that comes first logically or temporally and that may influence a later variable or characteristic. One's racial group membership may influence how one votes on a referendum, so race is an independent variable.

Index A way to measure a concept. Often an index is composed of several different measures. An index of corporate sexism, for instance, might include components based on promotion statistics, content analysis of company brochures, and self-reported job aspirations by male and female employees. Correctly assembled, such an index is more accurate and more believable than a measure based on only one item.

Index of dissimilarity, D A single statistic that summarizes the amount of inequality in the distribution of a variable over individuals or groups. Like the Gini index, it varies from 0 (complete equality) to 1.0 (total inequality). It is often used to measure segregation (for example, the distribution of blacks over census tracts) because it is easily calculated and explained.

Inferential statistics (A term with two closely related meanings.) When describing a population, such as all job applicants at Redneck Tanning Company since 1980, based on a sample of fifty files pulled at random, inferential statistics are procedures that allow the social scientist to generalize to the population, with a known level of likely error. When comparing two samples or populations, such as white and black job applicants, inferential statistics convince the social scientist to choose between the null hypothesis (no significant difference between the groups in hiring rates) or the alternative (race does affect hiring).

Interpolate To approximate the correct datum between two known points. For example, we wish to know the percentage black in the working-class labor force in 1978, the year our plaintiffs claim they were not hired owing to their race. We have countywide data for 1970 and 1980. We interpolate to find 1978. Usually straight-line interpolation is simple to do, easy to explain, and accurate enough.

Interrogatory Written questioning put by the opposing attorney before trial as part of the discovery process. Written answers must usually be supplied, which must be careful and responsive to the questions but should not volunteer information in a misguided attempt to persuade the opponents of the error of their ways.

Intervening variable A variable or characteristic that is neither independent nor dependent, but is intermediate in the chain of causation. Medical doctors disproportionately produce medical doctors among their children, for instance, but they do not do so directly. The most obvious intervening variable would be medical school; progeny who attend it become doctors while those who don't, don't. Intervening variables may exist that explain discrimination. For example, a test may lie between racial membership and employment as a firefighter. If whites pass it while blacks mostly do not, then this intervening variable is an important link in the chain of causation and may itself be actionable.

Level of significance The strength of a scientist's confidence that she is right in rejecting the null hypothesis, for example, and asserting that some factor, perhaps discrimination, must be involved to explain the observed difference between two groups. Usually the 5 percent or 1 percent significance levels are cited. The 5 percent level means that if the analysis were repeated 100 times and the scientist rejected the null hypothesis each time, she would be wrong and chance variation could have produced her results in five of the analyses. The 1 percent level means she would be right 99 percent of the time. It is a more stringent criterion.

Lorenz curve A way of graphing the distribution of a variable over a population. Common examples are incomes for a population of families, or nonwhites for a population of census tracts. *See also* Gini index.

Macroethics In social science, ensuring that moral use is made of research. This can be aided by the scientist's sensitive phrasing of her results, by her active participation in making use of the findings to promote greater justice in society, and by choice of topics and methods in the first place.

Mean, $\bar{X}$ The arithmetic average; a way to describe the center of a distribution of parametric data. $\bar{X} = \Sigma X/N$; add all the scores (or incomes or whatever) and divide the total number. *See also* Median.

Measures of central tendency Numerical ways to summarize a distribution by telling where its center lies. *See also* Mean; Median; Mode.

Median A way to describe the center of a distribution of parametric or ordinal nonparametric data. Arrange the scores (or incomes or whatever) from smallest to largest and select the middle case; its value or score is the median. If there are an even number of cases, then the median lies halfway between the two middle cases. For these six incomes: $1,000, $2,000,

$4,000, \$10,000, \$12,000,$ and $\$1,000,000,$ the median is $\$7,000,$ halfway between the two middle cases.

Microethics In social science, ensuring that the people encountered in doing research or from whom data are collected are not harmed but are treated morally. Anonymity is part but only part of this process.

Mode A way to describe the center of any distribution, parametric or nonparametric, by grouping the scores (or incomes or whatever) into categories. The mode is the category with the most cases.

Multiple correlation Determining the combined effects of two or more variables on a dependent variable. In a way, multiple correlation is the opposite of partial correlation. If age relates positively to income (so that older adults tend to make more money) and if education also relates to income, then age and education together may have a higher r than either does alone.

Noise in the system Variability that sneaks in to interfere with even strong relationships because it is hard to locate and eliminate. Examples include measurement error, nonresponses in a survey, misunderstood questionnaire items, and countless other idiosyncratic or larger-scale problems in research design.

Nominal A scale (or property space for a variable) whose categories do not relate to each other in any particular order. Examples include marital status (never married, married, divorced, widowed) or ethnic group (Polish-American, WASP, Afro-American, and so on).

Nonparametric A scale that is discrete or not quantifiable, or whose numbers, if numbers are used, do not connote real numerical relationships and cannot legitimately be added or divided. *See* Nominal; Ordinal.

Normal curve The bell-shaped curve as in figures 6-2, 8-1, and 8-2. Its importance comes from the fact that it resembles the binomial expansion, as in figure 6-1.

One-tailed test Applying an inferential statistics test in a directional way, so that one is not ascertaining if blacks face a different loan-approval rate than whites, for instance, but if they face a lower rate.

Operational definition The way a concept is actually measured by the social scientist. The concept *racist,* for instance, may be operationalized by a three-item attitude scale on which a respondent who answers any two of the items in what has been determined to be the antiminority direction is defined racist. Even everyday terms like *responsible employee* or *good credit risk* are usually given operational definitions by careful social scientists and by most bureaucracies as well.

Ordinal A scale (or property space for a variable) whose categories relate to each other in a definite order, but are not quantified precisely. Examples include freshman, sophomore, junior, senior, and all Guttman scales.

Overlapping percentages A way of avoiding the ecological fallacy by using group data to make valid inferences about the behavior of individuals in the groups. It requires groups that lean overwhelmingly (90 percent or more) to one alternative of a dichotomous variable.

Parametric A scale that is continuous and numerical, so that data can be added, divided, and so on. With such data, a sample can be characterized by its mean and standard deviation, which are called its parameters.

Partial correlation Analyzing the statistical association between two variables while removing (partialling out) the effects of a third. To take a famous example, there is said to be a correlation in Europe between neighborhoods with storks and neighborhoods with lots of babies. Obviously storks bring babies, it was said. Storks live in rural areas, not industrial cities, however, and cities have much lower birth rates than farming communities. A correlation between number of storks and birth rate in each neighborhood, with degree of urbanity partialled out, will reveal whether there really is a relationship once rural/urban effects are statistically eliminated.

Partialling In table analysis, controlling for a third variable while assessing the effect of a first variable on a second. Partialling is done by looking at only part of the data at a time, that part within which the third variable does not vary. For example, to examine the relationship between family income and home ownership among whites only is to remove any racial effect.

Participant observation Studying an institution by assuming a role within it, covertly or as an announced social scientist. Many fine studies have resulted from participant observation, but it is problematic for courtroom use because it is slow and open to the charge of subjectivity.

Percentile Placing an individual score onto a comparative scale by giving it the number corresponding to the percentage of all scores that it excels. Thus the highest scores would fall into the ninety-ninth percentile.

Pilot study A small study done to explore a topic or institution, learn some fruitful and fruitless methods for studying it, develop operational definitions, and obtain preliminary data.

Population pyramid Using horizontal bars to show the age and sex distribution of a population.

Power of a test Tells how effective a statistical test is. In testing a hypothesis, a researcher may make two kinds of errors: (1) She may reject the null hypothesis and accept the alternative hypothesis when chance variation could have been responsible. This is a Type I error and its likelihood is told by the level of significance (for example, 5 percent or 1 percent). (2) She may accept the null hypothesis, concluding that no significant difference occurred, when something *was* going on and chance was not responsible. This is a Type II error. The greater the power of a test, the less the chance of committing a Type II error.

Prima facie On the face of it. A prima facie case of discrimination is a factual presentation that indicates inferior treatment of women or a minority. Officials of the institution may be able to explain the statistics or show that the treatment was justifiable, but until they do, they appear to have discriminated and the burden is on them.

Projection   A calculation forward in time beyond the last observed data, based on that data and prior data.

Random sample   A subset of a population, drawn in such a way that each member of the population originally had an equal chance to be chosen. The term is commonly misused where "uncontrolled sample" is meant; avoid this error.

Range   The largest number in a distribution minus the smallest one. As a measure of how spread out a distribution is, the range is inferior because it is affected by a single very large or very small item. *Compare* Standard deviation; Variance.

Redlining   Banks' refusals to loan in minority neighborhoods, regardless of the individual economic characteristics of the would-be borrower.

Regression   Fitting a line to a scattergram so that it best fits all the data (using the least-squares method). The regression line then compactly summarizes the relationship between the two variables. Its slope tells how much the dependent variable increases (or decreases) when the independent variable goes up by a given amount.

Reliable   Replicable. A measure or operational definition is reliable if it will come out about the same when measured again.

Scattergram   A visually effective way to show two variables at once, hence also making graphic any relationship between them. The scattergram is also the basis for correlation and regression and requires parametric data.

Significance   The likelihood that a finding did not occur by chance. *See also* level of significance.

Significance tests   Statistical analyses that reveal how likely a given outcome is due to chance.

Sociogram   A questionnaire or interview that asks people to list other people they feel tied to, such as best friend. Useful for studying the informal structures of organizations.

Standard deviation, s   A way to measure how spread out a parametric distribution is. The formula, $s = \sqrt{X_i - \overline{X}/N}$, is not completely distorted by one very large or very small number. About two-thirds of a normal distribution is found within one standard deviation of the mean.

Statistics of association   Ways to measure the effect one variable has on another. The correlation coefficient and gamma are two common examples.

Structured observation   Systematic recording of aspects of social interaction. Because operational definitions are specific and procedures are written down and replicable, the resulting data can be convincing in court. Examples would include noting use of courtesy titles by race in a social-services office or monitoring the ways a primary-school teacher elicits participation from diverse students in her class.

Survey Asking the same questions of many people via a questionnaire or interviews.

Unobtrusive measures Data-gathering methods that do not bother anyone, and so are not subject to the conscious respondent distortions that can vitiate surveys. Examples include compiling maintenance records to see which museum exhibits get more visitors or seeing if residents replace empty garbage cans quickly after collection as a measure of neighborhood caring.

Valid Measures what it purports to measure. When an operational definition meshes with the conceptual definition of a term, we have validity. *See also* Construct validity; Criterion validity; Face validity.

Variance, s^2 A measure of dispersion or spread in a distribution. *See* Standard deviation and square its formula (remove the square-root radical).

Venire Panel of potential jurors, often numbering fifty or more people.

Venue Trial site.

Index

Continuous, 220. *See also* Parametric
  variables
Controlling for third variables, 31–32,
  195–205, 220
Copus, D., 106–107, 216
Correlation, 71–77, 179–185, 192,
  220. *See also* Multiple correlation/
  regression; Partial correlation/
  regression
Couch, A., 152
Crain, R., 18, 162
Criterion validity, 175–176, 221
Cross-examination, 34–37, 209–212

Data base, 25, 28–29, 38
Data gathering, 28, 50–53, 59–64, 79,
  143–152, 188
Data presentation, 32–33, 39. *See also*
  Bargraphs; Mapping
Davis, B., 191
De facto, 156–157, 221
De jure, 156–157, 221
DeFunis, 169
Degrees of freedom, 139
Demography, 13, 87–89, 221
Denzin, N., 55
Department of Health and Human
  Services, ethical guidelines, 52–53,
  56–57
Dependent variable, 68–69, 181, 190,
  221
Depositions, 36–37, 207–208, 221
Descriptive statistics, 64–68, 79–93,
  221
Desegregation, 8–9, 18–19, 138–139,
  156–157
Deutscher, I., 56, 153, 216
Diamond, E., 107
Diamond, S., 122
Discovery, 28, 221
Dispersion, 221. *See also* Range,
  Standard deviation, Variance
Dothard v. *Rawlinson*, 96–97
Dollard, J., 50
Douglas, W., 169

Dummy variables, 72
Duncan, O., 191

Earley, J., 205
Ecological fallacy, 184–188, 192–193,
  201–202, 213, 222
Ecological regression, 181, 186–194
Economist, as expert, 10–11
Education, researcher in, as expert, 14
Educational Testing Service, 171–171,
  173, 177
Elkhanialy, H., 200–205
Ellison, K., 19, 122
Empirical, 222
Employment discrimination, 95–101,
  104–106, 169, 183, 195–199
Equal-N shading, 86–87, 214–215, 222
Ethics, 26, 30, 47–58, 225
Etzioni, A., 122
Experiments, 62
Exhibits, 29–30, 32, 34, 39, 79–82,
  84–88, 209–210

Face validity, 175, 222
Fallows, J., 177
Fees, witness, 26–27
Fiedler, J., 44, 153
Fiegel, J., 93
Finfrock, W., 45
Finkelstein, M., 77, 122
Four-fifths rule, 169
Fourteenth Amendment, 1, 18
Freedman, D., 77
Frequency distribution, 64–67, 222

Gallup Poll, 123, 128, 198
Gamma, 73, 222
Genz, M., 178
Geographer, as expert, 20
Gini index, 160–161, 222
Glazer, M., 56
Glenn, N., 93
Goldfarm, M., 93, 177
Goldzband, M., 18
Goodman, L., 45, 93, 153, 191

About the Author

James W. Loewen has testified widely as an expert witness in cases dealing with voting rights, unequal taxation, jury discrimination, municipal services, and other issues. Partly in recognition of this work, in 1978 he received the Sidney Spivack Award from the American Sociological Association for "sociological research applied to problems in intergroup relations." He coauthored a book on the history of Mississippi, which won the Lillian Smith Award for Best Southern Nonfiction (1975) and which also became the subject of a lawsuit (*Loewen et al.* v. *Turnipseed et al.*) won against the state of Mississippi regarding the book's use in public schools.

He received the Ph.D. in sociology from Harvard University and has been chair of the Department of Sociology at Tougaloo College in Mississippi, director of research for the Center for National Policy Review in Washington, D.C., and associate professor at the University of Vermont. He is currently lecturing on race relations and the law at LaTrobe University in Melbourne, Australia, on a Fulbright Fellowship.